WAR
EAGLES

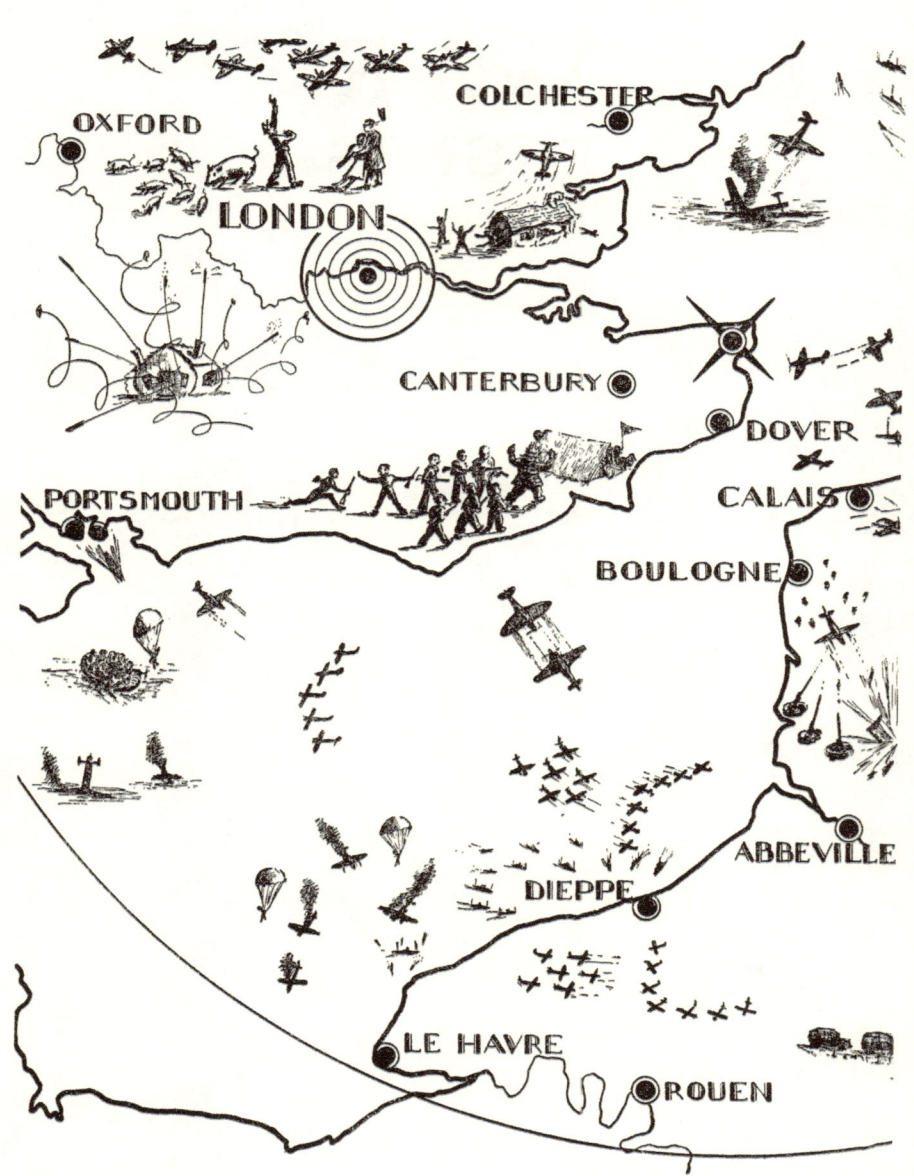

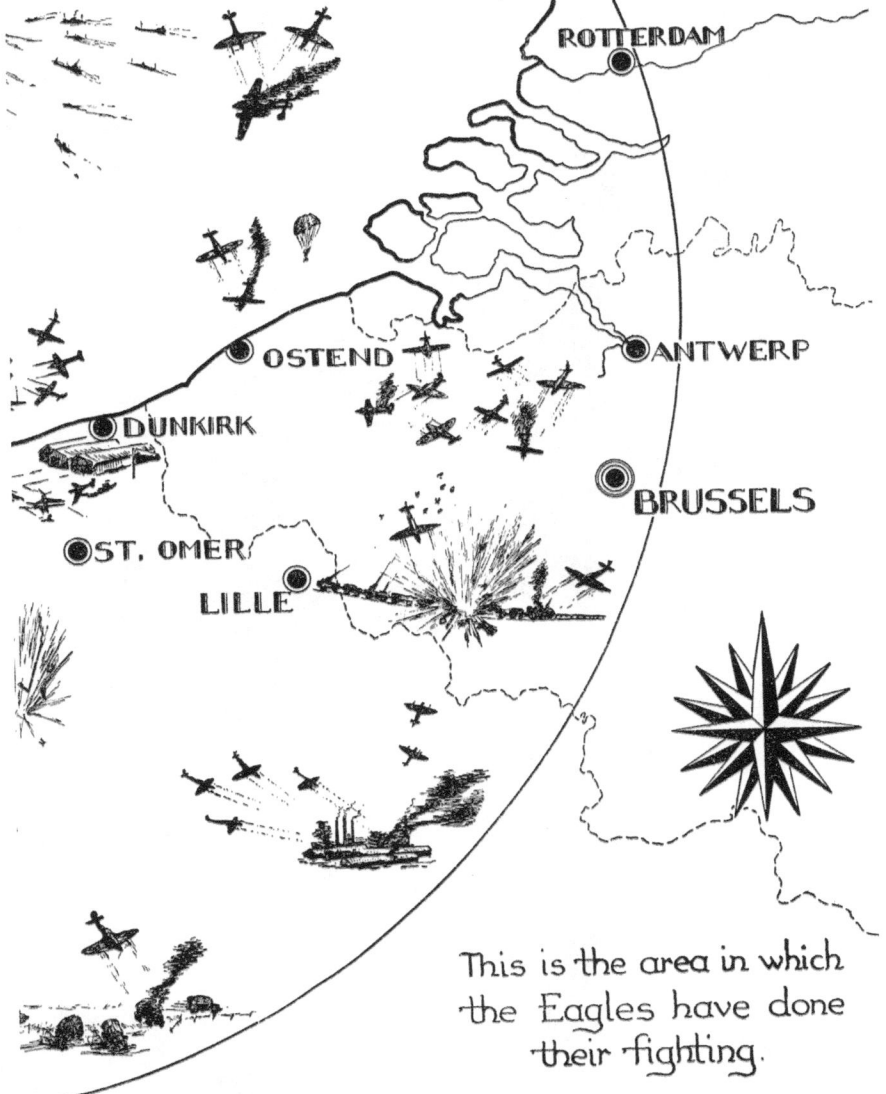

ROTTERDAM

OSTEND

ANTWERP

DUNKIRK

BRUSSELS

ST. OMER

LILLE

This is the area in which
the Eagles have done
their fighting.

EAGLE SQUADRON: The squadron flag flying at an airdrome in England. In the corner of the picture is one of the ground guns, constantly manned and ready to answer any German bomber or fighter who might attempt to strafe the drome.

WAR
EAGLES

*The Story of the
Eagle Squadron*

James Saxon Childers
Colonel, United States Army Air Forces

COACHWHIP PUBLICATIONS
Greenville, Ohio

War Eagles, by James Saxon Childers
© 2023 Coachwhip Publications edition

First published 1943
James Saxon Childers, 1899-1965
CoachwhipBooks.com

ISBN 1-61646-549-2
ISBN-13 978-1-61646-549-0

Acknowledgments

First, of course, I must thank Air Ministry for granting me access to official records of the Eagle Squadron. I should like to thank, too, all British officials, both of Air Ministry and elsewhere, who with characteristic courtesy and friendship have helped me in so many ways.

I suppose next I should thank Squadron Leader Robinson, Lieutenant Colonel Peterson, and Major Daymond, who read the manuscript and, in their editing, gave proof that they know more about the Eagle Squadron than any other three living men.

All the Eagles themselves were helpful, and I am grateful to them. I must particularly thank Captain Strickland, who took a month's leave and spent it in my home, working with me until late at night, writing and editing as enthusiastically and as carefully as if the book had been his own.

I should like to thank Linda Bramley, who made the drawings for the book. Miss Bramley, an English artist, has been forced by the war temporarily to put aside her paint brushes and now is working at Headquarters of the American Air Force. She takes dictation, types, files, draws superb illustrations, cheerfully sews on buttons, and precisely mends the uniforms of the men in her department.

James C. F. Mancuso, once a photographer in Cincinnati and now an officer in the American Air Force, took most of the photographs in the book. He knows that I appreciate his help.

The other photographs were furnished me by a most cooperative Photograph Division of the British Ministry of Information, by Peter Masefield, editor of *Aeroplane,* by Fayer, the London photographer, and others. I wish to thank them sincerely.

Finally, I must thank all officers and men of Intelligence Division, Headquarters, Eighth Air Force, who have listened so patiently as frequently I have talked of the Eagle Squadron, probably sometimes repeating myself while telling of these lovable and adventurous American boys who came over to see what it was all about, and remained to establish a record unexcelled in the Royal Air Force.

J. S. C.

A Letter

*A Letter from Major G. A. Daymond, DFC and Bar,
Commanding Officer, 71 (Eagle) Squadron*

Dear Colonel Jim:

I've just finished reading the manuscript of our book, and I'm proud of it. At last something has been written about the Eagle Squadron that is true and sincere. You've produced the best story I could imagine and it's a pleasure to read a record we won't have to live down.

Your description of our odd and assorted episodes is so accurate that I was filled with nostalgia as I relived those wonderful days with all my old pals. I especially liked the story of our invasion practices—never in the history of horse play have so many been so confused by so few. I honestly think you've got the spirit of the Eagles just right; in our seriousness and in our damned foolishness you've understood us and somehow you've managed to get it all on paper. Thanks, really, and from all of us.

Incidentally, when will we have the pleasure of your remarkable countenance around here again? It would be a particular pleasure to see you now because things are letting up a bit. I saw one squat, myopic dreg of the Luftwaffe the other day but I couldn't catch him before he leapt into a cloud, and so there was no fun.

We had a powerful "do" in London the other night. We all took in "Du Barry was a Lady." Afterward the usual dynamiting of the West End took place, and then came the bleary-eyed journey home. Sorry I didn't give you a buzz, but the activity was too intense.

Once again, Colonel, congratulations on title book, it's really good. You have our biggest vote of thanks. I hope to see you and Robbie soon. In the meantime, keep weaving.

Yours,

                                        Gus

1

We were at Robinson's. We were sitting there in the garden having tea. The roses and the hydrangea and all the
flowers were thick about us in their beds, and Daymond
was talking. He was looking up at the clouds, and he was
saying: "Those are good clouds up there today. I'd like to
be up there tearing around in those clouds."

"It was like that yesterday," Peterson said.

"Were you out yesterday?" Robinson asked.

"Yes," Daymond said.

"Get anything?"

"We didn't get any planes, but we had a pretty lively
time."

"What do you mean by that?" I asked.

"I mean I got to shoot my guns," Daymond said.

But I wasn't satisfied, and later as we were walking in
the garden I asked him to tell what he meant. Just as he
began to tell me, Peterson's wife—she and Pete had been
married for two weeks—pushed Daymond out of the path,
and he took out after her and chased her until he caught
her, and they tussled like any other pair of youngsters full
of life and playing. After Daymond had given Pete's wife a
whacking for having pushed him, we all went on walking
through the garden once more.

"What were you shooting at?" I asked.

"At an alcohol factory," Daymond said. He was straightening his tie after his tussle with Audrey. "It used to be a sugar beet factory, but the Germans took it away from the French. They've taken away all the sugar beet factories from the French, and now they make alcohol in them for munitions."

"And you shot it up?"

"Yes. The whole squadron went over to shoot up whatever we could find. We went in low, just over the treetops, and I found this alcohol factory and flew round it a couple of times firing at the condensation coils with my cannons and sort of blasted hell out of it, until brown smoke was pouring out and I knew it was finished. Then I flew on toward the coast and saw a man with a surveying instrument in a field, and I started to kill him and flew at him to kill him, but when I was about to push the button I saw he was a defenseless man without a gun of any kind, so I thought I'd let him live and I did. Then I flew on out, and I saw about fifteen men in a gun emplacement. I was flying low and coming at them from behind, and they didn't see me, and I opened with everything at three hundred yards. I flew straight at them firing everything until I was almost in amongst them, and arms and heads and legs were flying every which-a-way. There was one body that sort of leapt up into the air and looped the loop and the head went sailing off in the other direction. I reckon I shot that fellow up into a lot of pieces, all right. Then I flew on out over the Channel and came on home."

"That was yesterday afternoon," I said.

"Yes," he said, as he started chasing Audrey again because she had slipped up behind him and stuck a nettle against the back of his neck. They went running all over the field until he caught her again and this time tumbled her down and gave her a good spanking, both of them laughing and having a lot of fun playing.

2

Later that evening we were sitting before the fire after supper, and there were four others who had come in. The Eagles themselves and anyone associated with the Eagle Squadron are forever dropping in at Robinson's, coming in for a meal or to take one of the beds, and when the beds run out they take one of the cots that stand ready in the ballroom of the big house and the boys go in and help themselves.

Four others had come up: two more boys from the squadron, Oscar Coen and M. C. McPharlin—"Wee Michael"—and two WAAF officers.

These two girls had been stationed for a long time on the same station with the Eagle Squadron, and they knew all the Eagles, and I could see they loved to talk about them. Not that they were in love with any individual boy in the squadron, but they knew them for a picturesque, adventurous lot, and in their sheltered English life before the war they had never known or even imagined such boys as these lads who would come to the WAAF officers' mess and sprawl on the sofas or the floor, while the girls went on doing whatever they had been doing, even if it was something as feminine as drying their hair before the fire or polishing their nails. Before the war and before they met the American Eagles, these English girls and their parents would have been shocked by such a genuine relationship between boys and girls in their early twenties. The girls had never before known boys like the Americans, who would lie there and talk for a while and maybe drink some beer until it began to get late, and Newton Anderson from Chicago would turn on the gramophone and play the music he liked best; it was always good music, and the boys would listen without moving. Then maybe one of the boys—probably Andy again—would read some poetry, or maybe one of the girls would read, and by that time half the boys would be asleep because they were tired after the flying of the day and maybe some fighting. Then late the boys would get up and stretch and say good night and go off to their quarters. But the next night they would come back, and for a while they would talk about the big battle of the afternoon when Sam Mauriello—"Uncle Sam," an Italian boy from New York—had shot down a Jerry in flames, and they would tell how Sam did it, making swooping gestures with their hands to show how the German dived and twisted and took all kinds of evasive action, but Sam stayed on his tail until he got him in his sights and then gave him a two-second squirt with his cannons, and the German burst into flames and went headlong into the drink—"the drink" being the English Channel or the North Sea. Then after the battles of the day had been fought again before the fire and all the funny happenings had been told, the boys would quiet down and perhaps talk about Cleveland, Ohio, and Louisville, Kentucky, and California, until somebody turned on the gramophone.

Not that I meant it, but I said that the reason the two WAAF officers liked the Eagles so much was solely a matter of geography. The American boys were different from English boys. They spoke with a different kind of voice and used different words, and their slang was different They had stories to tell of long-horned cattle on the Texas plains where you could lose the whole of England. They talked about Florida and New York and places the girls liked to hear about. And sometimes the boys swaggered about their women because they were more experienced that way than English boys, and of course such talk interested the English girls; it seemed to make these young chaps glamorous and something like the swashbucklers of other days, the fellows who made a *beau geste* of piercing the heart of a man by day and the heart of a lady by night. I said that geography and a different background from English boys and a kind of unseen white plume in their hats, like the rakish white plume in Cyrano's hat, were the reasons the English girls, the WAAF officers, liked these American fliers who called on them at night and talked until they were tired, while the English girls listened and were fascinated.

But the WAAF officers denied what I said and would have none of it. They argued with me, and throughout the evening they struck back every chance they got, striking at me in their talk for saying they were interested in the Eagles chiefly because of geography. Three days later Robinson got a letter from one of the girls:

My dear Robbie:
I did enjoy last night. Such a lovely supper and such a wonderful bed. I love coming up to your home because I always know I'll have good food and a real bed, and while they are not the only reasons I come, I must admit they play their part.

I'm afraid we were no help at all to Col. Jim in his quest for the lowdown, from the WAAF point of view, on the Eagles. You know it's funny, but I wish he weren't writing a book about the Eagles—any other squadron, but not the Eagles, not my squadron. How can you put them into print? Surely the essential would be lost. Could you show

Mr. Smith of Memphis or Mr. Jones of New Orleans—as
Col. Jim said he wanted to—the Eagles as they really are?
Could you show, for instance, that Pete is really two per-
sons?

There is the Pete who grabs you and dances a whole pile
of records without stopping. And sits on the floor drinking beer and smiling in that boyish way of his, who likes
eating cheese with sweet biscuits and laughs the way people of our age—his and mine—should laugh. And there's
another Pete who is so much older than twenty-two, a Pete
that funnily enough I love best, when he stands up with the
squadron on their feet facing him, Pete in his boots and
Mae West, with that shockingly operational hat over one
eye, briefing the boys for the three o'clock bus service to
Lille or St. Omer or Abbeville, or wherever they are flying
that afternoon. A much older Pete, who doesn't smile but
whose eyes seem to flick over all those faces before him as
though by doing so he could see into their minds and find
out whether they have understood him. Then when he has
finished he might say: "Gray."

And Jerko would answer: "Yes, sir."

"Gray, this afternoon for Christ's sake keep up. You're
going to lag behind just once too often and they're going
to let you have it."

They'd all laugh and move toward the door of the dispersal hut and go on out and climb into their aeroplanes.
Then we girls at the WAAF mess would be standing on the
roof and we'd count them as they rose from the ground
and would wave to them as they flew low over us, flying
at us almost as if they were going to dive in amongst us,
then zooming up and going on off on the daily bus service.

After they had gone, flying a tight formation, we'd
come down and get on with our jobs, but before they were
due back we'd be on the roof again, smoking and talking
and pretending we were there for no particular reason.

We'd all be smoking a little fast and our laughs would be short and quick until we saw them appear somewhere in the sky. Then we'd wait until we could see the individual planes instead of just the formation, and we'd count them in. All of us would watch them come lower and make for the runway, and some girl would see the marking on the fuselage, the big letter painted there, and she would say: "That's 'G.' 'G' is back." And we'd all know that Shorty Keough was flying that particular plane that particular afternoon, and someone would say: "Shorty is back." Then we'd identify another plane and maybe some girl was fond of the boy flying that plane and you would see the tenseness go out of her and she would start breathing again. Then all the planes would land except one, and perhaps some girl was in love with the boy flying the plane that was missing and she would sort of stand there and maybe one of us would say something, maybe one of us would touch her and kind of bring her back, and she would manage a smile; but she never burst into tears or too much showed her feelings because we all knew that sooner or later each of these boys might get it, and then it would be some other girl standing there, and each of us would think that next time it will be me waiting for a plane that didn't come back.

And how could you put Oscar on paper? The way he had of coming up to you, and putting his hand on your shoulder and half turning you toward him saying, "Well, pal." And sometimes he would sort of give you a little pat, not in a too-familiar way, not in any way that meant anything it shouldn't, just a little pat that said, "We're really pals, aren't we?" And how could you describe his smile and the way he used to get tremendously excited? I remember the way he was the day we shot down five. I remember all the boys landing and climbing out of their planes and not even bothering to look at the bullet holes through

their own planes but rushing over to dispersal and standing there talking and fighting the battle all over with their
hands, making those gestures, and little Oscar standing on
the edge of the mob jumping up and down and showing
how he had "shot the literal hell out of the beggar who was
trying to get on Pete's tail."

And how can you convey the feelings I used to get
when I sat there listening to Lulu and Jim DuFour playing
duets, sitting there in their boots and Mae Wests ready for
a scramble, and then the signal coming through and they
dashing off to climb into their aeroplanes, leaving only
an overturned chair and an unfinished tune, which someone else, getting on with her job on the ground half an
hour later, would probably still be whistling unconscious-
ly when Jim and Lulu were at twenty thousand feet roaring
away toward battle.

Just a bunch of adventure-loving kids! Just a bunch
of palookas! Last night someone tried to explain them by
saying they were away from their homes and their fami-
lies and that we liked to mother them. And Col. Jim said
they appealed to us because they were out of their setting
and had a fascinating accent. That may be true, but the
Canadians are also away from their homes and to my ears
they have a very similar accent. No, Robbie, they may
be just a happy-go-lucky bunch of fightin' fools, another
gang of boys flying and fighting just for the hell of it,
but to us who really know them, they are special—it's just
one of those things. You see, a certain bunch of people
met another bunch of people and we were all friends. We
don't think the Eagles are heroes any more than our own
countrymen are heroes, but starting with the most awful
handicap of prejudice against them, they won first our
friendship, then our love, and later our very genuine respect for them as fliers and fighters with such guts as few
fighters have ever shown.

Gosh, I've got terribly long-winded over my squadron, but you understand. You, too, know the kind of chaps they are. And you're English like me, and like all the other English people who've met the Eagles we know there is something about them different from any other crowd of boys. Maybe it's because on the ground they're only boys, while in the air they're men and brave men pressing home their attacks until they give it to Jerry or get it themselves.

OUTSIDE DISPERSAL: At this airdrome in England the American boys built their own "Times Square" outside their dispersal hut. On warm days they lie about on the grass of the "square" waiting for the welcome cry of "scramble."

3

I went to a station where the Eagles were living, and after living with them for a while I learned something about the beginning of the first Eagle Squadron, how it came into being back in the middle of 1940.

At that time the United States was still neutral, but there were some American boys who wanted to get into the RAF and into the fighting. Technically, they couldn't, because we were a neutral country. But actually they slipped over into Canada and enlisted. Word got around about what was happening and other American boys slipped into Canada. From there they sailed for England, and the first of them landed at Southampton, August 21, 1940.

At first there was not much for these new boys to do. At the time, the Battle of Britain was on, and everybody was too busy fighting to bother about training new boys in battle tactics. Everybody who had ever flown a fighter plane in England was now up fighting the Germans that hourly swarmed over England to bring her to her knees, swarming over to carry out Goering's boast and blast a highway over which Hitler would ride as he came to that dinner he has not yet eaten in Buckingham Palace. For a long time, for months, the young Eagles sat around waiting. Until they became restless and went to the commanding

officers and said they had come to fight and not sit, and
what about it?

So they gave the boys training—as much as they could
with the instructors that were available. But most of the
instructors were still fighting. They were going up at daybreak and coming down to land and have their planes
refueled and going up again, carrying on like this from
daylight to dark and doing it day after day, until as their
planes were being refueled they fell asleep and had to be
waked to go up again to meet the new wave of fresh fighters that Goering was sending over: hundreds and hundreds
of them to be met by this handful of dead-tired pilots
flying their ragged planes, perhaps with a bullet hole or
two not yet patched from the last fight, going up to shoot
the Germans down, then land, refuel, and fly off to battle
again.

After a period of training, the Eagles were put on operational flying; they were told to stand by for the signal
that would send them up for their first battle.

"And will I ever forget that signal!" Gussie Daymond
said. "When it came through we all jumped up and started running, and most of us were just running in circles. I
fell flat on my face and all my maps spilled out, and I was
trying to pick them up but my fingers wouldn't work, so
I said to hell with them, and I climbed into my airplane
and took off without any maps. My throat was tight and
my lips were dry, and I was plenty scared because I knew
the whole damned Luftwaffe was upstairs just waiting to
pounce on us, and particularly on me!"

Their course on this first scramble lay to the south
across Canterbury and toward Calais.

"I was flying along scared and excited," said Oscar,
"when suddenly I was saying, 'Good God, there's France!'
I was having my first sight of France when *fruuump!*—
and a Messerschmitt 109 went past me. I felt him go by,

INSIDE DISPERSAL: *Above:* The boys in the old days when Bill
Taylor was squadron commander. Robbie is at the extreme left. Gus is in front
of the door, carrying on the "usual Daymond quack." Taylor himself is at the
extreme right. *Below:* A year later inside dispersal are all new faces. *Left to
right, seated:* Andrews; Boock; Sweep, Boock's dog; and Whitlow. *Standing:*
Leader, the dispersal hut telephone operator; and Mills. Even though faces
have changed, the costume remains the same: the inevitable Mae West and
boots as the boys wait for the order to "scramble."

and when I looked to see where he had come from, I saw another that had come from God knows where and was on my tail shooting the absolute hell out of me. Then the sky was full of 109's, and everybody was quacking like mad over the R/T"—the radio telephone—"and I cut away somehow and streaked for home."

That evening there was a lot of talk in the Eagles' mess. "We quacked late that night," Daymond said. "We sat around, and we reckoned the Jerries had tossed a pretty emphatic amount of lead at us that day, and we were scared stiff. Before we had gone up and got shot at, before we had been in battle, we'd thought we were pretty hot stuff. Now we knew just how green we were. Those Jerries had piddled on us from every angle and all we did was promenade around in the sky with our guns squirting off at nothing but the sky. We were damned lucky to be alive, and we knew it."

Their first experience in battle taught them, and aged them. Then they met death. And that taught them and aged them, too.

When the American boys left California and Texas, when they left Omaha and Richmond and New Haven, they had no thought of being shot down into the English Channel; they had no thought of dying. Death was to be no part of their adventure, and they gave it no consideration. There were to be airplanes and flying and fighting and glory, but not death.

Then in January, 1941, Phil Lechrone from Illinois was killed. They were all up that day, the whole squadron, flying at twenty thousand feet, when suddenly Phil fell off into a steep dive. The others followed him down, calling to him over the R/T and telling him to pull out. But for some reason he didn't, perhaps because his oxygen cut and he fainted. Anyhow he plowed in, and his pals, circling above him, saw him crash and his plane crumple like paper.

Not long after that day two of the Eagles, Bud Orbison and another man, were off somewhere flying when the weather closed in. The sky turned into a gray muck, and the clouds came down almost to the ground.

"No one can fly in such filthy weather," the other Eagles said, as they sat around dispersal waiting. "No one can fly in weather like this. Even the birds are walking."

Quick to detect their growing tension as the boys worried about Orbison and the man with him, their commanding officer ordered Robinson, the squadron intelligence officer, to begin a lecture on aircraft recognition, the art of recognizing a plane when it is still far off and determining whether it is friend or foe.

Robinson began talking, but he had hardly begun when they all heard two airplanes flying somewhere above them, circling the field low, searching for it, then going away. Only to come back again, coming in low, feeling for the landing field, then going away and the sound of the motors dimming.

Then from high above they heard the grinding, whirring rasp of a plane spinning down. One of the planes was out of control and was spinning until in the midst of the rasping sound there was a sudden silence.

"He spun in," said Mike Kolendorski, half rising from his chair.

"There's a lecture on," the English commander said.

And Robinson went on talking about aircraft recognition.

Then the door was flung open and the other Eagle who had been flying stalked into the room. He was dripping with rain.

"I've seen death," he said. "He spun in. Bud's dead."

"There's a lecture on," the commanding officer said.

And Robinson went on talking.

"SCRAMBLE"

"But he spun in. He's smashed to nothing. He's dead. I've seen death, I tell you."

"You're back just in time to hear the rest of the lecture. Sit down." He waited until the boy had sat down, sort of cowering there in the corner. Then the commanding officer looked back at Robinson. "Yes," he said.

And Robinson went on talking. . . .

These were the first two deaths in the squadron, and the Eagles left alive were shaken. For the first time they had looked on death among their own number, and they were a little unnerved. They had not yet developed that curious, bizarre attitude toward death which was to come after they had seen so many of their number shot down or dying in crashes. These first two deaths chiefly confused them and depressed them, and then, after each death, came the funeral.

The British made them state funerals, using the deaths of these two American boys to emphasize Anglo-American friendship, to make a gesture across the ocean just as we in America would have done had they been British boys killed in the United States. The whole Eagle Squadron and the officers of the station and high officials from Air Ministry lined up by sick quarters, and from there they received the coffin, and they placed it on a cart and covered it with the Union Jack. Dressed in service dress with black arm bands of mourning and marching slow time behind the gun carriage as the band played the solemn funeral march, the Eagles followed their comrades to the grave. But there was one of them who couldn't march slow time. That was Indian Jim Moore of Texas. This Indian boy could not march at the tempo the band played, and even in the funeral procession he walked with loping, springy steps as his Indian forefathers had walked over the plains of the American west.

After they buried their pals, the Eagles marched away in quick time, swinging along now to the quick march of living men. They all went back to the mess and to their tea, and, as the Cockney airmen about the station forever say, "Life went on."

But now it was a new kind of life. These boys had seen the "meat wagon" carry a pal's body away. They had seen death stride through their midst taking one of their number with him. They had looked into a coffin and into a grave, and not even the sound of the quick march could take from their ears the drone of the chaplain's voice, there beside the open grave.

These boys began, perhaps for the first time, to ask themselves why they had left Utah and Kentucky and Virginia to cross the ocean and risk their lives. For what? They began asking themselves that question: For what? And probably not one of them could answer. Or if he could, it was not the answer that was being published in the papers and spoken over the radio and used by the politician.

One night in London some of us went to the British premier of the Hollywood film, "Eagle Squadron." Never mind how completely Hollywood proved itself Hollywood in the making of the picture or how the Eagles themselves groaned as they watched the "bull unloaded." But the part of the picture that for the moment interests us is the opening, when Mr. Quentin Reynolds tells how these boys led the way across the sea, how in the vanguard of freedom they didn't wait for a declaration of war but came on their own to fight, that liberty might not perish from the earth . . . or some such stuff as that, even if those aren't the exact words.

Later that night Gus Daymond, who had been played up by Mr. Reynolds in the introduction, said to me: "You know they're going to keep on flinging that bull at us until some of it sticks. They're going to keep on telling us that hero rot until we believe it ourselves."

I have asked almost all the Eagles why they left the United States and came to England to enlist in the RAF. It is true that by no means all these boys are intellectually keen. Furthermore, one or two of them are blowhards that try to dramatize themselves and, as the British say, shoot a terrific line. But most of them are pretty savvy fellows: they know the answers. Yet not one of them has been able to tell me why he left home and joined the RAF. Two or three of these boys have positively brilliant minds, yet not even they can get into words why they left home. And I think there's a reason why they can't put it into words, why they can't phrase it.

You see, when a man is driven by a great ideal he knows why he acts. Paul said he heard the voice on the road to Damascus; he knew specifically why he changed his route, he knew the reason, and for the rest of his days he went about telling that reason. Joan of Arc heard voices. Any number of the other mystics have also listened to the voice within. Likewise, when a man seeks an ideal and doesn't find it within himself, he sets up a symbol of some kind and goes in search of it. The Knights of the Round Table sought, not the perfect life by name, but the Holy Grail. And the Crusaders sought not salvation but the True Cross.

The reason these boys scoff at talk of idealism, of their wish to keep the world free and make it noble, is that they left home for no reasons of idealism. They heard no voices crying out to them; they had no Holy Grail or True Cross to seek. And they are far too honest, too forthright, too damned near the ultimate truth of death, to forge in their own minds even a nebulous cup or cross. Nor is their silence prompted by the usual shyness of boys to admit idealism. The simple truth is that idealism played little, if any, part in their leaving home. These young fellows left home for the reason that young fellows have always left home.

There was for them, of course, the perennial excitement of what goes on beyond the horizon. There was, for these boys of their particular generation, the accentuated glamour of battle and heroes in battle. Loving airplanes as they do, they had read scores of books and magazines about the airplanes of the last war and the famous fighters who flew them. They all knew Guynemer and Foncke and Rickenbacker and Bishop and Richtofen; they could recite by heart the tales of the great air battles. And they dreamed of themselves some day becoming as their heroes had been. They knew of the Escadrille Lafayette with its thrilling history. And here was the Eagle Squadron. Here was another Escadrille Lafayette, a group of daredevil Americans going over to fight the Boche. Here was really a chance for them to play the lead in "Hells Angels," to play opposite alluring platinum blondes like Jean Harlow that they had seen in the picture and win them by incredible exploits in battle.

Besides this perfectly natural appeal of the glamorous there was another general reason why these American boys wanted to leave home and go to England. There was a Big Show going on, and they, like all normal boys, wanted to see it, to be a part of it. They didn't want to miss anything. So, a little more adventurous than the rest of the kids in the neighborhood, they packed up and left.

One or two of the boys had reasons a little more specific than a general desire to wander off in vague pursuit of adventure.

One was having girl trouble, and he thought the best way to rid himself of a troublesome girl was to join the RAF. Better the occasional battle in the air over England than the constant battle on the ground at home.

Another left home because he was a ne'er-do-well and owed a lot of money and couldn't pay it. He thought if

INSIDE THE COCKPIT: Having raced from the dispersal hut and leaped into his plane, the pilot is now ready to take off. The gunsight is immediately before the pilot's eyes and the firing buttons are within the small rectangle at his thumb.

he went abroad and proved himself, he could then return home and hold up his head once more.

There were others of the lot with equally personal reasons, but one of the main reasons they left home was that they, every one of them, are mad keen on airplanes and love flying above all else. They talk about gambling and whisky and women, the subjects all men talk about, and they talk of these subjects with a surety of knowledge and with the complete disillusionment that comes to the very young before the years bring back the solace and the excitement of dangerous companionship. But even their talk about women is calm. It is only when they talk of airplanes that their talk quickens and their gestures are sudden and involuntary and certain. These boys love airplanes, and the speed and the danger of airplanes, as men of quieter souls love their comfortable nightly wives.

A good number of Eagles wanted to fly airplanes in the American Army or Navy or Marine Corps. But they couldn't pass the tests. This one had a thumb and forefinger off. This one had bad eyes. This one was hard of hearing. This one had never been through high school, much less through college. They couldn't pass the tests, but they could fly airplanes and they were determined to fly them. They knew that England had no such reservoir of physically unblemished manhood as the one the United States could draw upon; they knew that England was taking men to fly its planes even if this man had only one arm and that one had no legs. Any one who could fly and fight was welcomed by England at the time when her whole men were being shot down like birds out of the sky.

Besides this love of airplanes, the Eagles were in love with speed. Some of them had driven automobiles on the race tracks of the world. Others had ridden motorcycles on the speedways. Still others had flown the fastest airplanes, and there was no way for them to experience more speed. But there was a way to add new excitement to the excitement of speed: they could add the excitement of battle. So they went to England and got into a battle plane that would dive at six hundred and fifty miles an hour, screaming down on to another plane, the guns blazing until the other plane burst into fire, and the boy behind the guns suddenly blacking out, the blood suddenly draining from his brain, and he, unconscious, falling until the blood was in his brain once more and he was flying level again, while still in the air the other plane was flaming as it plummeted toward the earth.

They may make some of that idealistic hero stuff stick some day. They may make some of the Eagles themselves believe it. But I doubt it. I doubt if they ever make these young fellows see themselves as noble dreamers going forth to free the world from tyranny and keep it free for democracy. If you tell them that, they will probably say: "Nuts, buddy, we came over here because we were tired of hanging around the corner drugstore at home and because we wanted to see what was going on. Didn't you ever hear of a kid running away from home to join the circus?"

4

Before the Eagles could prove themselves ready to be sent into battle, they had much to learn.

In the first place, most of them had to learn to fly. All of them could take a plane off the ground, circle the field, and put it down again. But they had to learn really to fly, to make an airplane answer their whim, their wish, almost their intuition. Some of them had lied about the number of hours they had flown in the States. They had said they were experienced pilots with hundreds of hours in the air. Back in 1940 England was so pressed for fliers that she didn't make too close an examination of an applicant's declaration, and some of the Eagles added a number of hours to their actual flying time and were then admitted to the RAF. Comparatively inexperienced, these boys had to be taught to fly, and to fly battle planes, until they could stand them on their noses and send them headlong toward the earth, until they could point them to the sky and climb so steeply that the planes seemed almost to hang by their propellers. They had to learn to twist and weave through the air, darting about, so that gunners from the ground couldn't bring them down with their ack-ack fire and Hun fighters in the air couldn't get an easy shot at a straight-flying target. And they learned fast enough, these Eagles. With their deep love of airplanes, they quickly

mastered even the tricky battle planes, and soon their flying instructors pronounced them ready.

But flying for the sake of flying only is for transport
pilots, for mail carriers, and for stunt pilots at air carnivals. Flying in battle is something else; it is a means of
getting armament into the air, getting aerial guns into
position to fire. A battle plane is to be considered not a
plane at all, but really a platform of guns. And though a
man be the greatest pilot in the world, he is worthless in
battle unless he is a good shot, unless he can hit a twisting, diving target at two or three hundred yards. Besides
learning to fly, these American boys had to learn to shoot.

And shooting from an airplane is different from any
other kind of shooting. You must hold your platform of
guns steady even though you may be diving at six hundred
miles an hour. You must reckon the speed of the other
plane and his angle of flight and his distance from you,
then you must aim at some point out in space where your
bullet will arrive at the same instant the enemy plane arrives and thus make the destroying contact. All this the
inexperienced Eagles had to learn.

They had to learn, too, the extremely difficult task of
controlling themselves, of restraining themselves. When
one first sees an enemy plane in the air, even though it
be half a mile away, the immediate desire is to press the
button, to begin firing at it. And while the cannon can
destroy at half a mile, the chance of a hit at that distance
is almost infinitesimal. So one must learn to nurture his
cannon fire and his machine-gun fire. The two cannon on
the most common type of English fighter plane are capable
of firing a total of only six seconds; the machine-guns, a
total of sixteen seconds. The excited pilot who blazes away
his precious ammunition at a distant enemy may quickly
find himself with empty guns, helpless before the attack of

some German who has been hiding in the sun and suddenly dives. These young pilots had to learn that any enemy aircraft beyond two hundred and fifty yards is out of good range and that the great aces of this war have held their fire, whenever possible, until they were within one hundred yards, two hundred yards at most, of their target. At that distance a quick squirt, only a second or two of fire, and the job is done: the enemy is destroyed.

One day at a station I was in the dark-room with some pilots of the Eagle Squadron. We were looking at combat pictures. Each fighter plane that goes up carries a ciné gun that operates as the cannon and machine-gun are fired. In this way a photographic record of each battle is made. In the dark-room, whenever a film was flashed that showed the enemy plane out of range, a far-off speck in the sky, the pilots made uncomplimentary sounds with their lips and razzed the pilot whose ciné gun was proving he had fired at only the horizon. But when a picture showed the full details of the enemy plane, even the Nazi cross fully visible at close range, the pilots would be quick to say their approval.

"That's the stuff."

"That's seeing the white of his eyes."

"That's where it ought to be—right up his behind."

One of the pictures opened with a German Ju 88, a bomber, at long range. But the Eagle pilot fired at it for only an instant. Then, dissatisfied with his range, he took his finger from the button. When next the film was exposed, it showed the Eagle guns almost into the German's tail fin. An instant later the enemy plane seemed just to fall apart and the parts to catch fire and blaze. The other Eagles in the room cheered such flying and such shooting.

"That's the stuff to give 'em. Get it up their bungs, then give 'em a squirt."

As the boys were crying out their approval, the pieces of the big bomber in the picture were falling to earth, blazing, and the fighter pilot was following: perhaps to make certain that nothing escaped, though nothing could have escaped from the burning wreckage that was plummeting down.

Besides learning to fly and to shoot, the Eagles had to learn the most difficult and exacting art of recognition: they had to learn to recognize airplanes when they are little more than specks in the sky. When a fighter pilot sees a distant plane he must know instantly whether it be friend or foe. If it is a friend, he can ignore it, but if it is an enemy aircraft, he must begin immediately maneuvering for the attack. The pilot who recognizes his enemy first, and who first maneuvers for position, has a terrific advantage in the coming battle. An air fight is something like a game of chess: one move is counteracted by another, but he who takes his opponent unawares, who makes the first thrust into enemy territory, has an advantage that may well lead to the checkmate of the king or the death of the enemy.

In a zone of battle, such as that over the English Channel, there are scores of planes that may be seen at any time. A fighter pilot must recognize each of them the moment he sees it. He must know at a swift glance if it be German, Italian, English, or American. He must know every plane and the distinguishing characteristic of each.

Learning these different battle planes seems a hopeless task for the beginner, but in time one comes to know them and to recognize them in the sky as old friends. I remember how I learned the difference between the Spitfire and the Hurricane. Of course now to me the difference is very apparent, but at one time I couldn't distinguish one from the other. I was sitting with a WAAF officer near an RAF station. A plane came out of the clouds and went back in again.

"Was that a Spitfire?" I asked.

"Oh, no," she said. "That was a Hurry bomber. Didn't you see? It was like a humped old man, all hunched up in the sky. While a Spitfire is clean and swift and beautiful like a bird."

The next time I saw a Hurricane I looked, and I saw the hump on its back. So I came to know that particular plane.

There is something equally distinguishing about almost every plane. The German Me 109E, for instance, is described by Gus Daymond as a cigar with two razor blades stuck in it for wings. And if you'll look at a picture of this plane you'll see that its body is long and narrow like a cigar, its wings rectangular and blunt at the end like razor blades.

Then there is the German Heinkel, with its two engines and its heavily-glazed nose absolutely in line with one another. And the German Focke-Wulf 190 with its carrot-shaped body. The Junkers 88 with its wings shaped like a coffin. The German Dornier with its heart-shaped nose and a body long and narrow like a flying pencil. And the Messerschmitt 210 with its hood like a whale's back and its tail fin like a clown's hat.

All these facts about these airplanes, and hundreds of other facts about other airplanes, must be known by a fighter pilot as a man knows his own name, without having to stop to think about it. The Eagles learned these facts. Forever in love with airplanes, they studied models and silhouettes and pictures until they knew the details of every battle plane that flies. Some of these boys became absolute encyclopedias of knowledge about airplanes, knowing instantly the wing span, the armament, flying speed, diving speed, climbing speed of any battle plane that could be mentioned. As a matter of fact, they discovered it was necessary for them to know all these facts: their lives depended upon it. Some day if they didn't recognize

HEINKEL 111

FOCKE-WULF 190

DORNIER 215

MESSERSCHMITT
109E

JUNKERS 88

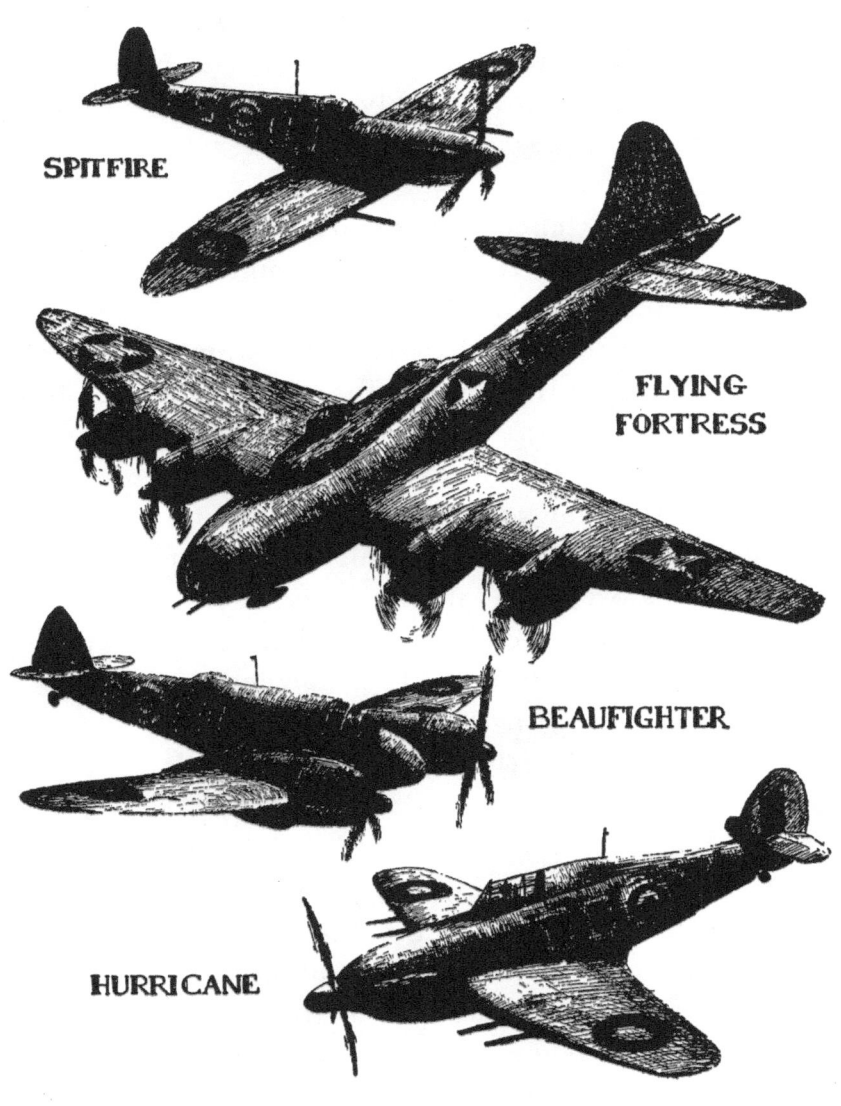

SPITFIRE

FLYING
FORTRESS

BEAUFIGHTER

HURRICANE

WAR PLANES

a "bandit" quickly enough, the Hun would spot them first and maneuver into position; then he would be on their tail and his guns emptying into them.

But even all this study and practice was not enough. Regardless of how well they could fly, or how straight they could shoot, or how quickly they could recognize the enemy, one factor was still lacking—they lacked experience in battle.

In their inexperience their greatest battle weakness was their inability to see. It has been estimated that even the most experienced pilot sees only seven or eight per cent of what goes on in an aerial battle. It all happens so terribly fast that sometimes it is over before the eye can see it and register it on the brain.

"A plane diving six hundred miles an hour past you—*fruuump!*—is past you and gone before you know it's there," said Sam Mauriello. "Your eyes just don't work that fast."

"But your bowels do," said another of the Eagles, then went on to tell of an embarrassing happening one afternoon when an FW 190 came from nowhere and an instant later was nowhere again.

Daymond told me that in the Squadron's first flight they were jumped by some Messerschmitt 109's. These German planes attacked. A battle was fought. The Germans withdrew. Yet when the squadron landed, four of the Eagle pilots knew nothing of the attack or the battle. They had not even seen a German plane, though a dozen of them had flown near enough to fire at them.

Peterson, who is one of the most capable and most canny of all the pilots, said that he flew on at least ten sweeps over France before he was able to look into the sky and positively identify a plane as a German plane.

"One of the hardest of all jobs for a fighter pilot is to train his eye to *see*," Peterson said. "Oh, I know everybody is up there looking as hard as he can. But looking and seeing is something different. You've got to look at one particular section of the sky and see it; you've got to know whether or not there's an enemy in that section. If there isn't, you move your eyes on to the next section. And so on round the circle. You're weaving your plane and shifting its direction so that you can forever be seeing new sky, and you're constantly turning your head and looking in every direction." Pete grinned as he said: "You've never seen a real rubber neck until you've seen mine when I'm flying over France."

Once they had learned to fly and to shoot, to recognize the enemy when he was far off, and to see him in his hurtling attack from above, below, or either side, then the Eagles were ready for battle; they were ready to prove themselves as fighter pilots in the Royal Air Force.

"ROBBIE"

5

Even after they had flown out to battle and actually been in battle, the Eagles still did not fully understand the seriousness of the new game they were playing. Before, it had been flying for the fun of flying, just for the hell of it. Furthermore, their guns had been fired only at meaningless targets. But now they were firing at men. Just as in return other guns were being fired at them. Like all inexperienced fighter pilots, they were slow to realize that they were actually being shot at. It is not easy to understand that somebody is trying to kill you, that somebody unknown to you is flying around in the sky waiting quite impersonally for a chance to slip up behind you and kill you.

"I remember the first time I saw a plane shot down," Gus Daymond told me. "We were flying above some bombers, and from God knows where some Me 109's dived past us, and the next instant they were in among the bombers shooting with all their guns. I saw the wings fall off one bomber and it went down, and I saw little balls of fire appear on the wing tips of another bomber, and then the whole thing was blazing and it went down, and I said to myself: 'Jumping Jesus, but this is a rough game.'"

A few days later the boys were over France again. This time they were flying with a Polish squadron, and suddenly

45

there was a terrific quacking from the Poles who had been jumped by some Me 109's. For a minute the Poles spoke in English, calling out over the R/T that bandits were approaching.

"Then things got really going and the Poles blew their gaskets and began to garble-garble among themselves in Polish, and we didn't know what the hell was happening," Daymond said. "I kept looking around with my head going like Donald Duck's, and the first thing I knew I saw a German plane going down with a Pole right on top of it shooting it into mighty small pieces. That Pole was surely in an ugly humor that morning, because he stayed right on the Jerry plane, and on the poor guy in it, and he kept on shooting and shooting. I told myself again that these guys were really playing for keeps. All at once it came over me that I was in the middle of a war, and for the first time I got scared.

"And it didn't help any about a minute later when one of our boys began to quack as loud as he could. A 109 had paddled up behind him and was smack on his tail shooting at him with cannon and machine-guns. And my pal—it was Sam Mauriello—was twisting and weaving through the sky yelling, 'Help! Help! This son-of-a-bitch is trying to kill me!'"

That night and for many nights afterwards, these boys from America sat around talking a little and thinking a lot. They had left home for travel and adventure and a date with a glamorous blonde. Instead, they found that each day they were near to keeping an appointment with the dark-eyed fellow who forever flew in, the invisible plane close behind them. Slowly they began to realize that the companion behind might some day fly nearer and take them into his plane, and then the Germans would announce that another body had been picked up on the

Dutch coast and was buried in Holland. This realization broke one or two of the boys.

One of them went up one day and turned back as the squadron left the English coast and started out over the Channel, the usual area of battle. He landed and reported that his engine had gone bad. The ground crew listened to the hum of the motors and heard nothing wrong, but they tuned it again just to make sure.

The next time this pilot went up, he turned back again at the coast. Again he reported that his engine had gone bad. Two days later when he turned back a third time, returning before the Channel was reached, every one knew what had happened. The boy himself knew at last. He understood that he could never go out into the battle area again: his nerves were gone. So he went to his commanding officer and admitted what had happened, and his name was taken from the battle list.

Then there was another who was also frightened, but he proved to be magnificent. Imaginative, forever looking inside himself, he knew quickly that he was afraid. His particular terror was the flak, the stuff the ground gunners shoot high into the air, the explosive shells that the gunners shoot at the planes and that burst in the midst of the formation, knocking holes in the wings and the fuselage and sometimes hitting the engine or the pilot himself; then the plane plunges down out of the sky, and sometimes it catches fire and the pilot is trapped in it, going down in the midst of the burning plane.

This American boy dreaded the flak. Strangely enough, he had no particular fear of enemy fighters. He said they were something he could see; they were tangible and he could oppose them; he could fight back and in the action of battle forget whatever fear might be within him. But this flak, streaking up from below, was an unseen hand reaching up to snatch him out of the sky, and he was terrified of it. Sometimes on the ground as he thought of it, he would tremble: his whole body would flinch as if drawing back suddenly from the exploding shells in the sky. But the next day he went up again and flew through the flak barrage. And the next day he went up again, flying over the German batteries, seeing the shells exploding about him like huge black flowers suddenly opening in the sky, feeling his plane rock from the force of the explosions, and sometimes coming down to find shell holes in his wings and fuselage. But next day he went up. And next day again. He was magnificent.

I have met this man. He is one of the bravest men I have ever known. He is still flying through the flak. And there are only four of us who know why sometimes as he sits quietly talking, he suddenly flinches and draws back.

While the realization of the imminence of violent death broke one or two of the boys, the others soon learned to go off to daily battle and ignore it. Death was something for the other guy, for the poor chap who got in the way of a bullet, who was unlucky. That couldn't happen to me, they each said. They tricked themselves by saying that, and they joked each other about who would get it first, each bolstering himself by believing: It won't happen to me. It'll be some other fellow.

Emboldened by such thinking, the young Eagles whose nerves had survived the first shock of battle went up for the second fight. And the third. And soon they began to win victories. One of the first of these victories was won by Gus Daymond, "Old Man Gus," who was nineteen years old at the time.

"There wasn't anything to it," Gus said. "This guy was just dumber than I was, that's all. He was sort of toodling along enjoying the view when I eased up behind him and gave him a squirt. Then like a dumb cluck he turned and exposed his belly, and I let him have it. It was so close I could see the details of his airplane, and I let go with everything, and the damned thing just fell apart.

"When I realized what I'd done, I sort of jumped and swallowed to get the lump out of my throat. There was a thrill in it, but at the same time there was confusion and remorse. I realized that I'd shot a plane and shot a man, and I was thinking about the poor guy being in trouble. I was sitting there sort of watching, hoping he would bale out, when all of a sudden some baby started to pour lead into me and I had to get powerfully busy to keep from getting my own pants shot off."

After this the squadron was fully operational and was in the thick of it, suffering its casualties and adding to its victories, running up a score that was to make the Eagle Squadron known and feared by the Germans and acclaimed in England as one of the greatest fighting teams in the history of the RAF.

One of the men chiefly responsible for the success of the Eagle Squadron is J. Roland Robinson. When the Eagles were first organized back in 1940, Robinson, who was an officer in the Royal Air Force as well as a Member of Parliament, was posted to the squadron as their intelligence officer. It was a job for which he was ideally suited. Knowing America and Americans and fully acquainted with the RAF and its traditions, Robinson was just the man to live with a bunch of rather temperamental, high-strung kids, each of whom in the beginning figured himself as pretty hot stuff.

A very wealthy man, Robinson allowed his wealth to play no part in his relationship with the boys of the squadron. Most of these young fellows were pretty hard up for cash, but Robinson let them work out their own financial salvation instead of acting as their banker and seeing them through their difficulties. Furthermore, when he was with them he cut his own living to the level of their pocket-books, and they respected him for it. Only when they went to his lovely home on the Heath high above London was there any apparent difference in their ways of living. But there at Robbie's home the Eagles found such luxury as some of them had never known. And, too, they found such a welcome as made their respect for Robinson turn into a kind of affection which is quickly apparent whenever these young Americans are with their slightly older English pal.

But if the boys themselves have an affection for Robinson, the Englishman has a feeling almost of love for these lads he lived with for a year and a half, sharing their hopes and their dreams and their fears, listening to them late at night sitting on the side of his bed telling the story of the day's battle, or the story of the girl back home who "has gone off and married another dude just because I'm not there," or the story of the well-hidden terror, the bottled-up fear that had to come out, and where better than in Robbie's room as the young pilot admitted he was almost funking the thought of the next battle with the Jerries waiting to shoot him down.

I've talked many an hour with Robinson, and a finer man I've seldom known. He is the perfect answer to this damned nonsense about the frigid reserve of Englishmen, about their lack of a sense of humor, about their superior attitude toward the boorish ways of Americans. He has given his heart and his keen brain to these American boys and would fight you, regardless of your size, if you made any slurring remark about their courage or their characters.

As an intelligence officer with the Squadron, Robbie's job was manifold. One part of it was "to brief" the boys each time they went out on an operation. He would meet them in the intelligence room and would show them on the wall-map the flight that was to be made that day. He would have the course drawn on the map and would show

them how, by flying that particular course, they would
avoid the areas where the German ground batteries were
the most numerous and the most deadly; he would show
how to fly between and around the ack-ack guns. Then he
would tell the purpose of the flight: to escort the bombers
on a bombing raid, or to sweep out over Occupied France
in a challenge to the German fighters to come up and
give battle. After he had finished his talk, the boys would
troop out of the intelligence hut and would go to their
airplanes, confident that good old Robbie had given them
the best information possible and knowing that his advice
about ack-ack, German fighter opposition and all the other
activities of the enemy was the best advice they could get.
Surely it was. Didn't it come from Robbie, their pal?

And when they came back from the sweep, Robbie
would be there on the field to greet them. He would look
at the planes as they were taxiing off the runways and see
which of them had fired their guns, which had blown the
adhesive tape from in front of the muzzles, the tape that
is put there to keep out dust and dirt while the aircraft
is on the ground. Seeing the planes whose guns had been
fired, Robbie would go to them and talk with the pilots,
listening to their stories of how they saw the Jerries and
how they dived on them and other Jerries got in the way
and then there was a hell of a scrap, planes turning and
trying to get into position and still other Germans coming
from somewhere and all of us taking a quick squirt and
the Huns blowing up or going down in flames. All this
being told not only with words but with the two-handed,
swooping, weaving gestures of the hands, one behind and
above the other, showing with the hands how the battle
was fought and won. Robbie would talk with all the boys
who had been in battle or had seen the battle, and he
would get the story from each of them. Sometimes there
would be as many as a dozen individual fights, and Robbie

would get them all. Then after the boys had quieted down, Robbie would go to his office, and write up the account of the day's fighting. He would write up each pilot's story, and it would become a part of the official history of the RAF.

With the most gracious permission of the British Air Ministry those records have been opened to us. This courtesy on the part of Air Ministry is but another of the hundreds of friendly gestures the British are daily making to American soldiers stationed in England. They are opening their records to me, an American army officer, that I may write about American boys who came over and fought wing-tip to wing-tip with British boys in our common Anglo-American fight. They are giving us these records in order that Americans back home may know how bravely these Eagles have fought, how fiercely they have smacked our common enemy, how well they have played their part in solidifying an essential relationship between British and American peoples. . . .

Before quoting from the records of the RAF, I should explain that when patrolling or going into battle a squadron usually flies in this formation:

		White		Blue
Red		I		
I				I
		II		
II				II
		III		
III				III
		IV		
IV				IV

The sections are named by the names of colors, and each pilot is called by his position: "Red III," "Blue IV," "White II," "Green I."

When two or more squadrons fly in formation, the formation is called a "wing."

Taken from RAF records, here are "Personal Combat Reports" dictated to Robinson by Eagle pilots immediately after landing from a battle in which they shot down five Huns:

SQUADRON LEADER MEARES, DFC

I was leading Blue Section. The squadron was flying as top cover for the wing; we were at 21,000 feet. We had crossed the French coast at Berck and were turning right over Hesdin when I saw about 20 Me 109's climbing underneath and ahead of the wing. The wing commander detailed 71 Squadron to attack.

I ordered Blue and Green sections to attack and using our superior height—about 3,000 feet—we dived on the Me's. I closed on the rear of one of the nearest section and gave a six second burst from dead astern. He started to pour glycol and I saw strikes all over the fuselage near the cockpit. He turned slowly to port and dived straight for the ground.

PILOT OFFICER McCOLPIN

I was Blue II in our formation. Just after crossing the French coast, going in at 21,000 feet, 20 Me 109's were sighted going south at about 18,000. They were climbing. Our leader gave orders for the attack, then dived on them himself.

While my leader was firing at the nearest 109 I overtook this plane from below and fired a half second burst at about 100 yards. The enemy aircraft then burst into flames due to my leader's firing.

I broke away to port and found myself in position for an attack on another 109E, so I gave him about 1½ or 2 second burst. He pulled up and dived with smoke pouring from him. He was seen to hit the ground, and as he was going down, I thought I saw the man bale out. Range of my attack: about 50-100 yards.

After breaking away I saw another Me 109 below, so I dived on him and followed him down to 3,000 feet, where I gave him a 1 second burst from 100 yards. Nothing happened so I followed him down, but he never pulled out and he hit the deck as I pulled up and left him.

I used only my cannon.

Pilot Officer Roscoe

I was Blue IV in the middle section of 71 Squadron. We crossed the French coast at 21,000 feet and observed a formation of 109's in front at about 17,000 feet. The Commanding Officer ordered Green and Blue Section to attack and we dived.

After Blue I and II had engaged, Blue III and myself observed two 109's off by themselves. We took after them and they dived away. I chased with full revs and boost and fired a short burst of cannon and machine-gun from long range. After several seconds the 109 pulled up and turned to port. I closed to 300-400 yards dead astern and emptied my cannons at him. I observed black smoke from his nose and I broke off due to lack of ammunition. I then went down with Blue III to about 1,000 feet and came home.

The Me 109 I had attacked was later seen to burst into flames and I claim it as destroyed.

Pilot Officer N. Anderson

I was Green I leading Green Black sections on an offensive sweep. Squadron crossed the French coast at Berck, and approximately eight miles inland Blue I reported bandits 3,000 feet below. I was ordered to attack the enemy's right-hand section.

I dived in to attack with Green and Black sections following in line astern. On approaching the rearmost bandit, a lone Me 109 crossed my nose. I decided to attack this aircraft and fired two bursts of approximately 2 seconds duration. These appeared to have had no effect, so I closed dead astern and fired many bursts, starting firing at 18,000 feet and following down to 4,000 feet. At no time was my range more than 150 yards.

At 4,000 feet I broke away to avoid collision with the bandit, and with my last burst, he noticeably shuddered and started straight for the earth.

Green II then fired a burst at the bandit and saw pieces falling from him.

This aircraft was seen to dive into the ground and it is claimed as destroyed.

PILOT OFFICER SCARBOROUGH

I was Green II. After we crossed the Coast of France the Commanding Officer gave the order to attack 109's climbing in front of us. My leader dived after one and I followed. He followed this Me 109E down to about 4,000 feet firing at close range.

I was afraid to fire before Green I pulled out, for fear of hitting him. When he did pull out I opened fire at 100 yards, and went on to close range. The right side of his tail came off and floated back past me. Next I saw an explosion on his right wing about three feet from the cockpit, and a large part of the wing came off and floated past me. I got another short burst into his left side and a large hole appeared in the port side of the cockpit.

I then pulled out and climbed back to 12,000 feet. But I could not see another enemy plane in sight so I came on home. . . .

THEIR BELOVED PUB—THE THATCHED: "The Germans have good cause to hate The Thatched."

In a history of the Eagle Squadron there is distinct humor in this particular battle.

It was fought October 2, 1941. The day before, an order had come through saying that weather reports were most unfavorable and that there would probably be no operational flying for at least a week. Orders were, therefore, that the older pilots of the squadron should be sent off for a week's rest. Elated, seven of the older chaps promptly packed up and left.

Next day the squadron, composed of virtually new boys, flew over France on merely a practice flight. No one dreamed the enemy would be out in such bad weather. Certainly no one dreamed he would be up in large enough numbers to give battle.

That night, some three hours after the battle had been fought, Pete and Oscar and some of the old boys sauntered into the bar at the Savoy Hotel. They'd already had a pretty good evening and were all set for further fun. Up rushed the Commander-in-Chief of Fighter Command. He took their hands and shook them hard.

"Good show, you chaps. Good show," he said. "Well done, Eagle Squadron. That's the stuff to give them."

The boys looked at him in bewilderment.

"It must have been absolutely terrific," said the Commander-in-Chief. "Tell me all about it."

"About what?" Pete asked.

"About what you did this afternoon. About all that stuff you knocked down this afternoon."

But all Peterson and his pals had done that afternoon was to go to a movie, and all they had knocked down was a few beers.

"What are you talking about?" they asked.

Then they heard the whole story with all its details.

They instantly rushed outside and went straight to Robbie's. There they waked Gus and Wee Michael, and an indignation meeting was held. Daymond was absolutely furious.

"Of all the bloody tricks," he quacked, stamping about the room in his pajamas. "Those little twerps shooting down five Jerries! They don't know their behinds from a hot rock, yet they shoot down five."

The old boys took it as a personal insult.

"What do they mean by doing that to us?"

"And we weren't even there to show them how!"

"We do all the hard work: we patrol until there're corns on our backsides, and nothing happens. As soon as we go away, the little squirts have all the fun."

"They can't do this to us. If they keep shooting down Jerries, there won't be any left for us."

And on and on into the night, bemoaning their bad luck at not having been in the battle, at not having had the chance to crack at Jerry.

6

While the older boys were holding their indignation meeting at Robbie's, the pilots who had been in battle that day were sitting at the station mess discussing the fight.

As the squadron had turned that afternoon to make its attack, turning in a downward, wheeling movement, the outside section found itself in an unfavorable position to attack. This section, therefore, was ordered to remain above and stay out of the fight. Strung out in line astern, the four pilots in the section could only stooge around above the battle, curse their bad luck at being left out, and count the Jerry planes as their pals shot them down.

"You guys did all right," said Pilot Officer Fessler that night. "Getting five was pretty damn good."

"Five!" said Squadron Leader Meares. "We put in claims for only four—the two McColpin got, the one I got, and the one Anderson and Scarborough shared."

"But what about Roscoe's? What about his?"

"Mine!" said Roscoe. "I didn't know I got one."

Then Pilot Officer Fessler and Flight Lieutenant Gilbert gave the evidence that enabled the squadron to make its full claim for the day. These two officers, sitting above looking down on the show, had seen Roscoe make his attack and they had seen smoke pour from the nose of the German plane. It was at this point in the fight, when Jerry's nose

59

was smoking, that Roscoe had to break off because of lack of ammunition. He did not see the end that was witnessed by Gilbert and Fessler; he did not see the enemy aircraft go down with smoke still pouring from it until suddenly it burst into flames and crashed. Had Fessler and Gilbert not been in position to see the complete destruction of the German plane, Roscoe would not have entered a claim for an aircraft destroyed, and the squadron, as well as Roscoe personally, would not have been credited with the victory.

Any claim for victory is made by a pilot immediately after he lands from battle. The squadron intelligence officer then takes down the facts, and, according to the evidence, he classifies the claim, giving credit for an aircraft "destroyed," "probably destroyed," or "damaged."

In the category "destroyed," the claim is allowed when the enemy aircraft is clearly seen to hit the ground or the sea, is seen to break up in the air or descend in flames, is forced to descend and is captured, or the pilot of a single-seater aircraft is seen to bale out.

The category of "probably destroyed" includes all enemy aircraft that are believed to have been destroyed, yet the actual destruction, though believed to be a certainty, is not seen.

The category of "damaged" covers cases in which the enemy aircraft is observed to be "considerably damaged"— the undercarriage is dropped, or the engines are stopped, or parts of the enemy aircraft are shot away. Damage may also be claimed if cannon shell, which are explosive, are seen to strike the enemy aircraft, even though no parts appear to be shot away or no flames are detected.

Daily we read in the newspapers that our fighters "destroyed" so many enemy aircraft. The figures reported in the newspapers are based, almost entirely, on claims made by the pilots themselves immediately after they come down from battle.

A pilot's word is itself sufficient to establish his claim, and no confirmation from any other source is necessary; if he said he shot down the plane, he is credited with the victory. An outsider might question the seeming looseness of such a system, might believe that frequently false claims are entered and credited. Actually, despite the natural keenness of each pilot to run up a big score, to become famous as an "Ace," there are probably few willful exaggerations of claims.

In the first place, the pilots themselves are honorable fellows, and lying merely for glory is too cheap a trick for men who are daily gambling with death. In the second place, there are numerous forms of confirmation, and if a pilot repeatedly claimed victories without any of them being confirmed, his word in time would be questioned. Ordinarily a pilot does not fight alone: ordinarily at least one other Allied plane is present, and the other pilot would witness the victory and confirm it. Then, too, there is the ciné gun: usually it is operating, and while it does not necessarily show every battle, it would sooner or later play its negative part in tripping a pilot whose camera never showed any enemy plane within firing range. Furthermore, if the fight took place over England, the wreckage of the destroyed plane would be found; or if it was fought over the Channel, some naval unit might well see the destroyed plane coming down, or, later, see and report wreckage in an area over which the pilot declared he fought. Finally, of course, there are the intelligence officers who first receive the reports and then the experts at Fighter Command who evaluate them; they are wise and experienced men who would be quick to detect the almost inevitable flaw in any false claim.

"During the time I was with the Eagles," Robinson said, "I do not believe a single battle was misrepresented. The boys were damned eager to have high individual scores and to add to the squadron's total victories, but I believe strongly that instead of exaggerating their claims, almost all pilots underestimate them."

After the intelligence officer of a squadron makes out his report with the claims included, the papers are sent to Group Headquarters and from there to Fighter Command. At either Group or Command any claim may be altered. For some technical reason, or for additional evidence received after the report was first sent in, the claim may be raised, reduced, or disallowed entirely. Of course, if a pilot flatly says he attacked a plane and it crashed in the sea, then no questions are asked. But if there are circumstances and facts which need evaluation, then the experts determine the category in which the claim is to be listed. For example, the original report sent in after the battle of October 2, 1941, showed Roscoe claiming only a "damage." But that night, after Gilbert and Fessler had reported seeing the plane crash, the original claim was altered to "destroyed" and was, of course, allowed.

One of the strangest of all claims came about as a result of a ciné film. A pilot had been in battle against a Focke-Wulf 190. He had dived on the plane and had opened fire. He saw pieces fly from the tail, but as he was firing, another FW 190 attacked him from the rear. Turning to look behind him, he still kept his finger on the button which fires the machine-guns and the cannon, and which exposes the ciné film.

When the pilot landed he reported the fight and made claim for only a "damaged." But when the film was developed it showed that in the moment the RAF pilot looked behind him yet still held his finger on the button, still fired his guns and exposed his camera, the German pilot had flung back his hood and climbed out. I saw this particular film, and one can plainly see the German jettisoning the hood of his plane and flinging off his helmet; then

A DORNIER IN ITS LAST DIVE: This photograph and the two facing page 45 were made by ciné cameras on the planes of victorious Allied fighters, the camera showing the German planes in flames or being shot to bits.

DEATH IN FOUR SCENES: A Focke-Wulf 190 has been hit and its undercarriage dropped. The object in the lower right-hand corner is the German pilot's helmet he has just jettisoned prior to bailing out.

The next exposure shows the helmet still not outside the camera's lens.

The RAF fighter has now gone in closer for the kill and is immediately on top of the plane.

The next instant the plane was blown out of the sky.

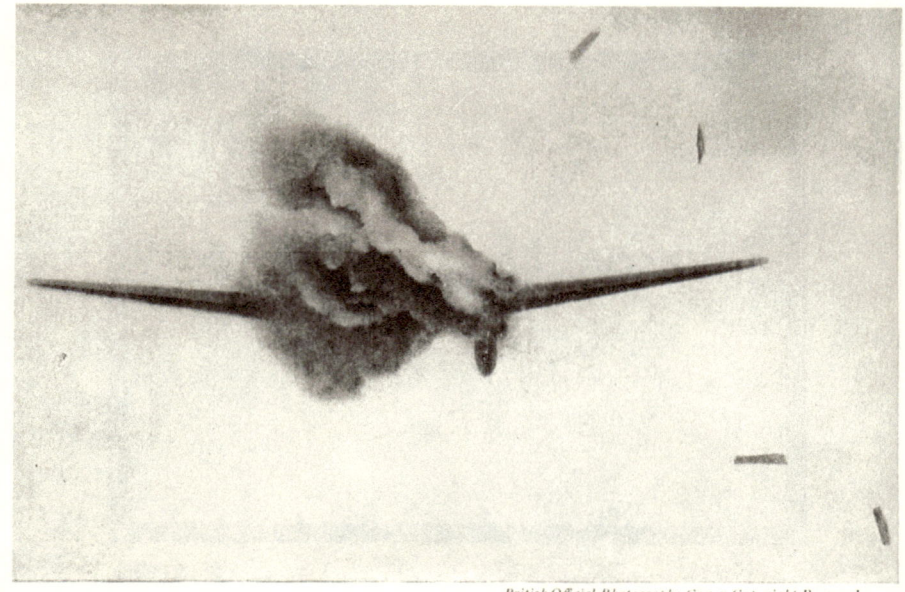

HEIL HITLER!

GERMAN BOMBER: With both engines on fire, its port engine bursting into flames, and with tracer bullets streaking over it, this German bomber is a death trap for its own crew in the night sky above England.

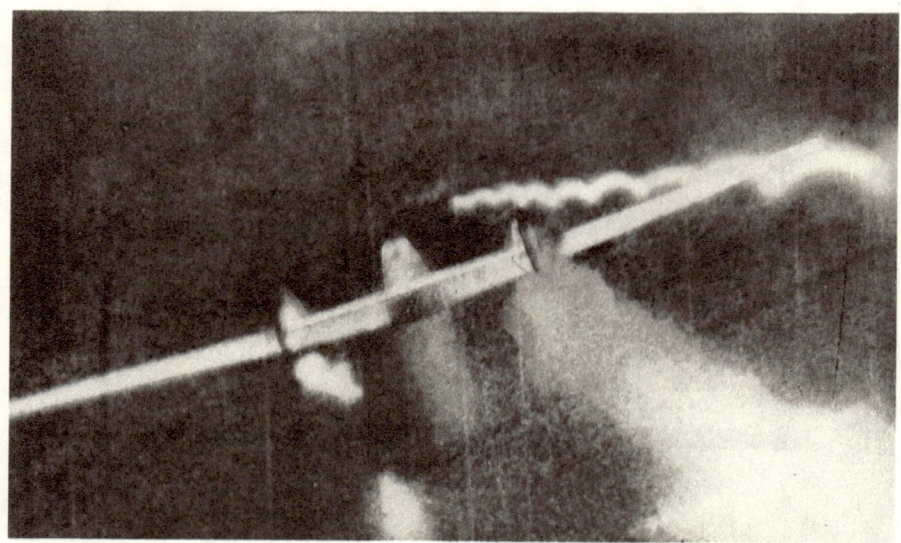

the helmet comes sailing back past the camera and the German pilot is half out of his plane when the exposure breaks off. Once the film was seen, the original claim of "damaged" was, of course, changed to "destroyed."

A claim made by Robinson for one of his Eagles was disallowed. In this particular fight the American boy shot the enemy plane at long range, but black smoke poured from it and it swooped down until one wing hit the sea. Then the Eagle—it was Gene Potter—in turning lost sight of the plane, and when he looked again, he saw no sign of it; it had disappeared. Robinson claimed a "destroyed." But Fighter Command ruled that while one wing of the plane was seen to hit the water and the plane itself almost certainly went into the sea, actual destruction had not been witnessed and the claim was therefore reduced to a probable.

With such careful examination given each claim, and with such severity of ruling on all of them, the chance of error is slight. The official Allied report of the day's fighting is, therefore, as near correct as it can be.

In contrast to the correctness of the Allied claims, some of the German operational claims are false and are known to be false when they are made. But strangely enough, the one German claim most commonly doubted by the general public is probably correct, according to the German way of scoring. The reports of the astonishing number of victories credited by the Luftwaffe to certain German fighters are probably accurate despite their almost fantastic figures. Yet while the famous Hun fighters have undoubtedly shot down many Allied planes and their score is truly high, there is no satisfactory way of comparing their records with those of the leading aces of the RAF. The reason is that the Germans do not keep score in the same way as the RAF; the Germans are not so precise in defining a "victory." Their classification is very loose, and a German ace may destroy three, probably destroy three, and damage three; yet he is credited with nine "victories."

Despite the inexactness in their claims, the German aces have been able to post astonishingly high scores even under RAF standards. There is a reason for their doing so.

The German Air Force disposed along the Western Front is made up of crack units, long experienced in all the practical aspects of war. Some of these units are led by pilots who have been on the battlefront almost constantly since they fought in Spain. Others are led by pilots who have been fighting since the first day the Germans flew over Poland. The operational pilots who today lead their staffels, their squadrons, against the RAF are usually fighters of long experience; many of them wear the Ritterkreuz, one of the highest decorations of the Luftwaffe.

English and American pilots who have fought against these German aces speak particularly of their outstanding ability at gunnery, especially their ability to shoot accurately at long range. One of the factors responsible for this accuracy at five hundred, even six hundred yards, is, of course, the high rate of fire from the German Mauser cannon—eight hundred rounds per minute, thirteen rounds a second—which permits a certain amount of "spraying." But the more important reason for the success of the famous German aces is that within the German staffels only the outstanding gunners are supposed to do the shooting.

While the other pilots act chiefly as guards, firing only when absolutely necessary, the chosen gunners are free to concentrate on their victims. For this reason the crack leaders of the Luftwaffe have almost phenomenal records of victories. Having the right to select the plane they wish to attack, and the right to place their companions in positions most advantageous to themselves, the master gunners can make their attacks under circumstances almost of their own choosing. It is the paramount duty of every other man in each staffel to protect the gunners. Regardless of what else is lost, the gunners must be saved: they are the absolute spearhead of the Luftwaffe's attack. This arrangement in fighting naturally leaves the other members of the staffel with less experience in gunnery, and makes them less able to defend themselves when not protected by their leaders' guns; but Goering believes the plan is good and he continues to use it. And the German aces, fighting under the most favorable conditions possible, continue to hand in reports of victories, while their defending companions are shot down about them.

Not all reports turned in by pilots of the RAF tell of battles in the air. Frequently pilots go off on low-flying expeditions, seeking any target that is important enough to be destroyed. Pilots who go on such trips frequently come home with a very varied bag.

There was, for instance, the report that Pilot Officer J. G. DuFour turned in November 5, 1941, after he had been over France:

> While flying north over France I encountered very heavy flak and in turning to avoid it, I got into a spin and came out in a dive directly above some gun positions south of Tingry. I fired at them with cannon and machine-guns at 450 yards, and in doing so hit a large hut, nearby. This hut proved to be an ammunition dump for it immediately went up with a blinding explosion.
>
> As I flew away I saw a convoy of army lorries on the road traveling north. I came down on the middle of the convoy and fired with cannon and machine-guns from 200 yards astern to point blank range at the first ten lorries. Three of them went off the road and

the second lorry in the convoy was left smoking.

On re-crossing the French coast, I fired a short burst and hit a listening horn.

I claim one ammunition dump and at least one motor lorry damaged.

Here is the report of another flight over Occupied France on which Pilot Officer DuFour and Pilot Officer Fessler attacked a variety of targets. The date was October 20, 1941. DuFour reporting:

Near Marquise I saw a freight train traveling north. I attacked with my machine-guns, giving a 1½ second burst from 150 yards to point blank range, but observed no results. I then turned and made a second attack from 300 yards to point blank range with cannon and machine-guns in a 2 second burst. The engine blew up and is claimed as destroyed.

Then Fessler takes up the story and tells of his activities:

I flew over a Hun landing-ground and saw between fifteen and twenty Me 109's on the ground. They were dispersed around the southern edge of the field, though there was one on the northern edge. I returned, and, flying at 300 feet, fired with cannon and machine-guns in a 1½ second burst from 350 yards to point blank at two Me 109's dispersed close together at the south end of the field.

I blew big holes in the first one and saw many pieces fall off the tail, wings and fuselage. The port wheel collapsed and the plane fell over. The starboard wheel then collapsed and the whole aircraft fell to the ground filled with holes. I claim this aircraft as destroyed on the ground. Large pieces fell off the second 109 which I claim as damaged.

I then crossed the field to the north and fired a 1½ second burst with cannon and machine-guns at another Me 109. I saw my fire enter the cockpit and the 109 burst into flames about 15 feet high. I claim this aircraft as destroyed.

On crossing the field I was fired at by about twelve or fifteen ack-ack guns without effect.

After leaving this landing field, I saw a goods train which I attacked. I gave a one second burst from 100 yards with cannon and machine-guns. The engine blew up and burst into flames. I claim it as destroyed.

As I was flying behind Calais, I saw ten barges and attacked them with a two second burst from my machine-guns from 200 yards, but observed no results.

In the midst of these personal combat reports are stories of experiences other than fighting. Here is a report from Fessler dated September 7, 1941:

When flying at 21,000 feet, after leaving Boulogne, Red I and I were attacked five times by four sections of Me 109's. The first four times we caused the German planes to withdraw by turning toward them to meet their attack.

During this time my oxygen mask kept slipping, and I continually had to put it back.

On the fifth attack by the Germans one of the 109's came close to Red I, and I was able to get in a second burst with my machine-guns and a 2 second burst with my cannon at 150 yards. I saw pieces blown off the 109 rear the cockpit and I claim it as damaged.

After this my oxygen mask slipped again, and I passed out. I am told that my plane went into a vertical dive and I recovered only in time to pull out of my dive within a few feet of the ground. Owing to the lack of oxygen at high altitude, I felt very nauseated, and did not fully recover until I was about half way across the channel. I crossed the French coast about one mile north of Boulogne flying at 50 feet. I landed to refuel at Shoreham before returning to North Weald.

Then there is the story of one of Michael McPharlin's battles. Wee Michael was fighting hunched down low in his seat, and something tragic almost happened. The fight took place April 4, 1942:

I was flying Blue II with 71 (Eagle) Squadron on a raid. After we had crossed the French coast I soon heard Blue I ask for permission to attack bandits below, and I saw four FW 190's beneath us.

I followed Blue I into the diving attack, maintaining a position behind and to his right. Blue I attacked one of the 190's. I was about to attack this same aircraft when I saw Blue I make a sudden turn, and thus come into the line of my gunsights. I was able to give the enemy aircraft a burst of only ¼ second with cannon and machine-guns from 200 yards range, and then I positioned my sights on a second FW 190 that was flying to the right.

With both hands on the control column to hold my aircraft steady in the dive. I opened fire, giving a burst of 1¼ seconds with cannon and machine-guns from 300-250 yards range. I observed strikes, a puff of black smoke and then a stream of white smoke pouring from the enemy aircraft. I claim this aircraft as damaged.

At this instant I caught a glimpse of an object approaching me from the right, coming more or less out of the sun, and I began to take violent evasive action even though I had not been able to identify the object as an aircraft owing to the speed of its descent.

I continued my dive and now was able to see that the object was an enemy aircraft which began firing, giving me a burst that went to my right. I continued diving, and looking back I saw that I had evaded the bandit. I then attempted to pull out of my dive. But I was flying in a crouched position and in some way my gear jammed with my hand on the control column, holding the aircraft in its terrific dive. It was at this time that, owing to the force of the dive, my panel blew out, and I thought I had been hit. In some way I managed to free myself from the locked position, and eased the stick back sufficiently to gain control of my aircraft again. I then came out of the dive and flew on across the French coast.

As I crossed the coast a barrage of flak was thrown at me. It burst on either side of me and two bursts appeared 300 yards in front of me, level with my aircraft. I continued evasive action, doing skidding turns until half way across the channel.

And here is the story Peterson told me of a raid that took him and Eddie Fletcher over the French coast one morning just at daybreak.

"We went on in," Pete said, "and were stooging along looking for something to shoot when we saw a train. It was longer than most trains, and I thought it looked worth knocking out, so I told Eddie over the R/T that we'd have a go at it. We began to dive, and then I saw that guns were mounted at different parts of the train and so I knew it was something special. I was mighty glad we found it, because they don't mount guns on just ordinary trains, and I knew this one was hauling special troops or special supplies, and I wanted to make mighty sure we got it. So we held our fire and they were shooting at us from the train with everything they had. The stuff was going past us plenty thick, but we waited until we couldn't miss and then we flew along beside the train and raked it with our cannons, getting in as close as we could and blazing away with everything we had at point-blank range. After we had fired the length of the train, I jerked up and began to climb.

"But Eddie acted like he wanted to ride on the goddam train and flew right at it, and when he was over it, all of a sudden it happened. That train just seemed to rise up in the air, all of it, engine and cars and all of it, and there was an orange and red glow as it lifted up in the air and disappeared, leaving a kind of pink haze over the place where there had been a train. You see, it was an ammunition train, and it blew up with the most God-awful bang you can imagine.

"And then Eddie began to quack. I've never heard such quacking over the R/T in all my life. Eddie had been so low over the train when it exploded that bits of it flew up and hit his plane, and one of the bits hit his engine and the glycol was streaming from it. With his cooling fluid pouring out, he knew his engine would soon be red hot and would freeze and quit. Eddie was quacking away telling me he had been hit and couldn't fly much longer and what the hell was he to do.

"I've never felt more helpless in all my life. There was Eddie, my pal, flying beside me, and I was in a perfectly good airplane and I was all right, but he was done for and I knew it, yet there wasn't anything I could do to help him. I could only tell him to jump before the blinking plane caught fire and maybe he couldn't get out before he himself was burned.

"He said: 'I don't see why the hell I ever left America,' and then I saw the hood of his plane go back and Eddie came tumbling out of it. He sort of twisted through the air, turning over slowly, and he was turning over that way when he went into a cloud and that was the last I saw of him until I saw him float out below the cloud, his parachute open as he drifted down safely."

If all reports were like those quoted so far in this chapter, the life of a fighter pilot would be exactly the kind of exciting life that the Eagles, and all fighter pilots, dream about. Unfortunately for them, English weather forces the dreary entry, day after day, in the squadron log book: "No operational flying."

Each day, when a fighter pilot wakes, he looks out at the weather, and if the sky is heavily overcast he turns over and goes back to sleep. But he can't sleep all day, and when finally he gets out of bed there is little for him to do. He can, if he likes, read, play chess, billiards, poker, shove ha'penny. He can sit in the mess and join the usual bull session; there. He can write letters back home and wonder how things are going with his girl—if she will keep her word and really wait for him until the end of the war. He can in these simple ways kill time for a day or two; but when bad weather sets in for a week or longer, as it frequently does during English winters, then life on a fighter station is a burden to these high-strung boys who can hardly endure the monotony.

Weather is not the only worry of the fighter pilot. Even though the day is good enough to permit flying, there is the continuous question in his mind: Will there be a battle today, or will it be just another damned patrol? When the boys patrol day after day, day after day, seeing nothing but sky and water, they become so fed up with routine flying that they curse the drudgery of it.

Patrolling over water in a land plane is always danger-ous, and in any plane it is frequently extremely difficult. When the sea is calm and when the clouds and water merge into one, the pilot loses his sense of reference. Many pilots have crashed because of the illusions and false horizons, the mirages, which appear over the sea. When patrolling a convoy, when flying around and around on the dreary patrol, a pilot repeatedly refers to the ships themselves in order to keep his sense of position, to maintain his relation with the sea and the sky, and to reject the false impressions that slowly steal into his senses. The strain of such flying is more tiring even than the strain of battle, and the mo-notony is maddening. But still such patrols must be flown. Day after day the pilots must go up, sometimes flying three or four patrols in one day. Next to no flying at all, it is the most wearing experience a fighter pilot can endure.

The report of the squadron's activities on January 4, 1942, for example, will indicate the monotony of routine patrol flying:

British Combine

ANTI-AIRCRAFT

LOADING ANTI-AIRCRAFT GUN

International News Photograph

ACK-ACK

LONDON AND ITS SEARCHLIGHTS

British Official Photograph: Crown Copyright Reserved

BRITAIN'S NIGHT GREETING TO GERMAN BOMB-
ERS: With shells and tracer bullets throwing their deadly ribbons into the
sky, Britain greets the Hun. In the background the great fire is a blazing
German plane the guns have brought down.

THE GUNS IN ACTION

THE GUNS BROUGHT THIS ONE DOWN: This Dornier bomber was swooping in low to machine-gun the streets of an English city when the ack-ack knocked it down and sent it sprawling in flames.

THE GUNS AGAIN: Here is another of Goering's pets, a Ju 88, that tangled with British guns and came off second best.

Acme

At 0600 hours [six o'clock in the morning] Red and Yellow sections were ordered to patrol a northbound convoy.

Shortly after Red and Yellow sections were airborne, "B" flight were ordered to readiness.

At 0735 White and Blue sections of "B" flight were ordered to relieve Red and Yellow sections who landed at 0735.

Green and Black sections were airborne at 0835 to take over from Blue and White who landed at 0845.

At 0715 Red section was ordered to scramble, but on landing at 0900 they reported they had seen nothing but water and a lot of sky.

Red and Yellow sections took off at 0930 to relieve Green and Black. This patrol was taken over by Blue and White at 1030.

Green section was ordered to patrol northbound convoy at 1115 and Black section a southbound convoy at 1130.

At 1215 Red section took off to relieve Green on the northbound convoy and Yellow took off at 1230 to take over from Black on the southbound convoy.

At 1310 hours Blue section was airborne to relieve Yellow. At the same time White took off to relieve Red.

By 1340 weather was closing in, so all aircraft were recalled.

By 1510 the weather cleared and Black section took off to patrol northbound convoy, being relieved by Blue at 1520.

At 1730 Black section was scrambled, but returned after 20 minutes. Nothing to report.

Green section was airborne 1730 to relieve
Blue on the final patrol and returned to base
at 1855.
No more flying for the day.

Such days as this are the trying ones for the young
fighter pilots. Flying only monotonous patrols, they
"patrol and patrol until there are corns on our backsides
and nothing happens."

Robinson told me that during long spells of bad weather some of the more nervous boys almost literally go ber-
serk. They gripe and grumble, and they swear they'll get
out of the bloody air force.

Then the weather clears, and they get a chance to fly
once more. It's wonderful just to be up in the sky again.
But soon, after a few days of merely patrolling a convoy,
the old routine flying isn't enough; the boys want battle,
and, failing to find it, they begin griping once more, cursing their luck and calling themselves ruddy fools for ever
having left home.

Until suddenly one day they run into a Hun formation
and the battle is on.

"They come back terrifically excited," Robbie said,
"talking as rapidly as they can, and making those swooping gestures with their hands. This battle, and the talk of
it, keeps them contented for a while. Then bad weather
sets in once more, and after a few days of inactivity they're
restless again, hating the dull days and swearing they'll get
out of the bloody air force.

"It's a strange life they live. Their days and days of boredom are broken at intervals by only a few minutes of in-
credibly swift battle. But for the boys those few moments
are enough; any amount of boredom can be endured if only
they can believe that tomorrow—*siempre mañana*—they'll
have a chance to risk their lives in a battle with the Hun."

7

In the beginning there was only one Eagle Squadron. Eventually there were three, but the second and the third stemmed from the first, and only the story of the first, the famous 71 (Eagle) Squadron is being written in this book. Anyhow, the story of one is pretty much the story of all: the pilots in 121 and 133, the later Eagle Squadrons, were like their pals in 71, American boys keen on adventure, in love with flying and fighting, and willing to take their chances of dying in battle. All three of the famous squadrons have seen extensive action, repeatedly making deep penetrations into enemy territory with the crack RAF wings, and all three have given memorable accounts of themselves. The 133 (Eagle) Squadron, commanded by Carroll McColpin, DFC, of Los Angeles, and 121 (Eagle) Squadron, commanded by Jimmy Daley, DFC, of Amarillo, Texas, have fully played their part in making "Eagle Squadron" a name to be honored in Allied countries and dreaded in Germany.

From the time of its formation in 1940 until September 29, 1942, when all three Eagle squadrons were transferred from the RAF into the American Air Force, the parent squadron, 71 itself, was commanded by seven men.

The first was an Englishman named Walter Churchill, DSO, DFC. He took command November 29, 1941. And

few persons would have envied him his job. The first of
these Americans who came over to fight in the RAF were
a picturesque lot, but they were not well trained as pilots,
and they hadn't even a remote conception of modern aerial
warfare. They just wanted to get up in the sky and give
'em hell, to have a lot of fun, and win a lot of glory; they
didn't understand that such paths of glory in modern air
fighting lead inevitably and quickly to the grave.

The Eagles had been at their first station only a week
when the Germans came over one night and gave the place
a good going over. Some of the boys were already asleep
when the attack began, and one of them was waked by being thrown completely out of his bed and sent sprawling
on his bottom.

"There was a hell of a flap going on," Daymond told
me, "and this type"—man, aircraft, anything at all in the
RAF is a "type"—"was running up and down the hall yelling for an airplane. He wanted to get an airplane and go
shoot the guy that had bombed him out of bed."

The young American "type" had been accustomed to
hitting back all his life. If somebody knocked you on your
backside, you got up and fought him. And this boy from
Illinois, along with most of the other Eagles in the early
days, simply couldn't realize that here was a new kind of
fight. He actually wanted to get into an airplane and go
after the Jerries who had bombed him. He didn't understand that he wouldn't have got ten feet off the ground
before they would have shot him into pieces.

Churchill's task wasn't easy. He had to take this mob
of wild cowboys, bronco-busters, most of them, and with
infinite patience and infinite tact, weld them into a fighting unit without destroying in the slightest their individual bravery and initiative. Curiously enough, he accomplished his purpose by the use of the most exacting military methods. He insisted on the boys' following the old

military custom of standing whenever he came into the room. He insisted on a smart salute. Careful dress. A soldierly bearing. The wrong man, and particularly the wrong Englishman, issuing such orders might have been answered by these young Americans with almost a revolt; at best he would have received only sullen acquiescence. But Churchill was the kind of man the boys learned at first to respect, then came in time to love like an older brother.

One of Churchill's most exceptional abilities was his power in reading. He could read an ordinary tactical report so that it became a fascinating adventure story. When he read to the Eagles in their little dispersal hut far down at the end of the landing field, the boys sat spellbound from beginning to end. And when he talked with them about his own experiences in the Battle of Britain, never boasting, merely using his own experiences to teach a lesson, the drop of a pin would have sounded loud. He was himself a great flier and a great fighter; he knew all the tricks, and he would take infinite pains to teach his boys how this man had won a victory, and that man had lost his life. Then he would lead his young American charges into the air and fly with them, giving them praise if they deserved it, and giving them unshirted hell if they deserved it.

The story of their feeling for him, their affection for him, is told in the fact that the Eagles all called him "Pappy" Churchill. Even after he had just bawled them out—which he often did—he was still "Pappy" to them. In return, Churchill was keenly loyal to his boys. He might criticize them when they deserved it, but no one else dared speak of them unfavorably. He knew that with all their faults they had great fighting hearts and that, once they learned the laws of the air and the tricks of battle, they would be magnificent.

Unfortunately, Churchill was troubled by really bad eyesight, though for a time he managed to hide his handicap. Then in January, 1941, he suffered a severe attack of sinus. The combined ailments could not be hidden, and he was relieved of his command and posted to a ground job.

Later, they sent Churchill to Malta because he was both a fighter and a leader. Soon after he arrived he went on one of the big raids over Sicily. He was shot down and killed. When the news got back to the squadron, the old boys, those who had known "Pappy," were an unhappy lot. They remembered that he had given them their initial training, that he had begun the welding of the Eagles into a fine fighting team.

The second commander of the squadron was W. E. G. Taylor, an American.

Older than most pilots in the RAF, "Bill" Taylor had traveled over the world and was something of a cosmopolite. He had served in the American Navy, and had been a transport pilot in the United States, flying between New York and Chicago. Before going to the Eagles, he had been in the British Fleet Air Arm, and had served as pilot on both aircraft carriers *Furious* and *Glorious;* he had fought in the battles of Norway. After his transfer to the RAF, this experienced American fighter was given command of the American squadron.

Having spent a great part of his military life in the Navy during peacetime, Taylor had ideas of discipline that were perhaps too severe for a flying squadron in time of war. He did not mix with the boys very much, because he believed that a good commanding officer should be the leader of all rather than friend of a few. Where Churchill had been able to humble his men with a reprimand, then play with them the next minute in a spirit of happy comradeship, Taylor delivered his reprimand and sent the offender away smarting under the rebuke. But along with these perhaps mistaken methods of discipline, Taylor was proud of his Eagles and was exceedingly ambitious for their success.

After he had led the squadron for a time, Taylor one day was called before the Air Officer Commanding at Group Headquarters and told that at thirty-six he was really too old to take an RAF Squadron into action over France. He was offered a promotion to the rank of wing commander and a job in a training unit.

Taylor was heartbroken, because actually the Eagles had become his life. He refused the training job. He would either have the Eagles and lead them in battle or he would resign his commission in the RAF. He was told that at his age he could not retain command of the squadron; he would either accept the training assignment or he would be permitted to resign his commission. He was given a fortnight to make up his mind.

Knowing that he was to leave, knowing that he had only a fortnight longer with the Eagles, he changed his severe treatment of them and his old Navy reserve fell from him. With his reserve and aloofness gone, he mixed with the boys on nightly parties, and at last they came really to know him. The better they knew him, the more they wanted him to stay as their commanding officer. There was a near riot in the mess at the end of the fortnight, but the Air Officer Commanding was adamant and Taylor handed in his resignation rather than go to the training post assigned him.

After leaving the RAF, Taylor went back to the American Navy, and was at Pearl Harbor.

The next commander of the squadron was H. de G. A. Woodhouse. And the Eagles didn't like his coming. In the first place, they wanted Taylor to stay. In the second place, they wanted to be led by another American, not by Woodhouse or any other Englishman.

Their likes and dislikes didn't trouble Woodhouse in the slightest. A calm, quiet, absolutely masterful man, he went to work on the Eagles and soon had them recognizing his complete authority. Strangely enough, he made them like it. In the past, the boys had managed to get in little remarks about their own wishes; they had even dared give opinions about orders from their squadron commanders. Woodhouse stopped all that instantly. He simply said how formations were to be flown, and that was the way they were flown, exactly that way.

Soon the boys came to understand that Woodhouse didn't care what they did on the ground, but he was relentless in his demands in the air. He would fly them again and again, practicing them over and over on each maneuver, tirelessly drilling them in formation. Before long the Eagles realized that "Paddy" Woodhouse was really the great teacher, the man who was taking twelve individual men and twelve aircraft and blending the whole into a perfect flying and fighting machine. When they realized what he was doing for them, they began to respect and admire this Englishman, this wise and careful leader, the perfectionist who was making Eagle Squadron the talk and the envy of the RAF.

Because of his success with the Eagles, Woodhouse was eventually taken from the squadron. In August, 1941, he was sent to Tangmere to succeed Wing Commander Bader. No greater compliment could have been paid, because only the very strongest leader could succeed the remarkable Bader.

Bader is probably the most famous pilot of the present war. He is already almost a legendary figure, like the Frenchman Guynemer, or the German Richthofen of the war of 1914-1918. Bader is a man without legs. Having lost his legs before the war when he crashed in a low-altitude acrobatic flight (he was rolling at low level and plowed in), Bader still insisted he not only could fly but could fight. He kept on insisting until the authorities

ALL-AMERICAN: The first All-American squadron in the Royal Air Force. This picture was made in February, 1941. *Left to right:* Sam Mauriello, DFC; Ed Bateman; Mike Kolendorski; Bill Taylor, squadron commander, now in the United States Navy Air Force; Nat Maranz; Andy Mamedoff; "Red" Tobin; Luke Allen; K. S. Taylor; Pete Provenzano; Gus Daymond, DFC and Bar, now commanding officer of the Eagles; R. Tongue, a British officer who was flying temporarily with the Americans; Bill Nichols.

Press Association

"RED" TOBIN: Killed in action

MIKE KOLENDORSKI: Killed in action.

finally gave him a chance to prove it. Immediately he showed himself a fine flier, and, despite his handicap, rose rapidly in the RAF until he was commanding a squadron. The men under him adored him. He was both a great fighter and a great spirit, and only the angels knew what he would do next. Men in his squadron have reported that he would string out a whole squadron in a line astern, dive at terrific speed and loop the twelve planes in a single great loop. They have told how the squadron would be flying alone, everything entirely correct; in fact, too correct for Bader. Over the R/T would come this command: "Over on your backs, you blokes." And the entire squadron would turn over and solemnly fly on its back until Bader righted them again. But such pranks were merely the play of a great leader, and in time Bader's extraordinary powers were recognized: he was given command of a wing, a formation of thirty-six planes. Already well-known in the RAF, Bader so brilliantly led his wing in battle after battle that in time all England came to know him and honor him.

In his last fight over France he attacked two Germans and shot one of them down. In swerving away from the aircraft he had just destroyed, Bader rammed into the other Hun plane, and, locked together, they started down. In some way the Englishman managed to free himself and bale out. He came down in his parachute, but in landing he smashed one of his artificial legs.

When word got back to England that one of Bader's legs was broken, a new leg was made according to measurements known in England. Then the RAF notified the Germans by radio that on a certain day a plane would fly to a certain spot over France and drop Bader's new leg.

On the exact minute, the plane took off from England, flew over the Channel, and on to the appointed spot. At the time scheduled, the plane tossed out a bundle. The top of it opened and a small parachute went drifting down, a leg fastened at the bottom. The Germans picked it up and gave it to Bader.

That night, to celebrate having two legs, the Englishman crept out of prison and was well on his way to a successful escape when he was detected and captured.

Woodhouse was followed by E. R. Bitmead, an English pilot who had been resting following an injury to his head in a flying accident. For a while after joining the squadron, "Bitters" would not fly with it in formation; he insisted on going up alone, testing himself to see if he were fit again. Then one day he came down and confessed that above ten thousand feet he had such pains in his head he did not think it fair to take the men into the air. So he left the station without having once led the Eagles into battle.

The next leader of the squadron was S. T. Meares. This tall, quiet Englishman was one of the men responsible for the success, and the resulting fame, of the Eagle Squadron. Meares had been with the Eagles only a fortnight when they knew he was absolutely tops. On the ground they found him friendly and considerate, and when he led them into battle they followed him without question; they knew he was right in all his swift decisions, and with no hesitancy they went in wherever he led them.

They had reason to trust him. This letter, written July 29, 1941, proves that they did. It is a letter written by Meares himself:

> My dear Mum and Dad:
> To-day we have a day off, so I am writing to let you know that I am well and fit after a very exciting week. We have been beating up the Heinies as you have probably read in the papers. During the last few days we have been into France as far as Lille, and haven't seen

a Hun within fighting distance. I think he is
badly scared, though during the first days of
the week we met quite a bit of opposition and
we had some grand fights, in one of which I
destroyed one more 109E, and damaged two
others.

I had a terrific fight with the one I destroyed. It happened over St. Omer, near Lille.
I had just seen the bombers drop their bombs,
when I saw a dog fight going on behind me. I
turned to join battle and, attacked a Me 109
who promptly dived vertically towards the
ground from 20,000 feet. I dived after him
and fired a one second burst at him. Then
I saw another 109 diving after me, firing as
hard as he could. I took violent evasive action, and in a few seconds was at ground level
doing about 500 miles per hour. Being well
out of the battle and about fifty miles inside
France all by myself, I felt a little lonely and
headed fast for home, but on the way back
I passed right over the middle of St. Omer
Aerodrome which had two 109's patrolling it.

I thought to myself that this was no place
to start looking for trouble, and continued
on my way. But the Huns did not feel like
that, and thought it would please Herr Hitler
if they shot me down, so they came after me.
They stalked me, but as I was flying below the
level of the trees I was able occasionally to see
them in the mirror of my plane. I waited until the first one was in firing range, and then
pulled the stick back, and turned as tightly as
I could, and to my "'orror and amazement" I

found the Hun was turning inside my turn, which meant he could fire at me and hit me. Then I started to perspire a bit.

I could not climb away, because he was slightly above me, and I could not dive because I was already flat on the deck, and suddenly it struck me that I was fighting for my life, which is the strangest of sensations. I knew with terrific clearness that unless I did something within the next split second I would be one of those who did not get home for tea.

I was flying about five feet above the ground, and I pulled the stick back so hard I blacked out for what seemed to be minutes, and when I came to again I was flying about twenty feet behind the Hun and he was obviously wondering where I had got to. Realizing how worried he must be, wondering where I was, I gave him a little squirt to let him know I was behind him. He then started to do the most amazing display of acrobatics I have ever seen, but I found it quite easy to follow him, and every time he made a mistake I squirted him. He bolted straight back to the aerodrome, and I chased him down his hangars, in between them, over the flying field and back again. He was trying to get his ground defenses to shoot me down. Then in desperation he turned on his back at about fifty feet, and I gave him a long burst and in he went; but it took all the rounds I had, and now I had empty guns.

Realizing that I was in a very unhealthy spot, I headed once more for home. But now

the second Hun had arrived on the scene.
So I had to turn and fight him without any
guns. This lasted for about ten minutes, and
every time I turned for home he came at me
again, and I was still about fifty miles from
the French coast. This continued until I was
almost exhausted, and in a last frantic effort
I got on his tail, and when he turned to shake
me off I went the other way and dived over
the top of a hill I had spotted. There I turned
as quickly as possible, and flew under the
level of the trees of a wood, about a foot off
the ground, and he never saw me again. I flew
at one foot level to Le Touquet, and then
home. I never knew how well I loved England
until I saw her shores again. . . .

Meares was a great idealist and frequently could be
seen alone in front of the fire in the mess, smoking his
pipe and thinking. "When I would see him sitting there
before the fire," Robinson told me, "I would think of that
marvelous description of John Ford, the old Elizabethan
playwright. Ford was a moody man and often would sit
in lonely contemplation. Someone once said: 'I saw John
Ford last night, sitting as usual with folded arms and mel-
ancholy hat.'"

After Meares had, commanded the squadron for five
months, after he had played his magnificent part in inspir-
ing the squadron to still greater victories, he took the boys
into the air one morning for a practice flight. In the air
Meares and one of the men under his command collided,
and Meares himself and the other pilot were both killed.

In a letter to Robinson written a few days later, Meares's
mother said:

I think death claimed him most mercifully—
a collision on a practice flight in close formation. They were flying at 5,000 feet. The
other Eagles saw the collision, and they circled round and round hoping each of the boys
would bale out. But none saw any effort to
bale out, and it seems a fair presumption that
both were stunned by the force of the impact.

We have agreed that he shall be buried
at Brookwood with the other Eagles who
have given their lives. It seems fitting that
he should rest among the men he so much
admired and loved, these young Americans
he had come to know as—and I quote him
exactly—"a grand bunch of lads whom I, an
Englishman, am proud to lead. They are absolutely magnificent fighting material."

In one of her later letters, Meares's mother wrote of
him:

He thoroughly enjoyed every minute of his
adventures, outwitting the Hun, braving the
flak to "beat up" the enemy, bringing down an
Me 109. He was able to do it all because he
had a real certainty in the essential rightness
and necessity of a passionate ideal.

In one of his letters he wrote: "I know
exactly where I stand. I have complete confidence in myself. I know exactly where my
duty lies, and I am ready to face death if necessary without fear and without regret. For
myself there will be no hate. I shall fight for
an ideal without which life would mean just
nothing.

"The invasion of Norway, Belgium and Holland with its pitiful stream of refugees, all the despair and destruction, brings home the truth of what we are fighting for. I feel as I expect most people feel, that this war will strike to the heart of each one of us, and that we shall not only have our backs to the wall, but our souls as well at stake.

"The hardest battle will come when destruction has destroyed itself, and when we have to rebuild the world again, 'remould it nearer the hearts desire.' We shall have to fight against the hate and fear this war is bound to raise to fever heat. We must keep our hearts clean from this, and fight now with determination and courage tempered not by hate and fear, but with wisdom and truth."

After Meares, came Squadron Leader Peterson.

SQUADRON LEADER PETERSON, DSO, DFC: Having damaged one Ju 88 in the morning and shot down another in the afternoon, and himself having been shot down in his second fight of the day, Peterson (at right) next day gets back to the station and makes his report to Pilot Officer P. Salkeld, the intelligence officer who followed Robinson with the Eagles after Robbie was posted to liaison duties with the American Air Force.

8

The alfalfa had just been cut on Brigham Peterson's farm near Santaquin, Utah. The field was bare, and a couple of barnstormers picked it out as a good place to land their rickety old airplane.

"We'd like to use your field for the time we're here," they told Mr. Peterson.

"Surely, boys. Make yourself at home."

But the next day Mr. Peterson went to the fliers and said he'd have to put a price on the use of his alfalfa field. "You see," he said, his arm around the shoulder of a slender, towheaded boy beside him, "this is my son, and he's clamoring for a ride. I guess there'll be no living with him if he doesn't go flying with you." Mr. Peterson was smiling in his friendly way as he said: "I'm afraid I'll have to charge you a ride for the use of the field."

The barnstormers thought it great fun that a nine-year-old boy wanted to go up in an airplane, so they took him into the air and introduced him to the sky. They did more than that—they introduced him to speed. As the plane took off, young Pete reached out to wave good-by to his father. The force of the propeller-wash almost snatched his arm off. After a glorious thirty minutes in the air, he came down talking about airplanes and flying and speed. From that day his devotion, almost his worship, was to airplanes and the speed at which they travel. From the day of his first ride, young Pete was forever looking at airplanes, wondering about them, trying to get close enough to touch them, then going home at night to talk with his Dad about airplanes, and going to bed to dream about them.

In due course, Chesley Gordon Peterson entered Brigham Young University. He did well in his studies and was popular with his classmates, but the smell of books in the library was not the thrilling smell of oil and gasoline in a hangar, and the drone of the professor's voice was not exciting like the drone of airplanes leaving on their pilgrimage off to the sky. Realizing finally that the strictly academic studies were not for him, knowing that there was one overwhelming love in his life, Peterson left the university after his sophomore year to become a candidate for commission in the United States Army Air Corps.

But Pete was still only a boy, and in order to enter the corps he had to overstate his age by two years. He was getting along well and was half through his training when an officer happened to discover the boy's true age. Regretfully, the officer told Pete he would have to be cashiered. A kindly lot, the dismissal board put him out of the army "for lack of inherent flying ability." Had the true cause of the dismissal been cited, Pete might have been court-martialed for misstating his age.

The boy was heartbroken. He was like a young priest dismissed from the seminary. He had given his brain and almost his soul to airplanes, and now they had been denied him. Along with two pals who had also been dismissed he went on a blind that lasted a fortnight, during which time the three wretched young fellows drank their way from San Antonio to New York and back to Los Angeles. In California Pete was maddeningly near one of the great airplane factories, and daily he heard the planes going over, hundreds of them; daily he looked up and saw the pilots flying their test flights from the Douglas factory. He couldn't stand it. As an employee in the factory he could at least be near airplanes, touch them and smell the dope fresh on the wings; he could hear the motors as the big planes moved down wind to the take off and came roaring back. Better the glimpse of a beloved woman, as tantalizing as that might be, than no sight of her at all. So he got a job in the Douglas factory.

In the factory he soon found other boys like himself, all of them talking, dreaming airplanes. Like himself, a number of these boys were ex-cadets who had been let out of the United States Air Corps for various causes. Somewhat in a spirit of bravado, in an effort to defy their disappointment, they organized the "Wash-Out Club." Membership was limited to boys who had been let out of the Air Corps.

Word got around. The newspapers got hold of it, and at the first meeting of the club more than a hundred persons were present. There was something fine, and something a little pathetic, about these boys banding themselves together to talk about airplanes, and at the same time to seek new ways of climbing back into the skies. Underneath it all, of course, was a desire to comfort themselves as they saw other American boys in the uniform of the Air Corps, saw them wearing the silver wings, the prayed-for accolade that seemed so far from the Wash-Outs.

At this first meeting, Indian Jim Moore of Texas was elected president. Pete was made vice-president. A subscription fee of a dollar was charged each person present at the meeting. With this money a stenographer was hired to do all the clerical work. And all the clerical work consisted of writing constant appeals to the War Department, asking that the Wash-Outs be given another chance to prove themselves worthy of pilots' wings.

Eventually arrangements were made for the boys to be trained as navigators and bombardiers, and about three-quarters of them took advantage of this offer. But some of them—Peterson among the lot—heard that certain Army officers of the last war, led by Colonel Charles Sweeney, were quietly recruiting volunteers to fly with the French. This was early in 1940, when Pete was nineteen. He offered his services to the sub-rosa organization, and with another boy he took a train for Toronto. But the American government had wind of what was happening, and in Toronto Pete and his pal, along with other young volunteers, were caught and turned back because the United States was not then in war, and the enlisting of American boys to fight against Germany was an unfriendly act against a nation that was, at least nominally, at peace with this country.

Pete and his pals returned to the Douglas aircraft factory, and lay low for two and a half months. Then they tried again. The same organization of old army officers was now enlisting for the Royal Air Force, and after a secret rendezvous, Pete and Indian Jim were smuggled out of the United States and on to Ottawa. From there they were sent to a port of embarkation, and were commissioned as officers the day they stepped on the boat, August 13, 1940.

After a time of training in England, they were posted to a new squadron—No. 71 (Eagle) Squadron.

As they flew together and lived together under the close watch of the British officers commanding them, the young Eagles began to prove themselves, to classify themselves. This one was a line shooter, a big talker and little more. This one was a fine flier but lacked the guts to make a fighter. This one was homesick and wanted to get back to his girl. This one was a wild man who liked nothing better than to plow into a dozen Huns and to hell with the danger. This one was quiet and determined, but lacked imagination and good judgment. As they showed themselves as individuals, and the old experienced RAF officers came to know them, the blond-haired young Peterson was showing qualities that made his senior officers watch him particularly. Soon they said he had the making of a great airman and a great fighter.

They said that in the air Pete was a good steady flier, and they knew that on the ground he was a careful, clean-living young fellow. When most of the other boys were broke, Peterson was spending within the bounds of his meager pay. At night when some of the others were going off on a binge, Pete would slip away to his room and go to bed at nine o'clock. After lunch, while most of the others were standing around gabbing in the mess, Pete would ease away to his room for half an hour's sleep. He learned early in his fighting that a man needs a rested body and a clear mind when he goes into battle. Peterson still says a man can't store up too much energy for that instant when he must have incredible energy, of both body and mind, in order to see, attack, and destroy all within an instant that is gone before it seems even to exist, leaving the body weak and the mind drained.

His steady ways and his quiet living did not mean that Peterson lived alone, away from his pals. Occasionally at night when a gramophone record was playing cowboy songs, Pete's eyes began to twinkle and his feet danced to the rhythm of the song. Sometimes later in the evening he would demonstrate his own particular dance, "The Utah Stomp." And other evenings when the crowd went to The Thatched, Pete was along, drinking his share of beers and competing for the girls. He was a good drinking companion, but he knew moderation, and he was mature far beyond his years. So in time the English officers made Pete a deputy flight commander. He quickly showed himself to be an exceptional leader, and soon he was promoted to flight commander.

At this time Peterson and Robinson were sharing a room at the station where the Eagles were living. And Robinson told me that Peterson's rise was no accident.

"It wasn't just one of those things that happen," Robbie said. "Pete had the natural aptitudes of a fine flier. He had inherent qualities of leadership. But his success is founded on work, hard work, and still more hard work. Since that first flight in Utah back in 1929, when Pete was only a little boy, he has worked at the business of airplanes, and flying airplanes, and fighting airplanes. They have been his life, and, in the air or on the ground, he has lived for them.

"At odd moments, instead of loafing around doing nothing, Pete would be off somewhere reading tactical reports. He would read how this man attacked a plane and shot it down. He would figure out how the victory was won; then he would change sides and figure out why the German lost the fight and was killed. He would sit reading and thinking, studying out every detail of the battle, until he had a full understanding of that particular fight. Then he would go on to the next report, and study it until he had learned all it could teach him. He would work out the details of the battle like a man working out some mathematical problem, until, finally, he arrived at the answer and could say why this man won and that one lost."

Whenever the bull session was about women or any other of the more common subjects, Pete would soon drift away from it. But when it turned to airplanes and tactics, he would sit talking for hours. He would discuss flying and fighting with anyone, at any time, debating, arguing, trying to learn from the other man and to clarify his own thinking on the multiple complexities of aerial tactics.

"But reading reports of air fights, discussing tactics in general, was not Pete's only way of teaching himself," Robbie said. "One of the best sources of instruction was his own fights. Whenever he came back after a battle he would stand around with the other boys and excitedly discuss it with them. Then, once the excitement and tension had died down and the other fellows were going to the mess for a drink, Pete would go along to our room. There he would lie down and quietly go over the whole fight, telling every detail of it. Lying relaxed on the bed, half the time with his eyes shut as if seeing it all over again, he would discuss the battle and the tactics he and his squadron had used, and the tactics the Germans had used. Impersonally, almost coldly, he would analyze the fight, pointing out mistakes on each side and praising a brilliant attack whether it had been made by an Eagle or a German. While I shaved and got ready for dinner, Pete would lie there, analyzing the whole battle until he was certain he had learned all he could learn from it. Then he would get up, stretch, and grin: 'Gee, but it was a great fight,' he would say. 'It was marvelous fun.'"

Some time after Pete had been made a flight commander the squadron ran into a period of terrifically bad luck. One day, the Eagles were jumped by the Germans, and the battle had hardly begun before more swarms of Huns began dropping out of the sky. That day the Eagle Squadron of twelve American boys fought two hundred and fifty Germans! Three Eagles were shot down. Tobin, Nichols, and Fenlaw went down, and Dowling was injured, his plane so badly damaged that while Dowling as able to lug it back to England, it was hopelessly smashed and had to be written off. One week after this "clobbering," this terrible beating, the squadron again ran into a sky full of Huns, and two more Eagles went down: Bill Geiger and

McGerty were lost. Within one week five men had been
shot down—two of them, Nichols and Geiger, were, and
still are, prisoners of war in Germany—and one, Dowling,
had been knocked out of action. Half a squadron had been
lost in a week.

Some of those who were left were a bit jumpy. The luck
of the Eagles was running out, they said. Each man flew
with a Hun on his tail—the terrible feeling that always
there is a Hun just behind, ready to press the button and
shoot you down. No one lost his guts, but some of them
began to get jittery and were flying on nerve only. It was
at this time that Pete showed himself a fine fighter and a
great leader.

Day after day he went up seeking the enemy. There
was no evidence in his talk or in his flying that six of his
pals had just been shot down. He went calmly on with his
job, and for a while he was the most successful man in the
squadron in seeking out the enemy and destroying him.
To Peterson's leadership and courage during this trying
period the squadron owes a great deal: in his run of good
luck he steadied the squadron until they were able to get
themselves together again, until they were able to fly and
fight with their old bravery and determination.

It was about this time that Peterson made the great
decision which was to combine with his other qualities
and eventually lift him toward the very top among the
truly great leaders who have fought in the Royal Air Force.

Again and again Peterson had heard pilots come back
after a sweep above France, and exult over what they called
the success of the day. They would tell how they had flown
over enemy territory, making a deep sweep over Occupied
France, and returned without losing a man.

I was talking with Peterson only the other day, and we
were discussing this attitude on the part of some fighters.
"I've no use for it," he said. "What the hell's the use of

going over there and promenading all over the sky and then coming home? What have you accomplished? I remember one day hearing some fighter pilots tell about going over, meeting some Jerries at six hundred yards, then coming home without attacking. What was the sense of it?

"It's not good enough merely to go over and come back. Our job is to go over, destroy the enemy, and then come back. Our job is to seek out the enemy and blow him out of the sky."

The all-important decision that Peterson reached early in his fighting days was that he, and the men under his leadership, must forever be on the offensive. Once he became sure that offense, and only offense, could win wars, Peterson began to talk it to the men under him. Day after day at the dispersal hut, night after night at the mess, he talked offensive.

"There's nothing gained by merely going out and coming back. All you've done is had a joy ride and wasted hundreds of gallons of petrol," he would say. "We've got to go find the beggars and clobber them, really blast them."

After weeks and weeks of talking aggressive action, Peterson so imbued the boys with his ideas and his enthusiasm that soon the Eagles were fighting with a new spirit that brought them victory after victory. By this time the other boys in the squadron, even those who had known Peterson in the United States and had come over with him, recognized his power of leadership and were willing and eager to follow him. They knew that Pete had studied the theories of battle, the theories of tactics, until he knew perfectly at all times what he was doing; he had studied aerial warfare until he was an absolute master of it. They knew, too, that he was a cool head in battle, that he always maneuvered until he reached the exact moment and position most advantageous to the squadron, then led the attack with incredible speed and fierce determination, striking in an instant and destroying the enemy.

I have listened to the Eagles talk about Peterson. Even now he is only twenty-two, but when he led the squadron into battle the boys under him looked to him as a man in whom they could put their full trust. "You see," one of the Eagles told me, "Pete never does anything foolish. He never falls into a booby trap, like diving at a stooge when there is a sky full of Jerries waiting to come *fruuumping* down and rub us out. He always knows what Huns are in the sky, and exactly where they are, and exactly the best way to shoot them down. Whenever he sees Jerries he knows just what to do and how to do it. And when they begin to maneuver against him, he knows how to out-maneuver them, and swoop in for the kill. He just naturally knows how to fight a battle, that's all. Whenever he sees Jerries, they'd better streak for home or Pete will turn them into cold meat."

One day I asked Peterson himself what he considered the qualities necessary for a great leader in modern air fighting. "Well, I'd say first he must know how an air battle is fought. That's his business and he must know it. You can't just stooge around in the sky and expect some dumb Jerry to fly across your gunsights. You've got to know how to see Jerries and recognize them, then maneuver into a position where you can shoot them down.

"But all this knowledge isn't worth a damn if you don't act fast. A good leader must know his job so well he doesn't stop to think what is the right thing—he simply does the right thing and does it instantly. I'd rather have a man do something wrong than do nothing at all. You might possibly get away with the wrong thing, but the right thing a second too late gives Jerry time enough to let you have it.

"Then, of course, a leader must be aggressive and must have the absolute confidence of his men. Furthermore, he must have a certain inspiration that carries him over that instant in battle which decides the way it will go; he must have something besides, and above, everything that can be named—and he must be able to pull it out at the right second and make such sudden use of it that maybe it surprises even himself." Pete smiled in his slow, easy way. "Then he's got to have good luck. If he isn't lucky he won't find any Jerries, and if you don't find them you can't shoot them down, you can't win any victories. Finally, he needs all the luck possible when he himself is fighting, or some new boy will get in a lucky shot from half a mile away, and then the best leader in the world goes down."

When Squadron Leader Meares was killed in a flying accident, Peterson was the inevitable choice to take the squadron. He was raised from flight commander to squadron leader, and November 11, 1941, he was given command of the Eagles.

Shortly afterward a number of new boys came to the squadron. In training these other American lads who had just come to him, Peterson particularly showed his leadership. He worked them in trial flights until he was satisfied that they were ready; then he led them into battle. Invariably he kept each new boy directly behind him, guarding and protecting him until the new boy had gained the necessary experience, until he had received his baptism of fire in such a way, flying close behind Pete, that his confidence grew and he was ready to be taken from under Pete's protection and given a more dangerous place in the squadron formation.

"During the time I shared a room with Pete, I learned something of the responsibilities and the anxieties of a man who leads a fighter squadron," Robbie told me. "Long after we had turned out the light at night, Pete would he there talking about the squadron and the men in it. He would tell how one man was losing his nerve and another was foolhardy. He would work out plans to encourage one, and plans to beat sense into the head of the other. Then he would tell how one member of the squadron had been shot down that day, and why. He would figure out how and why his pal had been killed: 'He wasn't weaving enough. . . . He wasn't watching carefully. . . . He didn't make a tight enough turn.' He would discuss how to use the death of his pal in teaching the other boys to avoid the same mistakes; he would plan how he could teach them and save their lives.

"Then he would go to sleep. But night after night he would dream about his men and their battles, and frequently would talk in his sleep. Often his talk would wake me, and I'd hear him encouraging some pilot, giving him sound battle advice, then suddenly he would be in a fight himself, fighting it all over again with the Hun. . . . 'All right, Tommy, all right. Never mind the damned flak. It won't get you. You're flying beautifully. Bloody good show, Tommy. . . . Closer in, Blue IV, closer in. You're straggling, and you'll be cold meat. . . . Christ! Well done! Well done! You've got the beggar. Well done!'"

One night Peterson met a girl named Audrey Boyes, a girl from South Africa. Then he saw her again. And again. On Thanksgiving night in 1941, Robbie entertained at his home, the Englishman giving the dinner partly in honor of the American Thanksgiving and partly to celebrate Gus Daymond's birthday. The table was lighted with candles. The center decoration was a large pumpkin with a big face cut in it and a lighted candle inside. They all ate turkey and sweet potatoes, sweet corn and pumpkin pie and ice cream. After dinner they played the piano and sang and danced. And Pete and Audrey knew, each of them, that there could be no happiness for either unless they had each other.

AUDREY

PETE

Throughout the winter they saw each other whenever possible. One day Pete flew from his station to Leicester to see her. "The next day," Robbie said, "the weather suddenly closed in and snow began to fall. We were sitting by the stove talking when somebody jumped up and said: 'Listen!' We all sat still until someone else said: 'Good God! It's a Spitfire. Poor devil, he's had it. Nobody can get downstairs in weather like this.' But there was an old pilot in the room, and he went on smoking. 'There's only one man I know who can land a plane in this storm. If it's Peterson, he'll make it. If it's anybody else, he's done for.' Ten minutes later Peterson came walking into dispersal, blowing on his fingers. 'Cold out there,' he said, and reached for the coffee pot."

In the spring of 1942 Peterson led the squadron with great inspiration. When the spring weather came, when the "shooting season" really opened, Pete led his boys over France at least twice every day. Some days he led them over as many as four times. Teaching and living his old belief in the offensive, Pete went into action with a courage and a vigorous initiative that brought the Eagles a particularly brilliant series of victories. His engagement to Audrey, instead of making him more cautious, somehow seemed to be an inspiration, and Pete himself started shooting them down until, in the big battle of March 25, 1942, he got two in one day.

On that day the Eagles were flying high cover over some Hurricanes, and Pete saw German 190's maneuvering to attack the bombers. Before they could get into position, Pete gave the order and led the Eagles in a fierce attack which destroyed five of the Hun planes, probably destroyed another, and damaged three more. The Eagles themselves lost only one plane and one pilot. It was one of the outstanding air victories of the war, and the squadron received a telegram of congratulations from the Air Office Commanding.

Then came June 26, 1942. Slender, black haired, the girl from South Africa was beautiful before the altar as she took her vows with the young American in the blue uniform of the British Royal Air Force. At the reception afterward at Robbie's home, the roses in the garden were in full bloom, and the sun was shining warmly. Gussie Daymond gave the toast to the bride and groom, and ended it by saying that he had seen Pete go bravely into many a fight before.

"And I believe he'll be victorious even in this long, hard battle he's beginning today," Gussie said, as Audrey and Pete cried out their protests.

Less than two months later, on the memorable nineteenth of August, the Eagles were fighting in the Battle of Dieppe when they heard the cry that stopped their hearts: "Mayday! Mayday! . . . Stardust Leader! . . . Stardust Leader! . . . Mayday! Mayday! Mayday!"

They all knew his voice, and, too, he had named himself by his position in the squadron—"Stardust Leader."

But Oscar Coen asked: "Is it you, Pete?"

"Yes," came back over the wireless.

There was a minute's silence, then the Eagles began to come in:

"Good luck, Pete."

"Cheerio, Pete."

"Meet you at The Swan to-night, Pete."

Then: "Mayday! Mayday! . . . I'm baling out. . . . Good luck, you chaps."

And all the Eagles came in: "Good luck, Pete."

A few minutes after Squadron Leader Peterson was heard to say he was baling out, the body of a drowning man was seen in the sea, all entangled with the cords of his parachute. His dinghy was floating about a quarter of a mile away from him. The Eagles saw this man and thought it was Peterson.

In that terrific Battle of Dieppe, five Ju 88's had been seen in the afternoon to dart in for an attack on the British convoy. Normally, a fighter pilot attacks a bomber from the side, making a beam attack in order to be safe from the fire of the rear gunner. But Peterson saw that these 88's were preparing for their bombing run over the ships, making ready for the moment of steady flight immediately before releasing their bombs. He knew if they were left free to make this run, they would be able to bomb and perhaps sink the British ships. Without waiting to maneuver himself into position for a beam attack, Peterson risked everything in order to save the ships. He made a fierce attack from full astern, going directly into the rear gunner's line of fire.

In his first burst, Peterson's cannon shells hit the German plane and the starboard engine burst into flames. Then the bomber was seen to jettison its bombs into the sea, making no further attempt to attack the ships and now thinking only of saving itself. Since there had been no answering fire from the rear gunner, Peterson thought he had not only ignited the bomber's engine but had also killed the German gunner. He therefore went in to destroy the enemy aircraft. But the gunner, having bravely held his fire until Peterson was only two hundred yards away, suddenly opened with everything he had. In the first instant of fire, Peterson's plane was badly damaged, but he continued his attack until his cockpit was filled with smoke and he was blinded. Duke-Woolley, his wing commander, saw him break away at the moment the flaming German plane crashed into the sea. Blind with the smoke, Peterson threw back the hood of his plane so that the rush of air might clear the cockpit. Able to see once more, yet knowing he would have to bale out, Peterson looked down and selected the fastest launch in the convoy. He then flew until he was slightly in front of it.

He took off his helmet, threw it overboard, and for a moment watched it fall. He then realized that he was carrying his revolver in his boot, and that it would weight him down once he was in the water. He hated to part with the gun, but he knew it had to go. He took it out of his boot, and held it in his hand, looking at it, as he said aloud: "Come to think about it, I never have fired you." So he stuck it up in the air and banged away until it was empty, then tossed it overboard and watched it go tumbling down.

By this time all the cooling fluid was gone and the engine temperature was rising so rapidly he knew he could wait no longer. He lowered the door by his side and jumped. Just as he left the plane, he saw it burst into flames and plunge downward.

Peterson did not pull his ripcord quickly. He rolled over several times, then straightened up and was surprised how slowly he seemed to be falling. When he got to about twelve hundred feet, he pulled the cord and an instant later was caught up with a jerk as his parachute opened.

All the time he had been falling, and now as he drifted down in his parachute, he was going over in his mind the routine he would follow once he hit the water. While floating down he realized that the weight of his flying boots would hinder him after he was in the sea, so he pulled up each leg in turn, took off his boots, told them good-by, and dropped them, watching them race him downward.

As he was going over his drill in his mind, practicing himself on what he should do, he touched the sea and was surprised with the gentleness of his going into the water. At that moment a puff of wind had got his parachute, dragging it along and causing him to be lowered gently into the Channel.

1. Peterson attacks four German planes
   and shoots down one.
2. Over the french coast he sees four
   Spits attacked and two shot down.
3. He himself is attacked by six
   Jerries, and is badly shot up.
4. He turns and fights, and his aircraft is still further damaged.
5. He gets a Hun all alone and
   blows pieces off him.
6. Peterson withdraws.

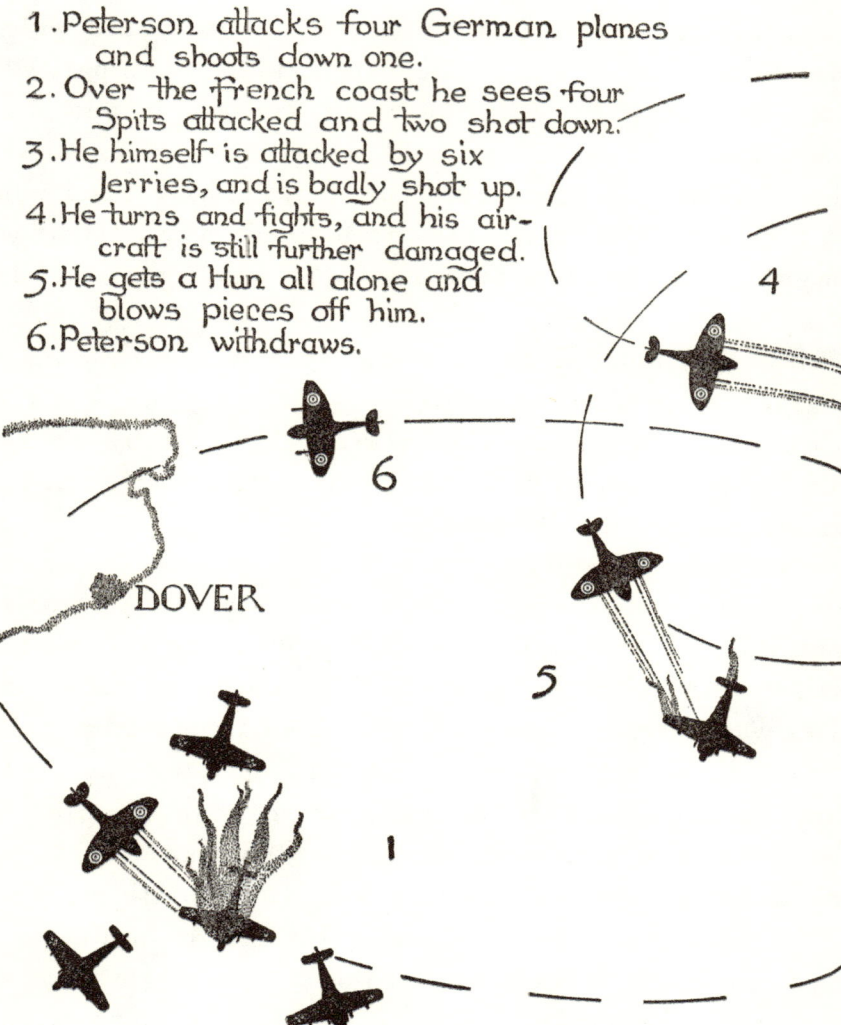

DOVER

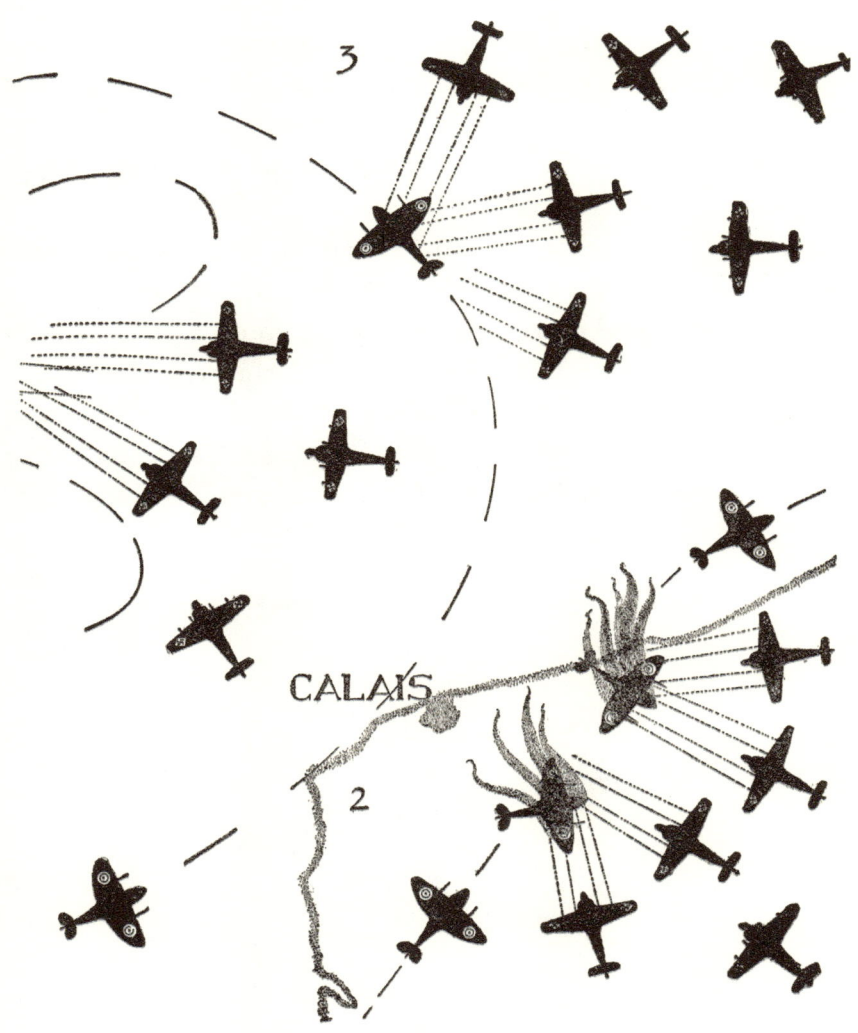

PETERSON IN ACTION

Once in the sea, he released his parachute. Finding himself rather low in the water, he realized that he had forgotten to inflate his Mae West. He then inflated the life jacket, opened his dinghy, and climbed into the narrow end according to routine. Having placed himself in position to come down near the fast-moving launch, he waited in the water for only fifteen minutes before he was picked up.

This same rescue boat also picked up a Canadian pilot who had been shot down, and the two fighter pilots, the Canadian and the American, sat on the deck of the launch talking with each other about the battle. As they were talking, a Focke-Wulf 190 suddenly dipped out of the sky and sprayed the boat with cannon fire. The Canadian pilot was killed instantly. Peterson was not touched.

9

Flying over enemy territory, taunting him, daring him to rise and fight, is but part of the varied job performed by a fighter squadron. Actually there are a dozen types of operational jobs that must be done by the fighters. Each kind of operation has its own particular name. Some of these names are military secrets, and I am, therefore, forced to substitute others which will sound strange to pilots and all people of the RAF; but they will, of course, be able instantly to identify the operation even though an unofficial name is given here.

First there is the operation we shall call the "Pineapple." It is the small-scaled harassing operation when a few fighters, usually only two, go over enemy territory and attack gun posts, trains, power plants, ammunition dumps, ground troops, airdromes, or anything else they can get near enough to destroy.

The "Rover" is an organized challenge to the Germans in which a dozen, three dozen, a hundred planes may sweep out over enemy territory, flying over Occupied France or the Occupied Low Countries in an effort to flush the Hun and make him fight.

The "Intruder" is the offensive night operation when our planes go over enemy territory between dusk and dawn in an effort to destroy whatever they can. These night

intruders particularly like to hover above airdromes, waiting to pounce on enemy aircraft when they come in to
refuel after their routine patrols.

The "Feint" is a small force of fighters which approach-
es the enemy coastline, then withdraws before it becomes
engaged with enemy fighters. But the enemy doesn't know
it's only a feint, that the fighters will withdraw without
giving battle, and he is constantly worried as the RAF
sends these feints from different directions, mixing them
with real attacks to give emphasis to the false ones. In following these tactics, the RAF forces the Hun to keep his
coastal defenses at the highest possible state of prepared-
ness and forces him to work under a condition of strain,
keeping him jittery and lessening his efficiency. And while
the War of Nerves is not written about so much as in the
early days of the war, it still goes on. Each side is forever
trying to work out some plan to unnerve the other. The
Germans drop bombs that not only explode but scream
like hysterical women as they fall. The English send over
a Commando raid that rushes ashore, snatches a few prisoners, and races away: it's done not only for the sake of
capturing the prisoners, but also for the unnerving effect
on the Germans left behind—they don't know what dark
night the English are going to swoop down and bang them
over the head.

Of all the aerial operations, the two most important are
the "Carnival" and the "Poker." They are combined operations in which both fighters and bombers play their part.

In the autumn of 1940, the time of the Battle of Britain, the Germans came in hundreds, swarming through
the sky. And the RAF rose to meet them. Day after day the
Germans came over, formation after formation, flying over
England to destroy the little island. But day after day the
RAF met them, until there came the day the Germans lost
one hundred and sixty aircraft and pilots, and then the

day they lost one hundred and eighty-five aircraft and one hundred and eighty-five pilots. After that, the Hun lost his guts and stayed home. After that, the German fighters stayed near their home airdromes and virtually never crossed the Channel, never dared cross the English coast and fight over England. So the RAF carried the battle to German territory: they went sweeping out over France, defying the Hun and daring him to rise.

At first he did come up in answer to the intrusive sweep, meeting fighter plane with fighter plane. But as his losses became greater and greater, and he knew he couldn't stand such a rate of loss, he finally ignored the intruding fighters: he simply sat on the ground and let them fly around, burning up their petrol and their energy.

So a new kind of operation was invented. If the fighters alone could not flush Jerry, then bombers were attached to the formation and the combined force went on parade over enemy territory. Now the Hun was in a quandary! If he didn't rise and fight, the bombers went on through and bombed some important military target. If he did rise, he had the dreaded job of shooting it out with the fighters of the Allied Air Force. And Jerry has no stomach for meeting the Allied fighters on anything like equal terms. He still remembers the days when the RAF shot him out of the skies back in 1940, and he well knows he must fight with the utmost care, he must conserve in every way possible in order to meet the steadily increasing production of planes and pilots from both England and the United States.

The statement that the German airmen do not like to meet Allied fighters on anything like equal terms may sound like orthodox national boasting. It is, of course, true that men of every nation consider themselves better fighters, braver fellows, than men of any other, and we Americans and English, goodness knows, have no accentuated modesty when it comes to an estimate of our prowess in battle, but I have found that the American Eagles are not a boastful lot. The man who has repeatedly been in battle, who is accustomed to seeing death all about him, who knows that he still has his own life by only millimeters, who can measure and see that the bullet missed his body by only millimeters, such a man does not bother to boast. Boasting is based on at least partial lying, and the man who has fought day after day has no cause to exaggerate: he need merely tell the truth; the truth itself is dramatic, exciting enough. Nor do such men commonly belittle their enemy; they simply appraise him and report their findings. As a group the Eagles are rather conservative in their judgments, and I have never heard them unduly praise themselves or blindly belittle the Germans. They have fought the Hun in the air for two years, and there is no trace of panic or patriotism in their estimate of him as a fighter. Their evaluation of him, based on battle after battle, should therefore be reckoned with. And their estimate of the Hun, their belief that he must have the advantage before he will fight, partly explains the need for the combined fighter-bomber operation that simply forces the Germans to rise and give battle.

Peterson, who is truly a great leader and a man very experienced against the Hun, told me he would gladly lead his squadron against a German formation any time he could get odds of two to one against himself. Basing his decision on experience, he figured that with the ratio of two Germans against one American, the odds were then even. He said further that with anything like a slight tactical advantage, he would unhesitatingly lead his squadron of twelve men against three times that number of Germans.

"The individual Hun is a good flier, and some of them are excellent shots. Their leaders have a keen tactical sense and understand how a battle should be fought. Furthermore, they are all well trained. But the really important fact," said Peterson, "is that they lack individual initiative. They have been reared and trained as part of a national machine, and so long as they can maneuver and fight as a machine, they're excellent. But once something slips out of place, once something goes wrong—and something is always going wrong in battle—they lose their mass initiative. Thrown on their own as individuals, they are not as a rule effective fighters.

"I have fought against formations of German fliers that fought superbly, then I've seen the formations broken, and immediately the Jerries started racing for home. Don't misunderstand—there are any number of German fighters who have no lack of initiative. I've seen some of them with brilliant, aggressive minds in battle, minds that worked like lightning, and I've seen some of them attack fiercely and come back to attack again."

"So have I," said Daymond. "I've had Huns chase me all the way from France to England, attacking every chance they got. I'll never forget one Hun—he not only had the usual Nazi markings on his plane, but he had a red Maltese cross painted on the cowling in front of his windshield—who shot the hell out of me all the way from Dunkerque to Dover. He had all the determination and all the guts in the world, and he was fighting absolutely alone."

"But such Jerries are exceptional," said Peterson. "I think that most experienced RAF fighters will agree that the average German fighter lacks initiative, and lacks an instinct for sudden, unexpected attack; he doesn't have the knack of suddenly doing the unpredictable and catching his opponent off base. It's that knack which makes the American and the Englishman so successful in air fighting."

As Peterson was talking I remembered a story that General Asa North Duncan, of the Eighth Air Force, had told me only a few days previously. General Duncan was a fighter in the 1914-1918 war. One day he and George

C. Kenney—now Major General Kenney in command of
the American Air Force in Australia—got in among some
Germans and shot down three of them. That night Duncan
began to figure out the mistakes that he and Kenney had
made. He thought they had better talk it over. So he went
into the mess where Kenney was playing bridge.

"Let's talk about this," Duncan said. "We made some
mistakes today. Let's figure out what we'll do if we ever get
in the same position again."

But Kenney went on playing bridge and said he didn't
want to stop.

"This is important," said Duncan. "We should make a
plan. We should decide what we're going to do."

"Listen," Kenney said, "go on and let me alone. What's
the use in deciding what to do? If we don't know ourselves,
then the Hun won't know. And while he's trying to figure
it out, we'll shoot him down."

That same spirit of leaving it to chance, waiting until the instant of action, and then making a split-second,
almost instinctive decision, is partly the reason the American Volunteer Group under General Chennault has been
so successful in China against the Japanese. Japanese avi-
ators that have been shot down and captured have said
they hated to fight against the Americans. They have said
they could predict the action of some of the other pilots
they were opposing, but the Americans were wild men,
and never did the same thing in the same way, and therefore they were hard to fight against.

Peterson went on talking: "Yet here is something
strange, and it proves Jerry can be the very devil in the
air when he forgets to follow plans and rules laid down by
Goering and the High Command.

"On the day after the night of our big one-thousand
plane attack against Cologne, the Germans fought like
tigers. That day we ran into a formation of them and they

met us head on, instead of turning away as they usually do, instead of refusing to fight unless they have a tactical advantage. Furthermore, after we broke their formation on this day they fought as individuals, and they fought damned well. That day Jerry was mad, and his heart was in the attack. The night before our bombers had blasted one of his big cities, simply plastering it with bombs and flattening whole sections of the town, and the Hun was out to get revenge. He fought magnificently, and we figured we were in for a period of real fun; we figured Jerry at last was going to stand and give battle. But the next time we met him, it was the same old story again: he wouldn't fight unless he had the advantage. After we broke his formation into small units, he was the same as before Cologne—in a big hurry to get back home."

The Rovers, the great fighter sweeps, and the Carnivals, the combined fighter-bomber raids, are staged chiefly to prod the Luftwaffe and bring it into the air, forcing it to fight. The Poker, the other major operation in which the fighters engage, is primarily a bomber show. Each Poker is a carefully planned attack against some military target which the bombers are sent out to destroy; in these attacks the fighters go along merely as escort, as protection. In the Poker the fighters do not seek battle; they are in the air solely to guard the bombers, to take them to their objective, watch over them as they drop their bombs, then bring them back home again.

There are many kinds of bombing raids, but the two kinds that obviously differ most are those made by day, and those by night.

When the raid is at night, the bombers go without fighter escort. This is for several reasons. In the first place, the need for escort at night is infinitely less than during the day. In the second, the fighters could not fly formation in the dark without navigation lights, which would, of course, betray them to the enemy. Finally, the most important reason is that night targets ordinarily are well beyond the flying range of fighter planes.

The big bombers can fly thousands of miles. Some of them carry a gasoline load of eleven thousand gallons, the entire contents of an American tank car. But the little fighters can carry no such load, nor can they travel such tremendous distances. When therefore a Poker, the bomber operation with fighter escort, is planned, the target can never be beyond the range of fighter planes. Up to the present that range has been about one hundred and fifty miles in and one hundred and fifty miles out, a total of three hundred miles—about an hour and a half, or an hour and forty-five minutes, in the air.

Of course, if the fighter flew at a slow cruising speed in a steady direct flying line, he could fly much farther, but there is never slow cruising or direct flying when a fighter is airborne. He is constantly flying at fast speed, and is forever "jinking" all over the sky, twisting, turning, weaving, trying to avoid the flak from below and to prevent any enemy aircraft from sneaking up behind and shooting him down.

Of the total three hundred miles flown on an ordinary fighter sweep, only a small part is flown over enemy territory. Suppose a fighter station in England is seventy miles inland, then that distance has to be covered before the Channel is reached. And the Channel has to be crossed, and the same distance flown back. Therefore, a great part of the total distance is merely going and coming, leaving only the much smaller part for flight over enemy territory, only a comparatively few minutes.

I am writing to-day in a small English village on the seacoast in Kent. Occupied France is just over there, just a little way across the water below my window. As I write, the air raid siren is wailing. Jerry is coming over to pay us a visit. He was over last night and banged us a bit, and here he is again this morning.

With the siren still going I look out of my window and I see the old gardener bending over his vegetables, working with them, not even bothering to look up and see if the Germans are coming in high or low, coming on only a "nuisance" raid or coming in force to give the place a real beating up.

Two women and a man are working in the yard building pens for some rabbits. They go on working and talking. None of them stops for a minute.

Out in the street the people continue on their way, paying no attention to the sirens. One or two glance up, but the Huns are flying high and can't be seen. So the people carry on. Nobody pays any real attention to the Germans up above.

Last night I had dinner at a WAAF mess, and I was talking with the WAAF officers, English girls who have come from castles and tenements to put on the blue uniform of the Women's Auxiliary Air Force.

"You people here get considerable bombing, don't you?" I said.

"Oh, we get our share," a girl of twenty-one told me.

"What do you do when the siren goes?"

"Do!" She looked at me in surprise. "What do you mean?"

"I mean if you're out on parade, for instance; if you're parading your airwomen, inspecting them—what do you do?"

They looked at me, a little puzzled. "We go on parading. What do you expect us to do? I mean, what the hell? You can't stop your job every time some silly ass German comes over to drop a few bombs; You couldn't win a war that way."

"Anyhow, this is nothing," another girl said. "You should have been here at the time of the Blitz;." The girl who was speaking couldn't have been much more than twenty. She was small, with big, brown eyes and a child's voice. "You should have been here then. I was a fire watcher in London, and I'd stand on my post and listen to the bombs come whistling down. As I'd hear each one coming, I knew that one was for me. Then is when your stomach ties up like a knot and your legs turn to water."

"It was terrific, wasn't it?" said another little girl across the table, sitting there in her blue uniform and her blue shirt and tie, her blond hair cut short like a boy's. "Sometimes the whole street would be blazing, and the bombs would be coming down and blasting things, and we'd be standing there at our posts, knowing any minute we might get it. It was really a rather extraordinary experience."

As I listened to these English girls talk, I thought that a nation whose women are so magnificent, so utterly superb, would be very difficult to conquer. And I said to myself that, despite our ancient jealousies, despite our irritating economic rivalries, we Americans are stupid if we don't take these British people into closer friendship, into full political alliance, so that together we, America and the British Commonwealth of Nations, can control a world that we must control, else through subtlety and force it will itself first control, then destroy us both.

Since we are writing primarily of the Eagles, a fighter squadron, we shall ignore the night bombing raids; we'll let the big fellows go their way alone in the darkness, penetrating without fighter escort deep into Germany, carrying their two thousand, four thousand, eight thousand pound bombs—and, God knows, we wish them well.

We shall write only of the bombers that go by day, the bombers that must be protected by the Eagles and other fighter squadrons, that must be in the center of a great cluster of fighters to guard them against sudden attack by the Hun.

When the day bombers are going into an area, an advance guard of fighters is sent to that area with instructions to sweep the enemy fighters from the sky. In particular, this advance guard clears the way directly over the target, because over the target is the place of greatest danger for the bombers. Usually the big planes fly more or less straight, in boxes of four, even through the flak, but the last few seconds immediately before the actual attack is made is the time of their greatest danger. It is then that the bombardier takes command of the plane and calls for a steady, absolutely unswerving course in order that he may "pinpoint" the target, that he may take careful aim and get the target exactly in his bomb-sights before releasing his bombs. If there were numerous enemy fighters nearby, they could attack at this moment of unswerving flight when the bombers would, of course, be easy to hit and destroy. So the advance guard clears the sky of the enemy directly over the target, thus allowing the bombers to make their "run," their few seconds of steady flying during which the bomb dropper can take steady aim.

Besides the advance formation, there are numerous other protecting planes with the bombers. These other fighters fly as close escort immediately beside, above, and in the rear of the big fellows.

And no fighter pilot likes to fly escort: it is the hardest job he can be assigned. The escorting planes are not allowed under any condition to leave the bombers. They must stay in exact position, and they may go into action only if enemy aircraft seek to break through their protecting wall. What little action they get is usually for an instant only, and it is almost never a fight to the finish. Ordinarily, as the enemy aircraft approach, the escort need only turn and fire a short squirt; then the enemy withdraws, just as any man draws back when struck at. But the escort must forego the fun of following and carrying on with the fight; it must turn back into position and stay with the bombers. So the pilots hate the escort job, because, while they fly in the very middle of action, they are never allowed to leave their assigned positions and attack an enemy, even though he is flying alone and in a lazy, tempting manner. Actually, the lone Hun plane is probably sent there by the German commander as bait, to provoke an attack, to draw off some of the fighter escort, thus breaking their formation and opening a gap through which the Germans could dive and get the bombers.

Besides the close escort, besides the planes hovering immediately about the bombers, there is still another formation of protecting planes. High up above, like a man in the Crow's Nest on a ship, is a formation that keeps constant watch, ready to report the first sight of danger. Pilots like to fly in this high protecting cover because from there they not only watch but may be ordered down to attack the enemy if he draws too near the bombers.

With planes in front, on each side, behind, above, and still higher above, the bombers are in the center of a swarm of fighters. Lumbering along at only three or four miles a minute, the big bombers go their way, and they are completely surrounded by the little planes, weaving and turning, holding back their speed in order to stay close by the big fellows who, despite their size and their many guns, need to be chaperoned.

When word arrives at a fighter station that a Poker is scheduled, the station "Tanoy," the loud speaker, calls all pilots to the briefing room. There the wing commander announces the operation and shows on the map the route to be followed and the target the bombers will attack. He tells the squadrons in his wing the time each will take off and the height each will fly. He tells the precise role that each squadron will play in the operation. And he explains exactly where and when the wing will rendezvous with the bombers, exactly where and when the fighters will meet the bombers in the air—possibly fifty miles away, twenty thousand feet up, at nine minutes and three seconds past five o'clock!

After the wing commander has outlined the details of the Poker, he then makes a few casual remarks and says nothing more. There is little more he could say. These men have flown Pokers before: they know their business, every detail of it. Nor is there any need to emphasize the route to the target and the route back home. They have all flown over Occupied France so many times they know it as an ordinary man knows his own backyard.

"We go in here," the commander says, pointing at the spot on the map. "We fly this course to the target. We come out here."

That is all—unless there is to be some new policy in the fighting. If some new plan of attack or defense has been worked out, he will outline it and order that it be followed. Otherwise he merely nods dismissal, and the pilots troop out of the briefing room.

Then, in small groups, they go to their individual squadron dispersal huts. Each of the squadrons in the wing, each of the squadrons on the station, has its own hut, and the pilots go there for a final word from their squadron leader. He may add a few suggestions to what the wing commander has said. He may make some criticisms, pointing out that in the battle of the day before there has been some ragged flying.

But the chances are he will say almost nothing. These chaps have been through it so often that detailed instructions would be silly and a pep talk an insult.

At the exact minute—and on one of these combined operations everything must be done on the exact minute, or men get killed—at the second agreed upon, the first section, the first four planes of the squadron, sweep down the field together and take the air. Then four more. Then the final four. All three sections are now airborne, and the planes circle the field, making their squadron formation. By this time the other two squadrons are airborne, and the three squadrons maneuver into wing formation; then the thirty-six planes fly away to keep their rendezvous with the other fighters and with the bombers themselves.

If one stands below a rendezvous point a few minutes before the time set, he sees one formation of fighters coming from one direction, another coming from another, and he sees the big bombers trundling along through the air, all coming to keep their appointment. For a minute or two they may turn or circle, jockeying for position; then the formation is made over the bombers, and the planes swing out above the Channel and on toward the German military installation, the target for the day, that is to be destroyed in Occupied France or the Occupied Low Countries.

From the time the planes are airborne, during the time they are flying over England and over the Channel approaching France, complete radio telephone silence is maintained; there is no talking whatever among the pilots in the air, or between the pilots and their control stations on the ground. If this silence were broken once, the Germans would instantly hear, and the presence of the formation would be betrayed.

Nor is there any need for talk, for discussion of plans of action, because before the aircraft left the ground every detail of the operation was worked out and thoroughly understood, even the direction of the turn the formation would take after the target had been attacked. Usually the turn is into the sun, so that the pilots can maintain a forward lookout into the great danger spot in the sky, so that they may heed the endless warning: "Watch out for the Hun hiding in the sun!"

With every move fully understood beforehand, the pilots fly without speaking until they know they have been detected, until silence is no longer of value, and then they begin to talk. Usually the first remark is a warning.

"Twelve bandits at nine o'clock." (All positions in the air are obtained by considering the area on all sides as a clock face. A plane directly in front is at twelve o'clock. Directly behind, six o'clock. Directly to the left, nine o'clock. To the right, three o'clock.)

Then a moment later: "Those aren't bandits. They are Spitfires."

Whenever this is said on the R/T, and it often is, somebody invariably wisecracks: "Famous last words"—for many pilots have been shot down because of improper identification, inability to distinguish between friendly and enemy aircraft.

Then silence again while the formation flies on toward the target, and listeners at home stations back in England wait tense, ready to record every word spoken.

And listeners at German stations send out reports of the number and location of the oncoming planes, and send out orders for Hun fighters to rise and intercept.

Then out of the silence comes the voice of a squadron leader: "Stardust Blue IV, you silly bastard, get back into formation."

And silence once more.

Then comes the real thing: "Eighteen bandits at three o'clock, four thousand feet below."

The escort immediately draws in closer about the bombers, like a hen tightening its wings about its sheltered chicks.

Then: "Twenty-four bandits at ten o'clock, two thousand feet above."

"Twelve bandits at one o'clock, three thousand feet below."

"Christ, the sky is full of the beggars."

And the calm voice of the wing commander: "Careful, you chaps. Steady now."

"Look out, Stardust Red IV—look out! He's just behind you."

Then silence again as the attacking German plane draws back from the quick squirt that Stardust Red IV has sent at him. (Each squadron has a code name—Stardust, Otter, Hercules, etc.—and in the air when five squadrons, for example, are in formation there are five Red IV's, or Blue II's, or White III's. One of the absolute laws of battle is that in naming a plane it must not only be named by position—Red IV—but be named by squadron as well; it must not be called merely Red IV, but be given its full name, Stardust Red IV. Otherwise every Red IV in the formation would think a Jerry was on his tail and would unnecessarily take accentuated evasive action.)

The bombers drone on toward their target, flying through the flak that is being thrown up from below, the explosives that are bursting nearer and nearer as the ground guns get the height and the speed of the bombers.

Then: "Jesus, look at that bomber!"

"He's had it, all right."

"Good God, look at him burn."

Silence for an instant.

Then: "There goes one baling out."

"There's another."

After a minute as the burning plane goes down: "The rest of them have had it."

And the quiet voice of the wing commander: "Escort wing in a little closer. In a little closer to the bombers, you fellows."

"There goes another one."

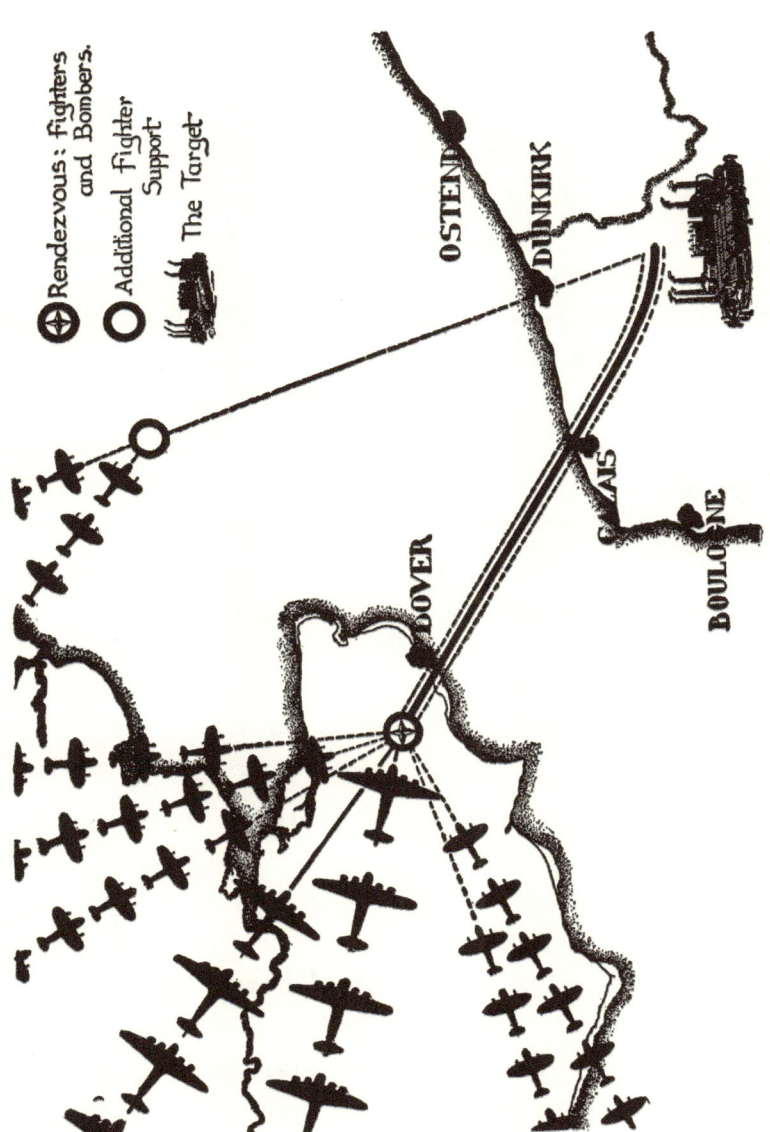

RENDEZVOUS AND TARGET

"Christ, look at him blow up."

"That flak is getting plenty thick."

"Hercules Blue IV, look out! Bob, Bob—look out! For Christ's sake, watch what you're doing. That 109 was right on top of you."

"Yeah, but he's not there any longer. I got it right up his behind."

Then from high above, from the high cover escort: "Otter Blue Section—Otter Blue Section—there are two bandits at eleven o'clock one thousand feet below. Otter Blue Section—attack."

As the four planes of the cover escort peel off to attack the two bandits at eleven o'clock, the main body of the German fighters makes a determined advance, seeking to break through and get at the bombers. But the close escort turns toward the Huns and drives them off, firing short bursts at them and forcing them back, then swinging into position, taking their places close beside the bombers once more.

The Germans reform and come back.

"Here the bastards come again."

"I wish to Christ they'd get within range."

"There's one within range now. Hercules White III, he's just behind you. Look out!"

"I've been hit. And the son-of-a-bitch is coming again. He's on my tail and . . ."

"Jesus! Poor old Ted."

This time the Germans do not draw back. They press their attack bravely, and soon a real battle develops. The high cover escort, free to attack where they will, dive to support the defending fighters, and planes from both sides go down, some of them wobbling down like birds with broken wings, others bursting into flames, still others exploding and flinging fragments far in every direction.

From one of the planes going down, a boy jumps. Then a parachute opens. A great white mushroom suddenly appears in the sky and goes drifting down, a black speck dangling beneath it.

Driven back, the remaining German planes dive away and the escort instantly goes into close formation about the bombers once more, the rear planes in each section moving up to take the place of those that have been shot down.

In the air all pilots fly with their transmitters turned to "Receive." They are constantly ready to receive any message sent them by other pilots or by the controller from their base back in England. Only when a pilot wants to speak does he press the "Send" button. One of the worst of all crimes is to forget and fly with the transmitter on "Send." If this is done, no one in the air on that frequency can speak to anyone else on that same frequency; all communication on that frequency is stopped. Occasionally, though, a pilot does forget and flies with the wrong button pressed. It happened not long ago when the Eagles were out on a big show. While the pilot in the air and the listeners on the ground were tensely waiting for the first word that would indicate the beginning of the battle, they heard a homesick voice singing mournfully about a very distant part of the world:

"Home, home on the range
Where the deer and the antelope play;
Where seldom is heard
A discouraging word
And the skies are not cloudy all day."

Another pilot one day left his transmitter on "Send." In each plane is a red button descriptively called the "tit." It is the button that, when pushed, gives the boost, the extra speed, that sometimes is needed. But "pulling the tit" is bad for the engine; it puts a strain on the motor, and the engineers beg the boys not to do it unless they are really hard pressed. One day one of the Eagles, who was very much in love, was trying to get out of France, and the coastline flak guns were throwing up a terrible lot of stuff at him. He finally got through the barrage, but the gunners were still peppering the sky with their shells, and the plane was wobbling and jerking from the explosions. Finally the boy, deciding that things were a little too hot and remembering his date for that night back in England, was heard to say: "Nuts to that engineer—I want to see Kathleen." So the listeners knew that the tit had been pulled, and the young Eagle was flying at extra speed away from the German gunners and toward his beloved Kathleen.

Another time a most unheroic conversation was taken down by the listeners on the ground, who, of course, record everything that is spoken in the air. Two pilots from the Eagle Squadron were flying patrol over a convoy. One of the most reprehensible of all offenses is to break R/T (Radio Telephony) silence over a convoy, because in so doing the exact location of the ships is betrayed to the enemy. But this day out of the silence from the skies suddenly came this unmistakable voice from Carolina:

"Andy—Andy—mah belly hurts."

No answer from the other pilot on the patrol.

Then: "Mah belly hurts and mah tooth aches and Ah'm a-goin' home."

A single infuriated word from the other pilot: "Scram!"

The ailing brother departed for home, but ten minutes later he was back. "Andy, Ah'm a-gonna stick by you. Ah ain't gonna desert you. But mah tooth still aches and mah belly still hurts."

Another unnecessary R/T conversation, and one without excuse at all, not even excuse of a belly-ache, was recorded by an indignant signal officer.

A pilot on patrol broke silence with this silly remark: "How are you, old chappie?"

"Why do you call me old chappie?" asked his companion in the air.

"Because you are an old chappie."

Admitted that these boys were simply bored stiff with their dull flying over the convoy, yet no amount of boredom justified their breaking silence. When they landed, they were sent for by their commanding officer, who already had a full report of the conversation. Their C.O. blistered them, then next day put the report of the conversation on the squadron bulletin board. He wrote the names of the offenders on the report. He also wrote: "Each day these officers will read this and each will say to himself: I am a ——, spelled with a capital S.'"

One of the greatest uses of the R/T is made when a plane has been attacked and so damaged that the pilot must bale out. Of course, if he is going down over enemy territory, he simply tells his pals good-by—if there is time—and jumps. But if he is over the sea, and is going down into the sea, he presses the "D" button in his plane, and that puts him on a wireless channel that is used only in emergency. There are four channels used by the fighters, four frequencies, one of which, channel "D," is kept clear until it is desperately needed.

When, therefore, a pilot is about to bale out over the sea, he switches to "D" and calls: "Mayday! . . . Mayday! . . . Hercules, Blue Three. . . . Hercules Blue Three. . . . Mayday! Mayday! Mayday!" The cry is the international sign of distress and actually is the French supplication: *"M'aidez! M'aidez!* Help me! Help me!" But the English have corrupted the spelling, and now one ordinarily sees it written as simply "Mayday!" After he has made his cry, the pilot then counts slowly: "One—two—three—four—five—six—seven—eight—nine—ten."

The sound of his voice in the slow counting carries to three different radio stations in England. At each station the listeners draw a line from their station in the direction the voice came from. These three lines are then swiftly plotted, and where they cross is the spot the pilot descended into the sea. "Air Sea Rescue Service" is then notified, a boat is immediately despatched to the spot, and the pilot is taken from his dinghy and brought back safely to England.

Sometimes when a pilot bales out under five hundred feet, his cry is not effective because the radio signal does not carry properly if sent from so low an altitude. Then his pals, who have seen him jump, climb to two thousand feet directly above him, and send out the distress signal for him.

I was on a station with the Eagles one day when one of them did a particularly brave job in protecting two pilots and summoning Air Sea Rescue Service to take them from the sea.

The boys were returning from France and were low on petrol, having made a long sweep by Dunkerque and St. Omer. At Cap Gris Nez many German fighters followed them out, looking for stragglers. Helgason, flying Blue IV, and watching behind to see that he wasn't bounced by the Huns, saw two boys from another RAF squadron shot down and bale out. They were behind the Eagles and far below, and Helgason knew if he took his eyes off the two falling boys for a second, he would lose them. He instantly broke away alone, dived beneath the numerous Germans, and covered the RAF pilots after their parachutes had opened and they were plainly visible to the Huns. Helgason circled the men as they went down, and he saw them hit at about the same time; he saw both of them go deep into the cold water of the Channel. There was a fair sea rolling, and at times, as they struggled with the harness of their chutes, the two pilots disappeared from view under the whitecaps breaking over them.

When at last the boys in the sea inflated their dinghies, they climbed into them. And Helgason circled above, flying so low that his camouflaged plane could not be seen by the Jerries who were searching for the two pilots, trying to find them and kill them as they sat in their dinghies.

After a time most of the Jerries returned to France. But three of them remained, still searching for the boys in the sea. When there were only three Huns, Helgason figured the odds were in his favor; so he rose to give battle. The Jerries must have figured the same as Helgason, because all three of them turned and fled. Helgason climbed on up and gave a fix. A minute later the Air Sea Rescue launches were on their swift way to pick up the pilots in the sea.

By risking his life to save two men, Helgason actually saved ten men.

The night before, a bomber had been shot down over the sea. The plane had been destroyed, but the entire crew of eight men were safe, floating about in their dinghy. Three times during the day they had seen rescue boats, but they themselves had not been seen, and now the dinghy was leaking badly and was sinking. The boat that came out to rescue the two men Helgason had guarded, sighted the bomber crew, and all ten men were saved.

After the big bombers on a Poker have been taken to their destination, and after they have done their jobs, dropping their bombs and blasting the target, the whole formation wheels and starts for home; the Poker starts back for England.

Once Occupied France is cleared, once the Channel is crossed and the English landfall is made, then the wing commanders and the squadron commanders begin to ask if every one is all right. Maybe some man has been hit, but says there's no need to worry; he can make it back to his base station all right. Maybe some man says he has been hit and is bleeding badly. He says he is landing at some forward airdrome; he is going down at the nearest landing field.

After the men have been checked, the commanders then ask about petrol; they ask if every one has enough to get back to base. And the pilots come in with their reports: "Twenty-three gallons. . . . Twenty-one gallons. . . . Twenty-four gallons."

Satisfied that all is well with man and machine, the commanders order the fighter wings and squadrons to break off from the bombers, leaving the big fellows to return alone to their base, while the fighters go back to their own stations in time for tea.

And another operation has been completed.

10

In the early days of their fighting, the Eagles were not of much value. They were so poor, in fact, that the commanding officer of the station said they should be disbanded. He pointed out that the first Eagle shot down was very probably shot down by the Eagles themselves. In a scrap over the Channel, three Eagles lined up behind a Jerry and poured lead into him and, incidentally, poured an equal amount of lead into the RAF plane just in front of the Nazi. Fortunately, the Eagle flying in the English plane was not killed, but the aircraft itself was shot to bits and crumpled as it crash-landed on the English coast. A fighter aircraft is valued at $30,000, and while, of course, a fighter pilot himself could never in any way be evaluated, the training given him costs the Government approximately $125,000: the major loss, therefore, was not suffered, but the commanding officer still couldn't have chaps going around shooting down friendly aircraft even if they didn't get the pilot.

"The point," said the officer, "is that they'll never make a team. These Americans differ among themselves quite as much as they differ from us, from the English. They're not a unified group in their background, or their ways of living, or their thinking. And they'll never fit themselves into a fighting team: they'll never learn to fight as a unified group."

There were any number of individual reasons why the commanding officer despaired of the Eagles in modern aerial warfare. One of the chief reasons was Mike Kolendorski.

Mike was a Polish-American boy from New Jersey. He was a complete individualist and to hell with the rules of modern air fighting; he hated the Germans and he wanted to get at them. He meant to fight them in every way he could. Flying a fighter plane, Mike couldn't carry bombs, but he improvised some bombs of his own. Before a flight he would fill his pockets with brickbats and stuff beer bottles here and there. Once he was over some German camp he would chuck out his brickbats and beer bottles, hoping that some of them might crack a German or two on the head. One day Mike had an idea of which he was mighty proud. What was the sense of carrying over empty beer bottles? So in grim humor he filled one in his own particular way and swooped low over an Occupied city to hurl the bottle and its beer-looking contents into the midst of some Germans who were dining at a sidewalk cafe. Mike thought that the greatest fun he had ever had.

He was a wonderful fighter, this Kolendorski. The other boys in the squadron said he would be the first to win the Distinguished Flying Cross, or he would be the first killed. They were right.

The squadron leader warned Mike over and over again. He told him if he didn't fly in formation the Germans would shoot him down. He said that darting off alone was simply offering himself for cold meat. But Mike said to hell with it. He came over to fight Germans, and he'd fight them in his own way.

The next afternoon he was flying with the squadron and saw a lone Hun stooging along. The squadron leader gave a warning over the R/T, calling out that it was a trap and for everyone to stay in formation. Mike held back as long as he could, but he couldn't stand it and he dived.

Then from out of the sun came the Germans that had been hiding there. They dived on Mike from every angle, and they shot his plane to pieces and shot the pieces to pieces. Mike tried to jump, but they killed him as he was climbing out, and he fell like lead, never opening his parachute. The next day the Germans broadcast that his body had been picked up on the Dutch coast, and that he was buried in Holland.

Individualists, a little cocky, these American boys were hard to whip into a team. They still thought of air battles as they were fought in the last war, when their heroes went out singly and won their exciting victories. They didn't realize that Guynemer, Foncke, Rickenbacker, and all the others were like the knights of feudal days who went forth and fought in single combat, challenging an opponent to individual battle and fighting him according to the rules of chivalry. They didn't understand that now the individual pilot has become a part of a mass aerial formation just as the knight has been lost in mass troop movement. Nor did they understand that the aerial chivalry of the last war is gone in the complete killing of the present.

Once the Eagles learned there was a new kind of war being fought, once they realized their old ideas of chivalric air fighting were outmoded, they gave up their individuality in the air, and fought together as a team. Under the instruction of Churchill and Woodhouse and Meares they learned to fly and fight as a closely-knit unit: each man in the air surrendered his love of individual adventure and became part of the squadron.

But on the ground no Eagle surrendered anything. These swashbucklers of the early days of the squadron, the picturesque fellows who came over first, could never lose the individuality that has made them, and tales of them, part of the rich tradition of the RAF.

One of the most memorable of the early Eagles was Andy Mamedoff. This bizarre fellow was a White Russian. By devious routes that had led him into strange parts of the world, Andy finally showed up in Miami. There he made a living by taking people up for joy rides in an old hack that long ago had been discarded by an aviation transportation company. But this aerial hacking was much too tame for Andy, and when finally he had the opportunity to enlist and get out of his humdrum job, he packed up, went to England, and joined the RAF.

He was a good flier and in time proved himself a good leader. They made him a flight commander. But Andy had bad luck. For some reason he was never able to make contact with the enemy; he never found any good fights, though he was forever out looking for them. He was as brave as any one, but on the day Andy was flying over the Channel the big fight was over France; when he went over France, the fight was somewhere above the Channel.

Hunting in the air is like hunting on the ground. Some men are lucky, and they hardly load their guns before the deer or the bear or the moose come walking into the open. Other men may hunt for a whole season and not get a shot. Fighter pilots are constantly hunting, forever prowling about the sky looking for something to shoot, just as a man goes through the bush looking for game to shoot, but some of the pilots are unlucky and never get to fire their guns.

One of the most fortunate of the Eagles was a great hunter, even before the war. All his life he had loved it. "But you know," he said, "this is the finest hunting I've ever had. Before, I used to hunt rabbits down in Tennessee. Then I only had a shotgun. Now I got two cannon and four machine-guns—and the rabbits can shoot back."

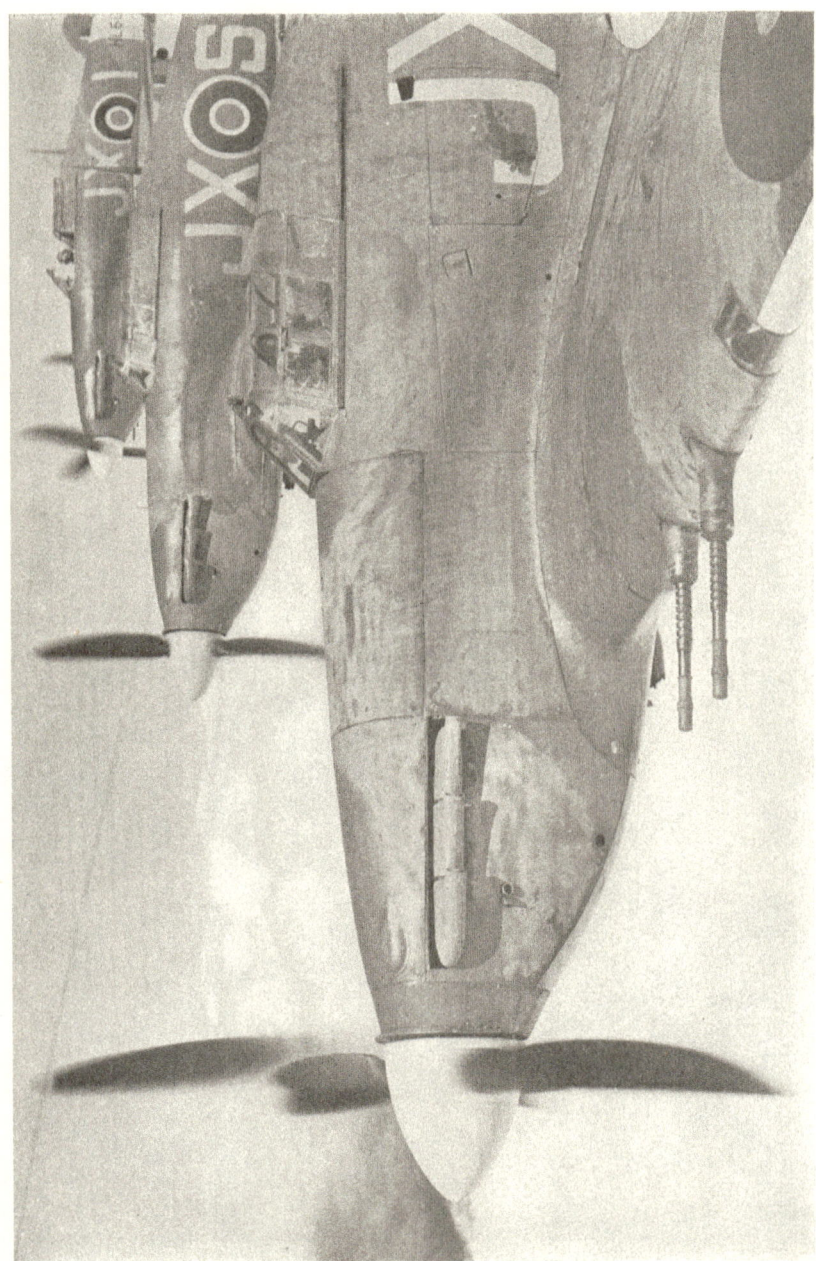

PACKED IN CLOSE: A really tight formation, when they're flying almost wing-tip to wing-tip.

PEELING OFF: Hurricanes peeling off formation before diving to the attack.

Sometimes the boys get so tired of going out day after day, hunting and finding nothing, that they frame up tricks to get Jerry to come up for battle. They bait the trap in various ways, and sometimes Jerry falls into it, but other times the ruse fails, and the Eagles fly home without having drawn blood.

One of the strangest of all efforts to pick a fight was made by a man named Humphrey Gilbert, an Englishman, who was with the Eagles as one of their flight commanders. Gilbert was one of the absolute best, though when he first went with the Squadron the boys didn't realize it. He was what unknowing Americans are accustomed to call a "typical" Englishman, though of course there is no more a "typical" English than there is a typical American. An Englishman from Yorkshire is as different from a man of Kent as a Maine Yankee is different from a Texas ranger. To the American who doesn't know the English, the "typical" Englishman is the monocled, buck-toothed, silly ass so commonly portrayed on the American stage and screen. While this dull and arrogant fellow does exist in England, he is, mercifully, extremely rare; certainly he is not the Englishman one ordinarily meets while living in England. Curiously enough, Gilbert actually was a little like the man usually depicted in Hollywood. He had slightly long hair, and he loved to smooth it back with a casual gesture while half reclining in an easy chair. And he had an accent that, for some strange reason, even the English call an "Oxford accent": that is, his "a" was very broad, and his speech had a faint suggestion of affectation.

When he first sauntered into the mess and spoke to the Eagles, they didn't like him. "To hell with him," they said, making the usual mistake of damning a "foreigner" because he was different from themselves.

But in time they came to know this man as a truly lovable fellow, a good drinking companion, and a leader

Above: ANDY MAMEDOFF and "SHORTY" KEOUGH, killed in flying accidents; "RED" TOBIN, killed in action. *Below:* MIKE KOLENDORSKI, killed in action.

T. P. McGERTY,
killed in action.

FLIGHT LIEUTENANT
HUMPHREY GILBERT,
DFC, killed in a flying accident.

stubbornly loyal to the men under him. They came to know, too, that in battle he had the heart of a lion. The Eagles still regard him as one of their friends and finest flight leaders.

One of the ways Gilbert won the boys was by his ability to sing. At night he loved to go to the pub and sit there with his beer mug before him and sing quietly. In England at the time were four American Negro singers known as "The Four Ink Spots," and they had won considerable fame. They sang in soft, whispering voices, and Gilbert liked to sing as they did. He was so good that when he sang all the Eagles gathered around close, and the other people in the pub stopped talking and listened.

This singing was at night. In the day there were battles to be fought, and no one enjoyed them more than Gilbert. Almost indifferent to danger, he was still a wise leader— except on one occasion when, just for the hell of it, he and his boys thumbed their noses at the Germans.

Gilbert was the inventor of the famous Eagle phrase: "Brave and calm, chaps." One day they were maneuvering to get into position to attack a German formation, and some of the boys were too eager; they swung out of line and hung poised, ready to dive. But Gilbert knew the most favorable position had not yet been reached, so over the R/T came his quiet voice, saying almost casually: "Take it easy. Wait a minute longer. Be brave and calm, chaps." Then the next instant: "Now! And let the beggars have it." It was Gilbert himself who dived first, leading his men into battle.

On the morning Gilbert and his flight really expressed their feelings about the Germans, they risked their lives, but they thought it great fun and wanted to do it again.

That morning Gilbert and his men had been flying over some of the most dangerous spots they could find, daring the Germans to rise and fight, daring them to come up. They followed the usual taunting tactics and flew over German airdromes, picking out airdromes where German fighters would be certain to see them, daring the fighters to come up and give battle. Finally, after having drawn a total blank, Gilbert led his men over St. Omer, one of the hottest spots in all Occupied France. Here the Hun kept some of his best fighters and kept them in large numbers. Surely, Gilbert believed, he and his boys could find a fight at St. Omer. So they flew over the airdrome. But no German planes rose. They flew over it again.

"I say, you bastards," called Gilbert over the R/T, drawling out the insulting word in the best Oxford accent, "don't you see us up here? Come up and fight."

But no German came up.

So the Eagles flew over the airdrome again. Again no Germans took the air.

"Very well," Gilbert said, "if they won't rise and fight, we'll jolly well show them how it should be done."

So he divided his flight into two sections of three planes each, and there, twelve thousand feet over one of the most feared airdromes in France, there in the midst of the German flak, he and his American Eagles fought a six-minute dog fight.

When the mock battle was over, Gilbert ordered his flight back into regular formation again and, brave and calm, flew away.

"Very unsporting of them," he said. "Very unsporting not to come up and fight. I'm afraid that, actually, Jerry is just a bit of a ——!"

There's small wonder that the Eagles adored this daredevil Englishman whose appearance and whose casual, almost bored manner so belied his character and his courage. Through Gilbert, and through hundreds of others like

him, the Eagles came to know that the English hide their
courage behind little mannerisms, that where the American is prone to talk and be fully honest about his ideas and
his emotions, the Englishman is rather a shy fellow who
is even willing to be considered effete rather than let you
know he can fight and die as brave and calm as any man.
Indeed, Gilbert had been with the Eagles for weeks before
they learned that in two of his battles, before he joined
them, he had been shot down into the sea. He was the kind
of man who might have had a dozen victories or been shot
down a dozen times, yet would never mention it.

Along with all his other abilities, Gilbert was an expert at aerial acrobatics. He particularly enjoyed climbing
above the Eagles' dispersal shack and diving down with
such force, and coming so near, that the hut would actually tremble. He came so close one day that he caused the
chimney to collapse. And he came so close on another day
that an even greater accident resulted.

The Eagles often shot at crows with a small shotgun
they kept in their dispersal shack. Indeed, they had a rather regrettable habit of shooting at all birds. So much so, in
fact, that the birds stopped flying near the hut. The birds
stayed away for so long that Gussie Daymond said they
had hung signs in all the trees near dispersal: "Flak Area,"
the sign said, according to Gussie.

"If you don't believe it," he said, "just look at any bird
that flies near here. Every damned one of them weaves as
he goes over."

One day an old crow didn't weave quite enough, and
Wally Tribken damaged his wing, even if he did miss the
fuselage. After he had shot him down, Wally took pity on
the crow, and took him into the dispersal shack. On the
roster sheet where records of combat were kept, Wally put
down: "Wally, One Victory."

Carefully he fed the bird and did his best to get Doc Osborne to patch up the injured wing so that the boys could keep it for a squadron pet. But Doc told him to get the bloody thing outta there—for sanitary reasons. Wally refused, despite the fact that after the bird had been around dispersal for three or four days, all the other Eagles voted in support of Doc's sanitary view. Still Wally wouldn't give in. It was his crow, and, by golly, he would keep it. Nobody was going to feed his crow to Eight Ball, the squadron cat that was always hanging around, looking at the crow and licking his chops.

Some one named the crow Geronimo, and he was always parked atop the flying locker where the boys kept their kits. The Eagles would sit in dispersal and scowl at Geronimo, and Geronimo would scowl back at the Eagles. Only Wally was his friend, daily bringing him water and food.

As I said, this Gilbert was really an acrobatic ace. When he beat up the dispersal shack, he didn't fool about it. Windows would shake. Ink bottles would fall off the table. He would come so close to the little frame building that the compression beneath his wings—the packing of the air against the ground—would actually make the building contract and expand with a frequency proportional to the four hundred miles an hour Gilbert was traveling. Then he would pull the stick back and his Spitfire would climb straight into the blue for more than two thousand feet. As he neared the top of these ferocious zooms he would often roll the Spitfire two and a half times. That would put him in an inverted position where he would again pull back the stick, dive, and repeat the maneuver. Each time, he would aim for the shack. Each time the shack would dance.

It was pretty dull that afternoon. There was plenty of ceiling, though, and there might be action. Anyhow, all

Peterson's Blue Section was on readiness. Everyone had his flying equipment and airplane at the ready.

But things were just too damned quiet to last. It wasn't natural for things to be quiet around the Eagles. Geronimo was perched atop Wally's footlocker. He, too, was having a dull day of it. Indeed, he finally got so bored with scowling at the Eagles that he turned around until his posterior was pointed into dispersal. Furthermore, he had the advantage of altitude.

The Eagles were dispersed around the small coal stove. Everything was dull . . . very dull . . . too dull. . . .

Four thousand feet above the shack, Humphrey Gilbert had pushed the throttle all the way to the gate and was starting down in one of his hell dives, straight for the dispersal shack. A Spitfire can't travel as fast as sound, but sometimes it seems to.

And this time there was no indication that the dispersal shack was collapsing until after Gilbert had pulled up. Everybody sort of involuntarily crouched, but still they knew it was a harmless beat-up. Everybody knew that nothing would happen to the roof itself. Everybody knew that Gilbert would miss the chimney—by six or seven inches. Everybody knew all these things, except Geronimo.

There were two reasons why the Eagles poured out of the dispersal shack that afternoon. One was to wave at the grinning Gilbert. The other was to get as far out of range of Geronimo as possible.

After Wally was made to swab decks for an entire afternoon, Geronimo was never seen again, whereas Eight Ball came out of the hut, washed her face with her paws, stretched out comfortably, and went to sleep in the sun.

Gilbert was a wild man in disguise. During the *Scharnhorst* and *Gneisenau* fight, on the day these ships were escaping and battles were fought all through the skies above the Channel, Gilbert attacked seven different

German fighters before returning with empty guns. While he was with the Eagles he did a lot for these American boys, teaching them the kind of men Englishmen really are beneath their rather stiff exterior. But, on the other hand, he embarrassed the Eagles: they were distinctly humiliated to discover that any one, especially an Englishman, could do crazy things in a crazier way than they could.

The Eagles were all fond of Gilbert, and they were truly unhappy when his plane crashed in a flying accident and he was killed.

While Andy Mamedoff, the White Russian with the Eagles, was brave, he was not calm. He would come in from a patrol swearing bloody murder. He would vow that he, alone, would fly forth for the glory of all the Russians, and he, single-handed, would attack the whole damned Luftwaffe. But despite his threats, Andy just couldn't find a fight with the Germans. Finally, rather bored with his bad luck, Andy turned to his second love. Next to fighting, Andy best loved to gamble. He was forever trying to get up a game of poker or red dog or twenty-one. Failing that, he would saunter over to someone: "Match you for a shilling," he would say. Or: "I'll cut you for a pound."

Andy gambled even on the day of his wedding.

He and his little English bride were married at the church in Epping. Afterwards, they went for the celebration lunch to The Thatched, the inn where so often at night the boys had drunk their beer and planned dawn raids over France.

But the lunch was a lonely meal. Andy and his young wife of a few minutes sat with only Robbie. None of the other boys was present. They had been kept at the station nearby on thirty minutes available. Andy knew his pals had tried to get free and come to his wedding, but the commanding officers had reminded them that a war was on and that fighter pilots couldn't be released from duty—

not even for a marriage ceremony. So Andy sat solemnly pondering the fate that had kept his pals from the church and from the celebration at lunch. The more he pondered his fortune, the more he drank, until finally the Russian boy was despondent even on the day of his wedding. Seeking excitement, he challenged Robbie to match him for a pound. Robbie matched him and won.

"I'll toss you again," Andy said.

They tossed again and Robbie won. And again and again, until Robbie had won thirteen pounds.

Then Andy said: "Mrs. Mamedoff, there won't be any honeymoon. The Mamedoffs are broke."

Where before there had been only despondency, now there was complete gloom.

"I'll toss you again, double or quits," Robbie said. "If you lose, you can pay me later."

So they tossed once more, and Robbie managed to lose, and then Andy was fully gay again. There would be a honeymoon, after all. In the midst of his gaiety, the swinging of his glass, and the singing of a Russian song, he paused and listened. Then Robbie, too, heard the sound. Together, with the little wife trailing them, they rushed out of the inn and into the street.

There could be no mistaking the sound they had heard: it was the shrill whine of the diving Spitfires. Andy's pals were coming to the celebration after all. The commanders might deny them the privilege of orthodox celebrations, but no one could deny the Eagles the right to climb into their airplanes and go flying. So they flew to Epping, and they swooped down until the leaves of the trees felt the blast of their propellers. They roared so low over the town that it is recorded that a sow, racing and squealing in terror, littered before her time near the entrance to The Thatched.

Adding to this pandemonium was the bridegroom himself as he stood in the middle of the street and cheered

and cheered, waving his arms at the diving planes that had
come to do him honor. "There are my boys." He pointed
toward them and lifted his hat aloft. "There they are."
As the screaming planes continued their brilliant flying,
Andy Mamedoff struck a mighty pose and beat his chest.
"They have come to do me honor. They have come for
the glory of all the Russians." Slightly crocked from all
the wine and brandy that Robbie had poured into him,
and even when sober a little full of Russian hooey, Andy
strutted and swaggered and shouted about his boys and
the glory of all the Russians, while young Mrs. Mamedoff
clung to Robbie's arm and wondered.

Then the planes were high again, and Andy made his
way back to the honeymoon vehicle, striding toward it as
if it were a royal coach. But it happened to be an ancient
and very asthmatic automobile that Andy had acquired for
the occasion. Attached to the car were all the tin cans the
Eagles had been able to collect for days past, and that Robbie had tied in places where they would make the most
noise. Andy climbed in, and beside him sat his wife. With a
great bow to his pals still in the sky, hovering over him, Andy
took his place behind the wheel and pressed the starter.

But the car was old and tired, and not even for the
glory of all the Russians would it start. Andy spoke to it
in English, in Russian, in the medley of tongues he had
acquired in his various journeys to distant places. But still
the car would not start. So Robbie drove into position behind the wedding coach and pushed it through the streets
of the village, while Andy carefully steered around the
extremely young pigs and nodded in royal condescension
to the bewildered onlookers.

Once the town was cleared and Robbie could give the
old car a long push, the motor caught, and Andy, with a
wave to his pals in the planes above him and his pal in the
car behind, chugged away on his honeymoon.

It was some time later, on a day of appalling weather, that a plane had to go north to Ireland. Andy volunteered to fly it. He must have got off his course somehow, because he flew into a hill, and they found him and his aircraft crumpled together at the bottom of it.

11

Once or twice the squadron didn't confine their hunting to Germans alone. Once or twice they turned on each other.

At a date unnamed, a new engineer officer, whom we shall call Jerome Brady, joined the squadron. This man came with a very great reputation as an engineer. Indeed, for some years he had been chief engineer for a great airline flying in and out of Santiago, Chile. But he had left his job because he wanted to fly airplanes, not merely work on their engines. Actually, he had flown a lot, and when he left South America after the outbreak of the war in 1939 he had gone to France, paying his own expenses so that he could fly and fight for France. But France fell too soon for him to fly with the French, and he made his way to England. There he offered his services as pilot. But his record showed his experience as an engineer, and he was commissioned as an Engineer Officer. Deeply hurt by being refused flying status, he nevertheless did his work so well that soon he became known throughout the RAF as one of the best engineers in all England. But his success meant little to him. He wanted to be a fighter pilot, and nothing else would satisfy him.

Jealous of the boys who were flying and fighting, he grumbled at them and said they were a bunch of little twerps who couldn't really fly in the first place, and who

certainly didn't care a damn about the maintenance of
their airplanes. Nothing further from the truth could have
been said about these lads who loved airplanes even more
than they loved women, and the pilots came to dislike him
thoroughly. That is, they disliked him until slowly they
realized why he grumbled and why he blamed them; then
they saw through his fraud and knew that he was taking
out his disappointment on them, using them as a butt for
his own unhappiness at being denied the chance to join
them in battle. So they broke down his barricade, and once
they got to know him, they voted him a very stout fellow
and took him along with them on their evenings to the
pub. Soon he became so regular a visitor that almost every
evening he could be seen with a pint of beer in his hand,
joining in the talk, yet miserable as the boys described
the big fight of the day, telling how the Germans came
up and gave battle and how they had shot them down.
One night at The Thatched, a half drunken pilot—not an
Eagle, by the way—called Brady a wingless wonder, and
that broke his heart. He had flown for more than five
thousand hours, yet here was a kid calling him a wingless
wonder.

Next day Brady again made application to become a
pilot. The application was refused because of the need for
an engineer of his remarkable ability and also because of
his age. From then on, Brady was perpetually threatening
to resign his commission. Every two or three weeks he
would stride into the office of the commanding officer
and hand in his final resignation, his absolutely final resignation. Upon the resignation being refused, Brady would
stalk out. Two weeks later the storm would break within
him again, and once more he would return to resign.

"And this time it is absolutely final, sir," he would say.

One evening in the summer, after a heavy day's work,
the Eagles having made three sweeps over France that day,

Brady, Robinson, and a new boy we shall call Bob Holloran, together with three girls, went to a country pub in Essex and there consumed fairly large quantities of beer. When at ten o'clock the pubs closed, the convivial friends returned to the station and picked up the commanding officer of the Eagle Squadron. Robbie also picked up a bottle of Scotch which he put in the back of the car. Then they all drove to a pleasantly secluded spot where they sat in the moonlight and talked.

Robbie and the Commanding Officer were sitting in the front of the parked car with the most attractive of the three girls. This worried Brady no end, for he wanted this little girl for himself. First he tried talking to her from the back of the car, but without success. Then he got out, walked around, and put his head in through the window; but however he tried, the solution was always unsatisfactory to him. He then grabbed Robbie's bottle of whisky, and before anyone realized what had happened, he had drunk three quarters of the bottle neat. Since he'd had no dinner at all, the whisky on top of the beer produced marvelous results.

Brady, standing on unsteady legs, made an oration in the moonlight. He recounted his life since he had joined the squadron. He brought the whole history down to the morning of that very day, leaving out no detail. And when he came to that day, his voice rose and fell in dramatic rhythm.

"Today," he said, "twelve planes went out over France. Twelve planes returned. And why? Why, I ask you, did they return? Because I, a wingless wonder, have kept those airplanes in perfect condition, so that these little twerps with only a few hundred hours of flying can go out over France and fight. Twelve airplanes up. Twelve airplanes down. No trouble. My job is successfully done, and done forever. I'll have no more of this sending other men into

the sky. By God, I'll get up there myself if I have to steal
a bloody kite. I'll have a go at Jerry if I have to fly a Tiger
Moth. Good night, Robbie. Good night, sir. I am leaving now. It is my absolutely final resignation. And I shall
never come back."

With that he walked slowly and unsteadily across the
field in the general direction of the English Channel, toward which he was going in order to start a new life, to
seek conquests more exciting than a mere wingless wonder
could achieve.

It was with the greatest difficulty that they succeeded
in getting him back into the car. And then they took the
girls home.

Afterward, as they went home themselves, they all felt
rather jolly and played about the village streets, with one
of them carrying a sandwich board up and down, trying
to sell imaginary cigarettes to non-existent people in an
empty street.

Eventually, though, they broke off their merriment and
drove back toward the station. Brady, sitting in front with
Robinson and the C.O., suddenly sighed, put his head on
the C.O.'s chest, and went quietly asleep.

"Robbie," the C.O. said, "he thinks I'm his popsy."

When they got back to the station, Brady was flat out,
and refused to be wakened.

"Let him sleep," someone said.

But Robinson made one last attempt to get him up.
Being well shaken, Brady finally woke, got out of the car,
and stared, wild-eyed, about him.

"Robbie," he said, steadying himself on the car, "this is
a bad business."

Thinking that Brady was referring to his condition,
Robbie said, "Yes, old boy, but you'll be better in the
morning."

"This is a bad business, Robbie. Either you or the C.O. has got my girl, my little popsy, and when I find out who it is, I'll shoot you on sight. I like you, and I like the C.O., but even a wingless wonder will shoot a man for his popsy."

Brady went upstairs and to his room. A few minutes later he came out with a loaded gun. Waving the gun before him, he announced that someone would die. Whoever had his popsy would die. Apparently he had forgotten completely that the girls had been taken home three-quarters of an hour earlier. Nor would he believe them when they told him that his popsy was probably already asleep dreaming of him.

While this was going on, a rather frightened adjutant slipped into the engineers room and took all the spare bullets he could find, but he could not get those from the gun that Brady was still waving as he repeated his declaration that someone must die. He, Brady, might be a wingless wonder, but he still was a man, and no one could take his popsy and live to brag about it.

Finally he went into the C.O.'s bedroom and pointed the gun at him. "Sir," he said, "in making this attack I am only seeking my popsy."

He then looked all about the room and under the bed. "Sir," he said at last, "it was a mistake and I withdraw. I do not retreat, sir, I merely withdraw."

After which he staggered along the hall to the bedroom of the wing commander, who had long been asleep. Flinging open the door of the sleeping man's room, Brady turned on the light, pointed his gun, and said: "Sir, you have got my popsy. I think she must be in your room."

The very startled wing commander sprang out of bed, and said: "No, positively not. You may look for yourself."

Brady then went from one room to another, searching for his popsy and threatening every one with instant death. Finally he came to the room of the man who had called him a wingless wonder.

Brady said: "Have you got my popsy?"

The man said: "You fool, you've got a loaded gun. Put it down."

"Have you got my popsy?"

"Give me that gun, you silly ass."

"Where's my popsy?"

"Don't stand there waving that gun, when you know you wouldn't dare fire it."

"Oh, wouldn't I?" said Brady, and with a laugh fired two shots between the feet of the man in front of him. Then, satisfied that he had done a good night's work, he went off to bed.

Next morning every one on the station was terribly amused, all except the officer who had been forced to dance to avoid having his feet shot off. This man went about breathing fire and fury and said Brady should be court-martialed.

Brady himself was mightily ashamed of the whole performance. He did not appear until five o'clock in the afternoon, and then he went to the C.O. and asked for a two days' leave in order to recover his composure. Before he went on leave, he found Robinson and gave him a parcel.

"Keep it for me," he said. "It has my gun and all my ammunition inside. You keep it locked up for me until I can get my flying status; then I'll carry it along on my first flight over France, and I'll bang it at those blooming Jerries. I'll show them who's a wingless wonder."

But he never got his flying status. The officials continued to talk about the need for engineers until they began talking about men passing the age when they're useful as fighter pilots. So one day Brady again turned in his final resignation, and they all thought it would be as before.

But this time he walked away and didn't come back. He joined the Commandos.

Brady was not the only man who shot up the Eagle Squadron mess. There was another member of the squadron who did some indoor shooting.

This man we'll call Dick Vaughn. He was forever talking about his adventures in Nicaragua, where he had been a marine. And his adventures in China, where he had been a sailor. And New York, where he had been a longshoreman. Most of his adventures had to do with women.

In his early days with the squadron, Vaughn did well, fighting bravely and showing himself a man of courage. Then his eyes went bad, and for a time he was grounded. Sitting around the mess day after day, seeing the other boys go off to battle, Vaughn grew unhappy. Once, after a drink or two, he went to the mess and, just to show the kind of fellow he was, took all the gramophone records and flung them about the place, smashing them on the floor, on the tables, on the piano. Then he went along to the bedroom of the commanding officer.

"Sir," he said, holding out a glass half full of whisky, "have a drink. You'll need it, after you've seen the mess I've made of the mess."

Things went on from bad to worse, until Vaughn became so troublesome that he was dismissed from the service.

"The night of his dismissal," Robbie said, "he returned to the mess and from somewhere got a tommy-gun. He was pretty drunk at the time, and he went from one room to another. He would walk up to the mirror in each room, take a good look at himself, and, lifting the tommy-gun, would say: 'Vaughn, you're a swine.' Then he would blaze away at the mirror and wreck it. He got rid of several mirrors that night before we could knock him down and take away the gun."

The next morning Vaughn went to Robbie's room, and poured out his heart. "I've never heard a man talk as he talked," Robbie said. "Before he left I was almost in tears. He told me the whole story of his life, how he'd never had a chance.

"'But now I am going straight forever,' he said. 'All the odds have been against me, but I'm not going to lose. I'm going to show the kind of stuff I'm really made of. This terrible experience has made a man of me, and I'll prove it. And now, Robbie, I want to give you a token of my esteem for you. I want you to have something to remember me by. It's something my girl gave me before I left America, and I want you to have it, so you'll never forget me, so you'll always remember your old pal, Dick Vaughn.'"

Robbie said he was deeply touched by all Vaughn was saying, and he was truly moved when Vaughn unwrapped a parcel and showed him a lovely wooden propeller with a clock set in the hub.

"Here, Robbie," he said. "I want you to have this. It was from my girl, and now I give it to you. It's my most treasured possession, and I want you to have it."

Robbie tried to refuse the gift, saying it was too expensive, and, besides, there was the sentiment of Vaughn's girl having given it to him. But Vaughn insisted.

"My girl will understand when I tell her. She, too, would want Robbie, my best pal, to have it."

So Robbie accepted the gift, and after Vaughn had left the station for his boat back to America, Robbie placed the propeller on the mantel of his office where he could look at it, and remember the boy who at last had seen the error of his ways and had gone out to live a new life.

It was two days later that the local police called on the commanding officer and reported that a wooden propeller with a clock in the hub had been stolen from an inn nearby.

"And, excuse me, sir," the police said, "but we heard that one of your officers was seen carrying it away."

So Robbie went upstairs and returned with the propeller given him by his old pal, Dick Vaughn.

GENE POTTER: Who turned over for an extra wink and missed the fun.

12

I was at the Eagles' station the other day and saw Jerko Gray play a lucky trick on his pal, Gene Potter of Chicago.

The night before, there had been a heavy bomber operation over enemy territory, and some of the bombing planes had been badly shot up over the target. Some of them couldn't quite make it home and had crashed in the sea, off Holland. All this was known by the RAF, and early next morning the rescue boats were racing over the sea looking for any air crew that might have escaped from a crashed plane and was floating around in its dinghy. But the rescue boats are vulnerable to attack from the air; they have virtually no defense against enemy aircraft, so fighter planes are always sent out as an umbrella over them, protecting them as they steer zigzag courses over the sea, searching from dawn to dark for wrecked crews.

On this particular morning, orders had come through for the Eagles to take off early and fly to a certain station near the sea. They were to operate from that station throughout the day, going out in sections of four planes each, relieving each other throughout the day as they acted as cover for the rescue boats, and at the same time themselves searching for the crews of crashed bombers. That morning Potter was supposed to be flying as Red II, but Potter turned over for an extra wink after being called,

171

and just as he came running out on the field he saw the planes taxiing to their position down wind; then he saw them turn and come skimming back and rise into the air.

"Who the hell is that flying in my position?" Potter asked.

"Jerko Gray," some one said. "He told us he was playing a joke on you. He was going to leave you at home."

After expressing his opinion of Jerko, and of all fellows who would steal a plane in an operation when there might be something doing, Potter went back to the mess and continued his grumble.

That night Potter's grumble became a roar as he stalked about blasting his luck.

Late in the afternoon Red Section was flying off the coast of Holland, and Red 1, who was Bob Sprague of San Diego, saw two FW 190's flying down low, just above the deck. He gave the order for the attack, and the section dived for battle.

They saw the two German planes below them all right, but they didn't see the other four that were hiding in the sun—in the direct line between them and the sun, so that they were hidden in its blaze.

Just before Sprague, got within range of the two Hun planes, he saw out of the corner of his eye the four Germans hurtling down from above, springing the trap they had baited with the two stooges.

"I saw 'em comin'," said Sprague, in that soft, slow way he has of talking, "but I was almost ready to attack the two in front and I wanted to shoot them down so bad I didn't care if those other guys were coming. So I held on, and when I opened fire I saw pieces fly off the rear German plane; pieces went sailing off his wings and off his tail, but he didn't go in the sea, and by that time the four 190's were shootin' at me pretty darned straight.

"Then I saw Jerko comin'. He was streaking up underneath the lead Jerry, the one who was shooting at me, and I couldn't figure out whether Jerko would get the Jerry or the Jerry would get me. I knew they hadn't seen Jerko, and I knew if I dived they would see him and he wouldn't get a shot, so I figured I'd better hang on for a minute longer and give Jerko his chance. You see, it was sort of like football when you're carrying the ball and a tackler is coming for you and one of your teammates is coming to take him out—you don't know whether the tackler will get you, or your teammate will get the tackler.

"About the time Jerry's cannon shells were getting mighty thick, I saw Jerko was in position and I yelled over the R/T: 'Let him have it, Jerko. Let the beggar have it.' And I saw streaks out of Jerko's guns, and then the Jerry plane sort of hesitated for a minute, sort of reared back its head as if the pilot had been hit and his hand had frozen on the controls; then the whole thing was on fire and was headed straight for the drink.

"When I turned, trying to get a fight out of the other planes, they were headed for home, going hell bent. And you know, sir, it was a funny thing. As I flew around low over the place where that Jerry plane had gone in, I saw it had kicked up a lot of spray, and in the spray was the prettiest rainbow I ever saw."

That night Potter was going about the mess cursing his luck, raising all kinds of racket because "the other guys get all the fun. I've been flying over that blinking drink for weeks and haven't seen a damned thing, then this Jerko takes my plane—and what's more, uses my parachute—and goes out and gets a Jerry. If that ain't a bitching, I never got one."

After Jerko landed, the other pilots gathered around and for a minute or two congratulated him and listened to

"JERKO" GRAY: He has just returned from battle in which he shot down a Focke-Wulfe 190. Robbie is taking Jerko's report.

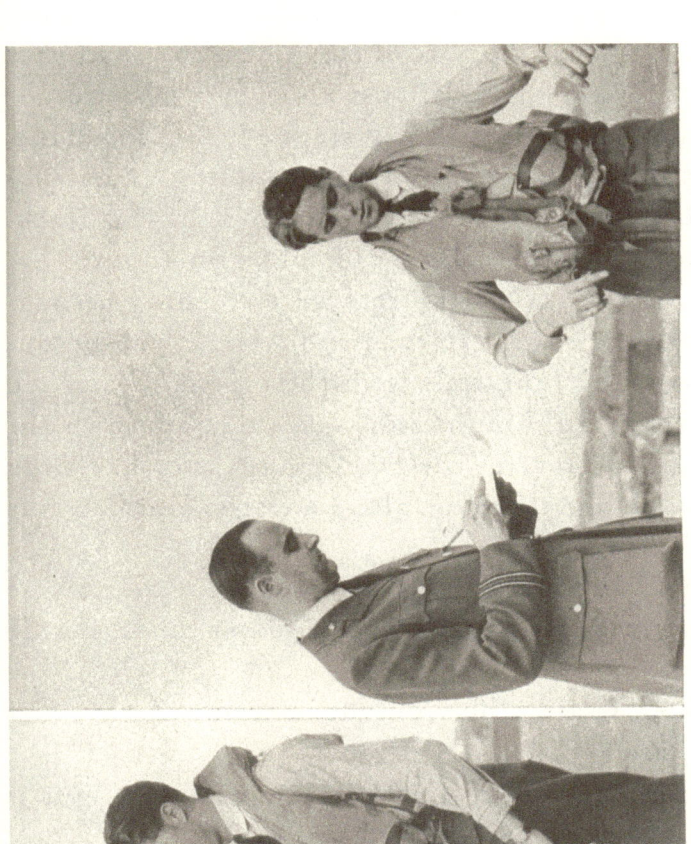

"Making the two-handed gestures that fighter pilots almost invariably make as they talk about planes in combat, showing how the planes maneuvered, turning and twisting and diving, showing with their hands how the battle was fought."

him tell how it happened. But they didn't cluster around him long. It was an old story to them. They, too, had shot down Germans. What the hell? Just another air battle.

Within ten minutes after he had stepped from his plane, Jerko had got on his bicycle and was pedaling as hard as he could, riding toward the mess to get some of the blackberry jam sandwiches the others had told him about.

As Jerko rode away, the armorers were cleaning his machine-guns with the short ramrods and were swabbing out his cannons with the long rods with the oily rags fastened to the end of them, rubbing the oily rags up and down the barrels, cleaning them after the two seconds they had fired that afternoon before the Hun plane and the German boy inside were blazing.

That night in the mess Jerko was sitting in one of the big easy chairs reading. I went over and sat down beside him.

"Well, Jerko," I said, "how do you feel now?"

"Fine," he said.

"Sleep all right tonight?" I asked. "Or will you fight it over again after you go to bed?"

"No," he said, "I won't worry about it. Except the mistakes we made. If we'd fought it better, we could have got four of the bastards."

I asked Jerko if he'd ever been in any other fights.

"Yeah," he said, "I been in several. I was in one damned good one. They shot me plenty that day. They were shooting mighty straight and they put a bullet"—he pulled the leg of his points free from his leg and I saw a hole in one side and out the other—"they shot one bullet through there. I reckon that was pretty close, all right." He was grinning "Couldn't have come much closer without taking my leg along with it, could it?"

I asked Jerko if he had ever shot down a plane before that afternoon.

BOB SPRAGUE: Who held on, even though "the cannon shells were getting mighty thick," until Jerko was in position to shoot the Jerry down.

"No," he said.

"How do you feel about it?" I asked.

"Swell. How else would I feel?"

I asked Pete one day how he felt after his first victory, after he had shot down his first German. He told me that on the day of the fight he had been leading Blue Section, and the squadron leader—this was in the days before Pete himself was the commanding officer—saw a Messerschmitt 109 flying along well below the Eagles and to the left. The squadron leader called out over the R/T: "There's a Hun at eleven o'clock, two thousand feet below." Having given the position of the Hun plane and knowing that the frequency over which he himself spoke was different from that used by the German, and that the German, therefore, had not heard him, the commanding officer of the Eagle Squadron then said: "Stardust Blue I, go get him."

That was the first time that Peterson, who was destined for so brilliant a career, was given an order to go into actual battle. He rolled off and dived. Three minutes later the Hun plane was a burning mass on the beach at Le Touquet, and Peterson had won his first victory.

"How did you feel about it?" I asked, as one night Pete and I sat talking.

"Well, I'd seen this Jerry and I wanted like hell to go after him. But one of the first laws you learn in the air is to stay in formation when you can help protect your pals and they can protect you. The guys who get into trouble are those who go off alone, trying to do something brilliant on their own. Impulsive and dumb fellows like that more often than not stick their heads into Hun booby traps—and get their heads shot off. You see, Jerry will send a single plane stooging along like a sitting target, just hoping that some emotionally unstable guy won't be able to stand the temptation and will break formation and attack. Usually before the sucker gets really started, three or four Huns drop out of the sky faster than he can see and they shoot him down.

"I'd seen this Hun, and, stooge or no stooge, I wanted to go after him; but I wouldn't have dared until I got the order. But the C.O. had seen that this was honestly a lone Hun, and he sent me down. When I went for him, the Hun flew along like a new boy, like some dumb kid just out of training who didn't know what it was all about. He was sort of floating along without even taking evasive action, and I doubt if he knew I was anywhere near him before I gave him a squirt, and he was on fire and going down."

"How did you feel as you saw him fall?" I asked.

"Well, to tell the truth I wasn't thinking about him so much as I was thinking about the plane. I've been loving airplanes ever since I was a little boy, and there I saw that beautiful thing, an airplane with its symmetry and its wings, a thing supposed to fly, to live in the air, I saw it falling and then it hit the deck. For a minute I hated to see it crash and crumple and burn, but then the ack-ack was throwing all lands of stuff at me, and I turned around and beat it for home."

Sometime later I was talking with Gussie Daymond and asked him about his feelings as he shot down Germans, as he saw their planes explode in the air or go down in flames.

"I don't know," he said, "exactly what I do think. Maybe it flashes through my mind that there's some poor guy in trouble and I'm sorry for him, but then I sort of say to hell with it, and start looking around for something else to shoot.

"I don't reckon I ever worried very much about anything I've shot down, except maybe the first bomber I got. It was a Dornier and it was flying low, right down over the drink. I went for it as hard as I could; I fairly beat the daylight out of my plane until I was within range, and then the Jerry rear gunner opened up and began to squirt lead all around me. I held on until I was pretty close; then I gave him a burst and after that the rear gunner was silent, so I figured I had discommoded him.

"That left the bomber without a rear gunner and it was helpless; it was just like a clay pigeon, and all I had to do was shoot it down. I had a funny feeling as I got closer, because I knew the crew were all inside just sitting there and waiting for it. When I got right on top, and knew I could make all my cannon shots count, I pressed the button, and the bomber dived and hit the water with a hell of a splash; but it bounced up again, and as it was bouncing I squirted it once more. This time it headed straight down and went into the drink, and a minute later there wasn't anything but a sort of white, frothy puddle on the water with some oil on it where the bomber had gone in. Then I knew I had killed the whole crew. I reckoned I had eradicated several people."

"I reckon you've eradicated a lot of people, Gus," Robbie said.

"I reckon I have at that," he said. He was not bragging; he was merely stating a fact. After all, his job, his purpose in life as a fighter pilot, was to kill Germans, to eradicate as many of them as he could. "But there was something a little different about getting this bomber," he said. "One minute the damned thing was there and the crew inside were alive and wanting to stay alive, and the next minute the plane was gone, and the crew were gone, and I had a mighty lonesome feeling as I thought about those poor guys down in the bomber trying to get out, and getting tangled in the wires, going on down with it as it sank, drowning as they went. I thought about that bomber and its crew for several days, and I can still see the frothy puddle with the oil on it."

I asked Gus if he had ever been like the crew in the bomber, an almost helpless target. I asked him if he'd ever been out in front of German guns, and not able to do much about it.

"Well, I wasn't exactly helpless," he said, and grinned. "There was something I could do about it. I could run like hell, and I did. But still I know how it feels to be in front of the other guy when he has all the advantage, and it's a mighty uncomfortable feeling. It makes you sweat."

It seems that one night at The Thatched, Gus and a chap named Johnny Flynn were cooking up a dawn raid over enemy territory. On this particular night a number of the boys were at the pub having a few beers and talking with, the barmaids, but over in one corner Gus and Johnny were bending across a table talking on more serious subjects than could be discussed with Thelma and Nancy, the girls behind the bar. Gus and Johnny were planning a raid.

Now a raid of this kind, the operation we are calling the Pineapple, is different from any other kind of operation; it is a strictly personal show. When the whole squadron goes out, it goes on orders from above, flying off on some mission that has been planned and ordered by higher commanders, but a Pineapple is entirely personal. Two pilots just decide on their own initiative that they'll go have a bang at Jerry. Usually they set out before daybreak and reach the French coast just at dawn, or they go out late in the afternoon and reach the coast just at dusk. And usually they go in bad weather—when there's a misty rain, so they can't be easily found by large numbers of enemy fighters, or they go under a low ceiling and stay close under the clouds, climbing into them quickly if they must hide from some unreasonably superior force. But if no large formation of fighters finds them and attempts to attack, they simply fly around until they see something worth shooting at, then they dive on it and press the button.

On this night at The Thatched, Gus and Johnny were planning a raid for the next morning. As a matter of fact, the Germans have good cause to hate The Thatched, because the destruction of any number of German gunposts and ammunition dumps and petrol depots and water tanks and power stations has begun at this pub as the boys late at night have felt their beer and talked of a raid for the next morning. Of course, many raids that were talked of at the pub, that were born in a bucket of beer, never came off; they remained talk and nothing more, because a Pineapple is a serious operation that can not be arranged casually at a bar. But sometimes the initial inspiration came while the boys were drinking at The Thatched; then later they went back to the station and worked out the intricate details about timing, course, and so on.

On this particular night, Gus and Johnny decided they would like to go over and shoot up some Huns or some Hun military installations. So they went back to the Station and got busy making the numerous necessary arrangements. That night they slept in the dispersal hut so they would be near their airplanes. Before dawn they were up and in their flying clothes.

When they took off, it was still night, and they flew toward the Channel. They crossed the drink, then crossed the French coast just as the sun rose. Over France they began their search; they flew around looking for something to destroy, anything that would hamper the Germans. But hunting was bad that morning, and they found nothing they thought worth destroying. Finally they gave up and were going out when they passed over an airdrome and saw two Messerschmitts taking off. Gus and Johnny promptly dived on them and took long squirts, but both apparently missed. Anyhow, they didn't see anything happen as they jerked up and began to climb.

Furthermore, they didn't see six 109's that had been hovering over the airdrome, and had dived as the Eagles made their attack on the two planes taking off. The first that either of the American boys knew of trouble was when these six 109's opened fire.

In the confusion that followed, Gus and Johnny became separated. Two of the 109's took after Johnny. They chased him out to sea, and there he managed to shoot one of them down. The other got away from him, but by that time Gus had completely disappeared, and so Johnny went home alone.

During the time Johnny was fighting and later while he was on his way home, Gus was engaged with the other four 109's. "And they were powerfully good," Gus said as he told me about the fight. "Those Krauts could really fly their airplanes, and they could shoot mighty straight. Every time I looked around, one of them was firing at me. It seemed as if fire was just streaking out of their planes in my direction. And they hit me plenty; they pretty much shot the hell out of my plane, all right."

The four Germans proved they had fought together often before and knew all the tricks of formation fighting. Two of the planes took their position behind and slightly to each side of Gus. The other two went farther out, one on each side. Gus, then, was in a kind of box with the four Germans closing in three sides of it.

"At the time they were all above me," Gus said, "but I didn't know when two of them might go down and attack from underneath; so I stopped that possibility by myself diving down to the deck." The deck is right above the water level, flying so close to the water that one day one of the Eagles, who at the time was looking behind him, didn't see a big wave coming and actually flew through it. "Once I was down to the deck I went all out, but they had me sort of headed off from home, and I knew I had to do something and do it fast because they had already hit me, and I didn't know when something was going to blow up or catch fire."

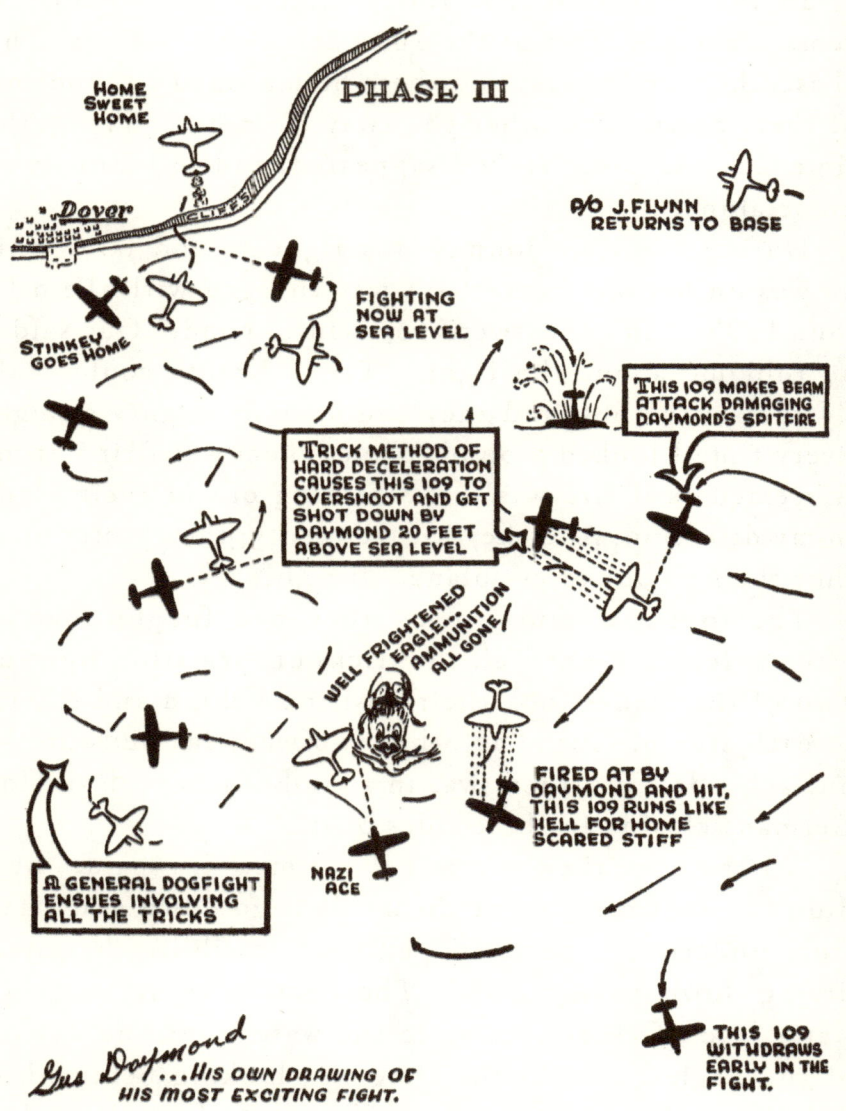

Gus Daymond ...HIS OWN DRAWING OF HIS MOST EXCITING FIGHT.

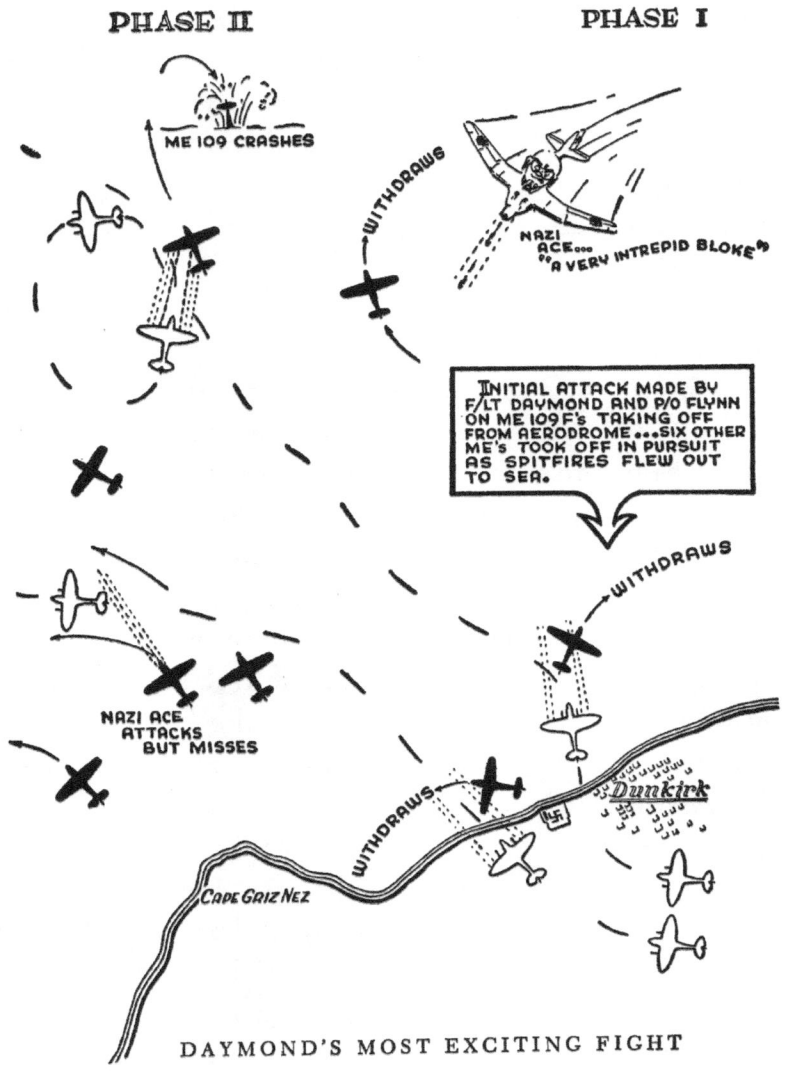

PHASE II   PHASE I

ME 109 CRASHES

WITHDRAWS

NAZI ACE... "A VERY INTREPID BLOKE"

INITIAL ATTACK MADE BY F/LT DAYMOND AND P/O FLYNN ON ME 109F's TAKING OFF FROM AERODROME...SIX OTHER ME's TOOK OFF IN PURSUIT AS SPITFIRES FLEW OUT TO SEA.

WITHDRAWS

NAZI ACE ATTACKS BUT MISSES

WITHDRAWS

Dunkirk

CAPE GRIZ NEZ

DAYMOND'S MOST EXCITING FIGHT

Then Pete broke in. "It was then that Gussie did about as brilliant a bit of tactical fighting as there is on record," Pete said. "With these guys coming at him from three directions, closing in on him, with them moving in at about three hundred miles an hour, Gussie cut his throttle and skidded his plane hard to the right, almost bringing it to a standstill. It so took the Jerries by surprise that they, going as fast as they could, overshot him; they flew over him and went on past."

"But as they went over," Gus said, "one of them blasted down with his cannon, and one of his shells blew the hood off my machine, and the hood was about six inches from my head. But after that, with them out in front of me, it was my turn, and I got a good burst into one and he went straight into the drink. I turned on another and got a squirt at him and sort of feathers began to fall off his wings, but I couldn't wait to see what happened to him. I think he turned around and went home, though he may have gone into the drink. The third chap turned and fled.

"But the fourth Jerry had managed to get back on my tail, and there he stuck. And, what's more, I had shot out of ammunition; I didn't have a single shell left in either my cannon or my machine-guns. And there was that Nazi behind me, squirting at me every chance he got.

"I knew it was my job to stay just as far away from him as possible, and believe me it wasn't easy. He was a mighty intrepid bloke, and he kept pressing his attack, shooting at me every chance he got. I suppose if he'd known I was out of ammunition he would have taken more chances and maybe would have shot me down, but he didn't know it and he kept his distance. But he was a damned good flier, and for about fifteen minutes during a running fight he simply shot my plane into a sieve. He stayed with me all the way to the cliffs of Dover, and when I climbed the cliffs he climbed after me, still shooting. He didn't break off until I was over the land. Then he rolled back and went home. And I never was so happy in all my life to get rid of a guy as I was to get rid of that one. I was mighty tired of looking at his guns with the flames spurting out of them."

PILOT OFFICER W. J. HOLLANDER FROM HONO-'
LULU: "And how can I convey the feeling I used to get as I sat there
listening to Lulu playing?"

13

Any man who is shot down over the sea, who has to bale out over water, must depend for his life on his Mae West and his dinghy.

When pilots are on "readiness" they wait at the squadron dispersal hut at the edge of the flying field. There in the midst of a poker game or a game of red dog or a bull session the telephone rings.

The next instant the operator calls out: "Scramble! Bandits"—Germans in the air are always "bandits"—"approaching from the south at fifteen thousand feet. Intercept them."

By the time the operator has said "Scramble," the unvarying signal for the quick get-away, the boys are racing from the hut. By the time he calls out the direction from which the Germans are approaching, the boys are running hard toward their airplanes that are standing with engines warmed around the edge of the field. Each pilot ducks under the wing of his plane and comes up with the parachute that has been perfectly placed, and as he climbs into the cockpit the parachute is fastened on. Then the starter button is pressed, and the plane moves out into position.

From the ringing of the telephone in the dispersal hut until the entire squadron is airborne, the average time is two minutes. Indeed, the Eagles have scrambled in one minute and twenty seconds.

"If they take longer than two minutes and a half," Peterson said, "they catch hell from their squadron leader."

It's at dispersal, when the boys are sitting around waiting for something to happen, for the signal to scramble, that they talk most. After a while they forget that you, an outsider, are present, and then they get really cracking and give out the pukka gen. . . . Gen—pronounced "jen"—is a term used by the Romany Gipsies: it means "information," and gen is one of the most frequently used words in that amazing vocabulary that has grown up in the RAF, the vocabulary that is distinctly something apart from the speech of ordinary folk who don't even understand the difference between "duff gen"—incorrect information—and "pukka gen," which is the real, the true information about anything from the blonde's telephone number to the flying speed of a new type of German aircraft

While on readiness at dispersal each pilot must wear his Mae West, the life-saving jacket which is compulsory for every man who flies over water. The bulgy jacket, named "Mae West" for most obvious reasons, is slipped on like a sleeveless coat and is tied fore and aft with tapes. It is naturally buoyant, can be inflated by a pilots blowing through a tube, and is yellow in color so that it can be more easily seen by the crews of the rescue boats. The Mae West also carries a packet of fluorescent dye which discolors the sea, forming a large green patch that is phosphorescent at night. Besides his Mae West, a pilot also has a flashlight and a whistle.

There is still another piece of life-saving equipment required of all pilots who fly over water—the dinghy. Made of rubber packed into shape like a cushion, it is attached to the parachute and the pilot sits on it. When he bales out, his dinghy goes with him.

Whenever a pilot is forced to jump, he makes about three motions: he pushes back the hood of his plane, unstraps himself, and throws himself clear. Within two seconds after making his first escape move, he is free of the plane and is going down. If he comes down on water, then his dinghy becomes his life-boat.

Immediately after going into the water, the pilot detaches the dinghy from his parachute and rips off the cover; then he inflates it with gas from a bottle which is attached. When inflated, the dinghy is pear-shaped, with high walls and a hollow center, and the pilot climbs in at the narrow end and settles himself in his rubber boat. He either lies back and waits, or he fits a little square paddle, like a duck's foot, to each hand and begins to paddle toward England, constantly watching for a rescue boat so that he may signal to it with his red distress flag. Should there be leaks, the pilot has plugs to seal them, and he can further inflate the dinghy by mouth. Waves sometimes splash over the sides, and then he must bail out the water as best he can, usually flinging it out with his hands. Like the Mae West, the dinghy is colored yellow, so that it may be easily seen in the gray-green water of the Channel.

The Eagle Squadron has one unhappy memory of the dinghy. Once there was a pilot in the squadron named Virgil Olson. He was the parachute officer. It was his business to see that "Jump-sack," the enlisted man charged with the care of parachutes and dinghies, kept all the equipment in perfect order. And it was Olson's duty, too, to see that every pilot took his Mae West and his dinghy into his plane each time he went into the air.

One day in a battle over the Channel, Olson was shot down. The other boys saw him bale out and saw his parachute open. Then they looked down and saw the rescue boats only three miles away, already speeding toward the spot where Olson would come down in the water.

But when the rescue boats got there, they could not find Olson. That night the squadron leader checked the squadron's equipment and found that Olson, the officer responsible for all parachutes and dinghies, had gone up that day without his own dinghy. And that is the squadron's one unhappy memory of dinghies.

Sitting on the dinghy throughout a long patrol is "powerfully uncomfortable to the behind," according to Gussie Daymond. None of the boys liked to sit on them, but there was one Eagle who particularly hated them. He was Sam Alfred Mauriello. There is no sense in permitting prudery to prevent us telling the kind of courage and stamina this man had: there is no mature reason why we should not tell that Sam suffered from hemorrhoids.

Sam Mauriello, "Uncle Sam," as every one called him and loved him, was one of the most picturesque of all the Eagles. He was born in 1908 in New York City, and his father, Anthony Mauriello, still lives at 2211 Twenty-third street, Astoria, Long Island. Sam has held all kinds of jobs, but the one he talks about most is his job as taxi-driver in New York City.

"Jees," he would say, "I may not be so hot in these Spitfires, but how I could weave through that New York traffic!" And Sam would show with his hands how he could weave in and out, making the two-handed gestures, one hand behind and above the other, that fighter pilots almost invariably make as they talk about planes in combat, showing how the planes maneuvered, turning and twisting and diving, showing with their hands how the battle was fought. "I could go through that Park Avenue traffic at six o'clock just like that—*fruuump!*—and I'd be through."

One reason everybody loved Sam was that no one in real life could possibly be as modest as he; it just couldn't be true. He had only two vanities: one was an occurrence in his taxicab in New York, the other was his brother.

SAM MAURIELLO, DFC: "Uncle Sam"

Sam's pride about the taxicab was owing to his belief that he was the only driver in New York who had ever delivered a baby in his cab. "But how was I to know the lady was in such trouble?" he said as he told me about it. "She told me to drive fast and faster and faster, and then all of a sudden she said, 'Too late.' So I pulled over to the curb, got out, and helped deliver the baby. Then we went to the hospital, and when her husband got there he gave me fifty bucks. But you know, it was a funny thing. That lady lived in the apartment where I used to have my stand outside, but after that she always avoided me. She wouldn't ride with me any more after that. I guess she was sort of shy."

After Sam got through driving a taxi he went in for flying and junketed around the country taking people up for rides and hiring out to carry passengers on long hauls in days before the great passenger lines were operating. Finally Sam grew tired of wandering around, so he got a job as airport manager at Binghamton, New York. He did his job all right and everybody liked him, but pretty soon he wanted to go wandering again, and this time he went to the RAF and joined the Eagle Squadron.

For a while he didn't have any luck. He went out on all kinds of operations, but he couldn't make contact with German fliers. Then one day he got into a battle and shot down a Jerry, but Sam's pals came back terribly depressed.

"Poor old Sam," they said. "He got one, but the others got him, for sure. They were right on top of him shooting with everything they had. Poor old Sam. He was a good guy."

Ten minutes later Sam came puffing in. His plane was well ventilated with holes everywhere, and Sam himself had been nicked. But he crawled out and said: "It was a hell of a scrap. When I got him in my gunsights I pressed the button and he just sort of went up like spray; everything seemed to come apart and he spewed up in the air."

Sam was the life and soul of every party. First, because he was such a fine, genuine fellow, and second, because he was a marvelous mimic. He could be a cow, lion, siren, motor horn—his favorite was to be a motor horn, going into the gentlemen's room just at the moment some gentlemen was actively utilizing the room, walking close behind him and going "Peep-peep" in such a loud voice that any gentleman would involuntarily swerve to avoid the oncoming taxi. Sam loved that.

But along in the summer of 1942 Sam began to look a little tired, though an occasional cable from home unfailingly brightened him. The cable was from his brother who was a prize fighter.

One day Sam had been out over the Channel and had been in battle; he had shot down one German, simply blowing him out of the sky, and had badly damaged another. When he landed there was another cable.

That night Sam went round the mess showing the cable to his friends. "That brother of mine is a great guy. He knocked out Kid McGuire in the third round. He's a wonderful guy, that brother of mine."

But Sam's flying in the summer of 1942 didn't have quite the snap and the precision that had distinguished it in the past. Sam's getting tired, some of them said. Sam's thirty-four years old, some of them said. Sam needs a rest, they all said. So one day the Doc called Sam and talked with him. "What's the matter?" the Doc asked. And Sam said nothing was the matter.

"Just let me alone and let me go on flying," he said. "Nothing is the matter."

But he said it so emphatically, so insistently, that Doc suspected he was not quite telling the truth. He ordered a physical examination. And they found that Sam had been suffering for months with hemorrhoids, that he had gone out day after day into battle, sitting on that hard, uncomfortable dinghy with all the pain it had caused him, enduring anything that he might have the chance to go up and fly and fight, that he might risk his life in battle. . . .

On the day of the great air battle of Dieppe, the day the RAF and the Luftwaffe fought one of the fiercest battles in the history of aerial warfare, Mae Wests and dinghies played important parts. In the fighting that began before daybreak and broke off only after the flames spurting from the machine-guns and cannon were visible in the darkness of night, scores of pilots were shot down into the sea. Two of the boys who jumped when above the Channel and went down into the water were members of the Eagle Squadron: Peterson himself and one of his deputy flight commanders, Wee Michael McPharlin.

14

The story of the Battle of Dieppe will be told in this book by two of the American Eagles. One of these boys was not ordered into the air at any time during the day; he knew of the battle only from the ground. The other Eagle fought from before dawn until almost night; he spent the day in the center of the most severe fighting.

There was a Big Show on, and we knew it. Of course we didn't know exactly what it was to be, but we knew something really big was planned. It might even be the Invasion, the day we were waiting for when we'd pile on to the Continent and see how hard we could kick the Hun where it would hurt him most. There were whispers and rumors, and senior officers asked questions with their eyes, and other officers nodded their heads and looked away, silently saying: Yes, it's about time now; in a few days we'll get cracking. Then the squadron was moved to a forward airdrome, to a station nearer the Channel. Then we knew, for sure, that it was time.

They moved the squadron down to the forward airdrome on Saturday afternoon, and if you knew the Eagles you could tell that they were tense and eager. They pretended they were just as they usually are, brave and calm;

but each of us was feeling the strain. We had waited and waited, we had flown Lord knows how many patrols, and now the Big Show was about to begin. We were pretty tense, all right.

That Saturday night we all left the station and went to The Black Swan, the local pub, to eat. Oscar, Hively, Stewart, Lulu, Andrews and myself all started for The Swan, and, too impatient to wait for the transport, we began walking. Half way down the hill, we were picked up by the transport and taken with haste the rest of the way. Nearly everybody cursed the driver for being late. However, our spirits were soon restored at the bar, where every one had a few drinks before eating. A strange cross-section of humanity frequents The Black Swan—shabby women and their men, young and hopeful girls searching for adventure, worn-out men with three days' growth of beard, drinking warm ale, children running around playing while their parents have "'arf a pint of bitter." The light was dim, but good enough to show me most of the signs on the walls, which were practically covered with posters and mottoes vilifying Hitler, Mussolini & Co.

We had a special dinner. It was Pop Darnley's best, for "his boys" of the Eagle Squadron—one egg each, ground ham, fried potatoes, salad, bread and butter and milk, served by his attractive red-haired daughter. Clever girl, Marguerite! She promises every pilot the delight of her charms, but none, so far as we have ascertained, ever got close enough to gain a victory—though one or two have put in claims for a "damaged."

Very quickly we devoured our meal, and afterward we settled down to do some conscientious drinking. With the drinks and with the air that was heavy with tobacco smoke and the smell of all the people, our senses must have got a little numb; though I was still able to notice that an orchestra was playing. The leader, a woman with a profile like a hawk's, sat playing the piano with her hat on, a cigarette in her mouth, and a mug of ale sitting precariously on the edge of the keyboard. While balancing herself on a stool and playing, her head tilted to one side to dodge the smoke from her own cigarette, she looked something like a witch riding a broomstick.

About this time Taylor and I felt the need of fresh air, so we climbed the stairs and went outside. But we had been there only a short time when Taylor remarked that too much air wouldn't be good for us, so we returned to the cellar. We waded through thick clouds of smoke, but soon our eyes were able to distinguish what was going on. Vincent was hanging from a water pipe in the ceiling and doing a monkey act, and Salkeld, the Intelligence Officer who came to the squadron after Robbie left, was giving his interpretation of the Hunchback of Notre Dame, going about begging for alms. Then Vincent became warm and proceeded to cool off by pouring a couple of glasses of ale on his head, and, stretching the belt of his trousers, poured the remainder down inside them.

When closing time came we all made a final rush to the bar, and, after hurried gulpings, we made for the exit. Mike McPharlin had lost his hat. So had Stewart. Vincent, who by then, was really no drunker than he had been two hours earlier simply by reason of having reached the saturation point, insisted on climbing out of the cellar via a beer barrel chute, with the result that when he slipped and slid back, he carried with him all the people who were struggling along behind him trying to get out. But that didn't bother Vincent. He attempted it again, and finally with a crash he pulled down the center railing, and with it seven or eight people who had been leaning over it watching the show. By this time Vincent was exhausted, or passed out, or something, and we carried him away, just a lot of absolutely dead weight.

Outside, cars were waiting to take us back to the station. Those who couldn't get in were lifted in by friends. The others climbed on wherever they could, on the motor hood, on the fenders, on the canvas roof. Then, shouting and singing and wrestling, we rode hell-bent for home.

On the ride home Rutherford knocked down Bill, then Lane, because he was afraid they might get hurt riding on the roof. In the knocking down, Rutherford himself almost fell out of the moving car three times. But he said it was all right, not to worry about him; he said that God would protect those who have no fear. When we reached the station we all fell noisily out of the car, and it wasn't long until we were sound asleep—Vincent in bed with his hat on, where it sat perched on his head until morning.

The next night was Sunday night, and we stayed at home and had dinner at the officers' mess at the station. Before dinner we had a couple of drinks, then after we had eaten we went to the music room where a visiting officer of the RAF was playing a Chopin Polonaise. Then he played Tschaikowsky's "Song Without Words." He played a lot more, and finally he played the Moonlight Sonata. All of us sat there listening to him, and enjoying it because he played beautifully.

Not much happened Monday. A section of "A" flight was in readiness when they were ordered out on patrol. Both "A" and "B" flights took part in the patrol. Anderson, who had been scheduled to go, was replaced at the last minute by Oscar, making Anderson cuss madly at the luck, but since Oscar was his Flight Commander, there wasn't much he could do about it. The anticipation of the flight with a possible battle with Jerry thrilled us all no end, but we drew blank. We saw some Me 109's but they wouldn't play; they turned tail and raced away.

After dinner Monday night most of the boys decided to go to bed early. As I was going upstairs I heard Oscar raising hell over the telephone with some poor sergeant who had scheduled a section of Oscar's flight for readiness at dawn. Oscar's complaint was that he was not going to be in readiness at dawn if nothing was going to happen. Unless the sergeant could guarantee him some action with the Hun, he'd be damned if he'd get up and be ready to fly at dawn. Oscar said he wanted action or he wanted sleep; he didn't want any of this just sitting around in the gray muck of morning.

Wing Commander Duke-Woolley, our winco and one of the absolute best, happened to be passing, and he took the telephone from Oscar and talked directly with Operations at our home station. He learned that "B" Flight was scheduled for readiness at dawn, and that settled it. Still, he handed the receiver back to Oscar and told him to go ahead and blow if he wanted to. Oscar, just a little fuddled by the winco's permission, nevertheless went in bravely to the attack. He took the receiver and bellowed: "What is all this bull about readiness at dawn?" The winco went away smiling and shaking his head. When Oscar finished with the phone, Stew, Lulu, and others, who had heard the conversation, congratulated Oscar on his bravery; to cuss as he had cussed before the winco was a damned stout effort, and they told him so.

I went off to bed, but about one o'clock in the morning I was awakened by McMinn. When I looked up he was standing there with one hand holding a bottle and the other shaking me.

"Shhh! Do you wanna drink?" He placed his index finger on his mustache and repeated: "Shhh!"

Tuesday morning Squadron Leader Peterson, our commanding officer, returned from a trip. And Oscar, Mac, and Stew went up to London. Not much happened until three o'clock, when word came that at four-thirty all pilots were to meet in the briefing room. Group Captain

Peel, DSO, DFC, the commander of our home station, and Wing Commander Duke-Woolley, DFC and Bar, were both at the airdrome, so we knew that there was to be a really big show.

At four-thirty we all went to the Intelligence Officer's room and were briefed by the group captain and the wing commander, who told us the plan of attack, the positions to be taken by the land forces, the approximate number of men and ships, the number of aircraft, and the parts they were to play in this gigantic Commando raid, the raid on Dieppe.

As we sat and listened attentively to our instructions, there were chuckles of anticipation here and there along the L-shaped briefing room. Group Captain Peel began the briefing by saying: "Here it is—this is what you've been waiting for." Then, very concisely, he gave us the story, the target, and so on. Some of the pilots were rubbing the palms of their hands briskly. All of us were very happy that action was forthcoming.

When the group captain finished, the wing commander followed with instructions as to formation of flights, time of take-off, what to cover, duration of patrol, and so on. A very short, softly-spoken speech it was. Then, with a smile on his face, he summed up by saying there was very little more that could be said: we pilots knew our job and we understood the danger of the mission, but whatever happened, please come back with reports of a jolly good day's hunting.

Group Captain Peel then warned every one to stay at the station that night and go to bed early. Also he said no phone calls were to be made or received. He said the element of surprise was of real importance, and since the Hun did not like to get up early, perhaps the surprise attack would do justice to the extensive plans made.

Briefing was over and we rose, but Squadron Leader Peterson announced that all pilots of Squadron 71 were to meet in his room at nine-thirty.

We had a very sober supper that evening: most of the pilots seemed thoughtful, and there was no talk at all about the events of the next day.

After supper we went into the library where Peterson and Strickland began their favorite sport: they began to play chess. They played until Pete looked at his wrist watch and got up. As if his rising was a signal, all the pilots of his squadron followed him up to his room. Oscar, McPharlin, and Stewart were still missing. They had left for London early that day, going up in search of a little excitement. They had not been present at the briefing in the afternoon, and I wondered if they would return early enough to get in on the fun. I knew they would be cursing madly if the show should come off and they missed it entirely.

As we entered the room—it was not Pete's room after all, because Taylor was already in red-striped pajamas lying in bed—Pete offered sticks of candy to us. We all accepted and started munching.

Then Pete began to talk, and every one hung on his words, which came calmly and quietly. He went over in detail the plan of battle and the part that 71 Squadron was to play in it. He repeated the code signals, compass reading, time, distress code words. He interrupted himself by looking at the stick of candy and saying: "Hmmm! Good." Then he summed up by saying he did not want any poor bastard to get lost or fall in the drink. (Of course Pete couldn't know that two of us were going to go into the drink the next afternoon: Mike McPharlin and Pete himself.)

Daymond checked the compass degrees to and from the rendezvous, then to Dieppe and return. Then the party broke up. It was about ten-thirty. Everybody disappeared fast. There was a few minutes' rush in all the bathrooms. Hively was shaving, as if he were preparing for a party.

At three o'clock in the morning we were awakened by the batman. We dressed hurriedly—no one took time to shave that morning—had a cup of tea in the library, and by three-thirty were having breakfast at the mess of the airdrome: eggs, bacon. Spirits rose at the sight of eggs, and we really piled into them.

It was yet pitch black when we went to dispersal. All planes were being checked by the ground crews. The pilots themselves were checking pistols, Mae Wests, parachutes, and were moving about in the dark, talking in low voices. There were quick steps and hurried instructions, and everybody was busy with something or other.

The squadron was divided as usual into three sections of four Spitfires each: Red, White and Blue. White section, with Squadron Leader Peterson in the lead, was in the center. Daymond led Red Section. Bob Sprague led Blue. They took off in the darkness of early morning and disappeared swiftly into the sky, climbing toward where the black was beginning to weaken into a vague gray.

I wasn't to fly on this first sortie, and, along with Sam Mauriello and some of the other boys, I walked over to the Control Tower. We thought we might hear of the arrival at Dieppe and hear when the battle started, though we knew that our pilots would keep R/T silence as long as possible and that we might hear nothing for some minutes. Everything was quiet at Control Tower, so Sam and I went back to the squadron dispersal hut. There we saw the ground crews squatting around in little groups, talking and waiting. One or two members of the ground crew were wrapped in their coats, dozing.

We waited until it was good daylight. Then the distant drumming of a propeller brought every one to his feet. It was a Spitfire coming back. It proved to be Strickland. He

landed and was immediately surrounded by a crowd, because we could see that the covering over his gun muzzles
was broken: his guns had been fired. It seems that he had
tangled with four FW 190's, had shot his wad, then beat it
back for home. He said he had possibly damaged one. He
was rather calm as he always is. Strickland is a lot older
than any of the rest of us—he is thirty-nine—and he's a
grand old man on the ground and in battle.

Soon afterward, one or two at a time, ten other Spitfires
returned. One didn't come back. One of them was still out
there, long overdue. We were worried about it, until we
learned that Morgan had crash-landed without undercarriage at Beachy Head, but he was unhurt. I was talking to
Morgan later about it, and he said that when he came in,
his plane all pooped out after having been shot to hell, he
had to crash-land in a hurry, and he couldn't take time to
pick his spot. As bad luck would have it, he came in smack
beside a Blenheim that had also crashed and was burning
on the ground. Morgan said he was scared pea-green because the Blenheim was blazing away and its bombs and
ammunition were exploding, keeping everybody far from
it. He said he got out of his plane and ran like the wind
for fear one of the bombs would go off and get him.

As the pilots came back from their first sortie, I noticed that they were all just about as they usually are.
Daymond was inwardly excited and was trying to cover it
up with a lot of his amusing talk. Pete was calm and smiling as usual. Hively was laughing and doing his customary
cussing. Sprague was quiet as always, never talking much,
but always saying a lot whenever he spoke. Sam Mauriello
was morose because Pete had told him there would be
no flying for him that day: Sam wasn't sufficiently over
his operation. Young Whitlow, very serious, was hunched
down in a corner of the hut absorbed in a book. Hollander
was running around playing pranks and enjoying himself.

AFTER THE FIRST FIGHT OF THE DAY: "The distant drumming of a propeller brought everyone to his feet. It was a Spitfire coming back. It proved to be Strickland. He landed and was immediately surrounded by a crowd be- cause we could see that the covering of his gun muzzles was broken; his guns had been fired. He had tangled with four FW 190's."

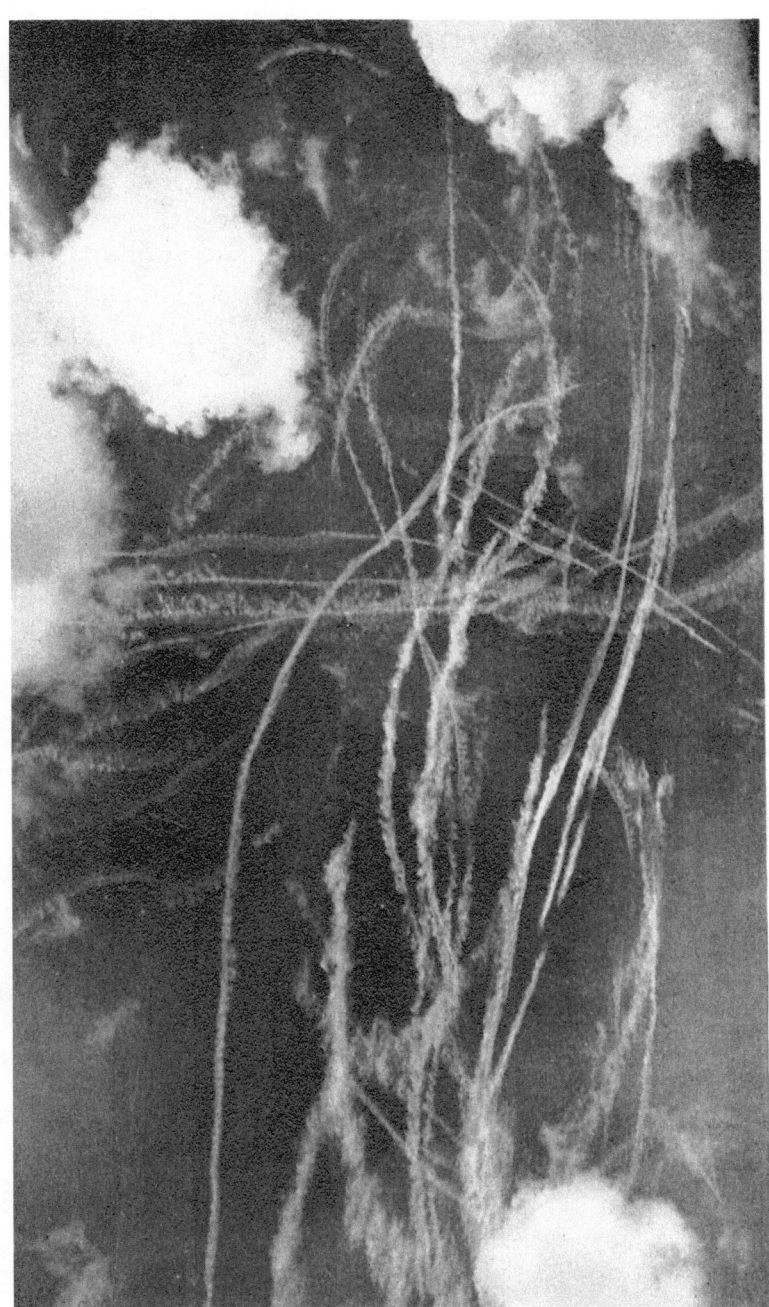

DIAGRAM OF A DOG FIGHT: "Owing to a form of condensation, a plane at high altitudes sometimes leaves a white streak behind it, a trail that clearly marks the path the plane has flown. Frequently from the ground the plane itself cannot be seen with the naked eye but the vapor trail can be seen easily." This picture shows the record of a dog fight, the vapor trails remaining for a time like a diagram in the sky after the actual battle has ended.

The refreshment truck was on hand with WAAF's to serve sandwiches and coffee. Most pilots partook of the nourishment, but while they were eating word came through for the squadron to take off for another sortie. With minor changes—which changes, worse luck, did not include me—the same pilots took off.

By now the battle of Dieppe was raging, and our fellows knew that this time they would see action. On this second sortie they were to fly middle cover—that is, the middle stratum of fighter cover, some squadrons above them, some below.

While they were gone this time, Morgan returned in the Maggie, a little plane that had been sent for him, and he told us how he had landed next to the blazing Blenheim, of all places!

It was about noon that the second sortie began to return. They landed, all excited and talking fast about the fun they were having. Each of them told his story, and they were all having a marvelous time, but still we knew it was pretty much hell out there. The enemy was mustering his forces, and a terrifically stiff battle was in progress. Pete probably described it best.

"It's like a goddam Fourth of July," he said, as he was climbing out of his plane.

It was about this time that Oscar, Mac, and Stew returned. They rushed to their Mae Wests like men possessed. They were swearing like mad because of what they had missed. Pete and some of the others went off to the mess for lunch, but they had no sooner sat down than word came for them to take off once more. They came back to dispersal in a hurry, joking about the good lunch they hadn't had.

In the early afternoon, the horizon became rather cloudy, and as time dragged on every one felt worn out with the already long day. We pilots on readiness were lazily sprawled around dispersal, Whitlow as usual reading a book, the others playing with their knives or their pistols, forever loading and unloading them. I was rather surprised that no accident happened.

There was a third sortie. And when they came back from this one, Daymond was swearing because some planes he had tried to attack wouldn't stay and fight. "They ran like rabbits," he said. Stew was telling how he had shot at an FW 190. We were all talking in the hut when word came that Peterson had been shot down and had baled out over the Channel. Then we heard that Wee Michael had jumped.

About this time Flight Lieutenant Robinson, our old intelligence officer, pulled in, having rushed down from London to get in on the show. When he was told that Pete and Mike were both missing, all he said was "Damn." But I'm sure he meant much more, because these two have long been his pals.

Most of us thought there was little chance for Peterson to be picked up at sea. And as for McPharlin, almost all of us felt hopeless. Sammy and I reasoned it out that he must have got lost and gone down over unfamiliar territory.

Even though your pals have been shot down, life goes on at an airdrome, and we sat around dispersal making plans for a real bender at The Black Swan that night.

Then came word that Mike was safe. He had baled out in the drink and had been picked up, two hours after. The story was that he had been shot and a bullet had hit his compass. His compass gone, he got mixed up and started flying toward home, he thought, when suddenly he recognized the French Coast. He turned around and tried to get back to England, but ran out of fuel and had to bale. Once he was in his dinghy he saw that his boots, which he had already discarded, were floating nearby and that from one of them his knife was still sticking out. So he swam to them to retrieve his knife, which was probably worth about sixty cents.

There was general good feeling about Mike's rescue, and we all set off for The Swan and a big feed. Also, most of us, after such a wearing day, were secretly planning to get a little stinko.

After I had sunk a few drinks at The Swan I suddenly felt mighty unclean. I hadn't had a bath since the night before. I hadn't shaved in two days, and, besides, that old witch on her broomstick was getting on my nerves.

So I decided to go over to the mess, have a bath, then come back and get really drunk in style.

I went out and got into the transport and returned to the mess. As I was climbing out of the transport somebody suddenly shouted that Pete had been picked up, had been lifted out of the bloody drink.

That good news sort of finished me, and instead of going back to The Swan I went upstairs and flopped into bed, and was asleep before I knew it.

15

This is an account of the Battle of Dieppe as told by an Eagle who fought in the battle throughout the day.

Because of the right combination of weather, wind, and the moon, we knew that conditions were right, and we knew that a large combined operation had been planned for some time, but it was not until the afternoon of August 18, 1942, that we knew exactly where and when the battle would occur.

On the afternoon of the eighteenth we saw Group Captain John Peel arrive at the forward station to which we had been sent; he was carrying an armful of maps and a long list of orders. We pilots were taken into the intelligence room, and the group captain addressed us there.

"This is *it!*" whispered O'Regan soon after the Group Captain began to speak.

The Commanding Officer explained the general plan of attack. On a large map he pointed to the coastal area— Berneval, Dieppe, St. Marguerite. He showed us the emplacements on the flanks that the Commandos would attack, and he showed where the South Saskatchewan Regiment and the Camerons would make the frontal assault. After the group captain had finished, Wing Commander Duke-Woolley then described the specific tasks for the wing as a whole and for each squadron. The 71 Squadron's part was easy to understand: we were to maintain air protection near the shoreline and prevent air attacks on our frontal assault forces.

That meant we would be in the thick of it. And that suited us.

After our commanders had finished, every one was ordered to remain on the post. Telephonic communications were discontinued.

Some very heavy dates at The Swan, The Ship, and other spots cracked up pretty badly that Tuesday night.

We rose early next morning and hurried to breakfast. We knew that during the day the Luftwaffe would meet us with strong fighter strength. We knew that the staffels, the German fighter squadrons, at Abbeville, Amiens, St. Omer, Le Havre, and Antwerp would join battle. We knew, too, that these fighters were some of the Hun's absolute best: he had kept his aces on the Western front to meet the sweeps that the RAF and the American Air Force were continually sending over. We were certain that during the day we would meet the Luftwaffe, and that suited us plenty. We had been trying for a long time to make Jerry come up and fight. With a show like this big raid striking at him, he would simply have to get off the ground.

When we started the Merlin engines of our Spitfires, we saw that some cloud patches had piled up in the east, making it very dark. We pointed our Spits into the breeze in tight formation of fours, and took off into the night; then we quickly shifted to line astern. We flew low over Kent on our way out, and, still flying almost on the deck, we arrived at our departure point on the English coast. Then we set our course for Dieppe, flying very low and close to the sea. Each of us watched his instruments carefully, for in the dark there was no horizon and the sea was flat.

It was still dark when we arrived to cover the dawn landing. Our troops were already ashore and were fighting hard. And the heavy guns of both forces were firing steadily: they were feeling for their targets. Whenever one of the big guns on shore hit one of our boats, we could see the flames leap up, and sometimes there would be an explosion. From where we were up above, we could spot the shrapnel bursts and the almost continuous streaks of red Bofors projectiles, rising and converging toward our Hurricane bombers that were ahead of us and flying low, making absolutely point blank attacks against the German gun posts, trying to knock them out so they could not operate against our troops that had already landed and those that were coming in to land.

Just as the first light of day was breaking, and the protective cover of darkness was disappearing, a bomber from our side skimmed in with his belly almost touching the water, and laid a smoke screen across the harbor. A very light wind drifted it toward the cliffs and into the eyes of the German gunners who were firing from there.

From the sea, hundreds of our corvettes, transports, destroyers, troop and tank transports, minesweepers, trawlers, and rescue boats were deployed. Those nearest shore were advancing doggedly through the Hun minefields and a strong artillery barrage. From time to time one of them was hit and exploded. Whenever there was an explosion, the boat disappeared below the water under a cloud of spray and foam, leaving an oil slick. Over the whole of the battle area there hung a thickening pall of smoke from the cordite, the smoke screens, distress flares, and exploding shells.

Our naval artillery action was having a particularly good effect. This barrage was gradually silencing enemy positions. High up above we could sit in the cockpits of our Spitfires and look down, and we noticed a slackening in the numbers of huge geysers that had been rising among our numerous sea craft. The enemy's primary resistance was slowly being overcome by our naval guns and by the attack of the Commandos themselves, who were capturing a number of positions in hand-to-hand fighting. As darkness changed into daylight, we could see that our fellows were advancing against the harbor's fortifications. We could also see that our troops were filtering throughout the town by means of hard street fighting. I can tell you it made us feel mighty good as we stooged around upstairs looking down and watching those troops advance into the teeth of all the Germans could throw at them. It was pretty dam exciting, and I reckon I was seeing one of the best shows any man has ever seen; it was mighty spectacular.

Pretty soon the full light of dawn came to Dieppe.

Curiously, our squadron did not encounter strong fighter opposition on that first sortie, and this lack of fighter resistance over the principal landing area surprised us a lot; we had expected the Germans to come up immediately and give strong opposition as soon as they realized the size of the combined attack we were launching. But in this initial stage of the battle, the enemy fighters which did rise were few in number, and they attacked in a very half-hearted manner. Only one of our chaps—it was Strickland—got a shot at a Focke-Wulf 190. He damaged it, and the other Huns nearby were so jittery they promptly whipped about and fled.

It was well after sunrise when this first sortie drew to its close, and we turned toward the sea, headed for home. We made our landfall, then steered for base, flying low over the beautiful hills and fields of Kent. The country lanes around Canterbury and Tunbridge Wells, winding among valleys, were filling with ground fog. We were glad that our drome was on a hilltop.

Before our propellers stopped turning, our splendid ground crew went into action, quickly refueling, rearming, and inspecting our craft. We heard the news of Morgan.

We pilots agreed that while enemy coastal resistance at Dieppe might be lessened when next we went over, we knew that air resistance would be increased. We knew that Jerry would simply have to come and give us fight. He could not sit at home on his duff while a show like this was going on. Hence we gulped our coffee and prepared for the second sortie.

As we were going out the second time, when we were about twenty miles off shore, we passed some of our sea craft returning with the first batch of the wounded.

When we approached Dieppe this time, we saw great fires and high columns of smoke rising: the harbor, the Casino, and some of the hotels that once were so famous at this resort were now blazing, while ammunition dumps were blowing up here and there. It was quickly apparent that our main forces had landed effectively, and had spread far afield. The work of the demolition squads was particularly apparent: they had blasted a number of buildings, and from time to time another would rise up into the air, shudder for an instant, then splatter. It was great fun to watch the demolition boys do their work.

As we were flying over Dieppe we were informed in the air that the Canadians had captured the racetrack, and that it was available as an emergency field if any of us had to crash-land.

This time when we arrived there were plenty of enemy aircraft in the air. As we approached the battle area we could see an absolute swirl of twisting airplanes. One hell of a big battle was going on in the air as well as on the ground.

Even before we got within range of the fighting, we heard the calm voice of the Controller-on-the-spot, the

Commander who was directing the fighting from the air, say: "Get that Dornier! Get him before he attacks that ship." Then we saw the Spitfires dive for him, and they literally blew him out of the sky, exploding him with cannon shell and sending him down in pieces.

Then Duke-Woolley, our winco, came in: "Warming up, chaps!" which meant we were to pour on the coal, to speed up and make ready for the attack. We split into three columns of fours. Blue Section, in which I was fighting, was ordered to climb toward a formation of Focke-Wulf 190's. We went for them, twisting and turning like an angry snake, maneuvering and counter-maneuvering with the 190s. But we soon saw they didn't actually want to fight; they just wanted to draw us away from the west flank of our convoy, thus exposing our ships to the bombers who were hovering around, waiting for a chance to get over the convoy and drop their bombs.

A Ju 88 did manage to get through our high cover and come in. Pete, our C.O. who was leading White Section, immediately spoke over the R/T: "Hurry up! Get that 88."

Right away we saw Red Section begin firing at the bomber. And we saw White Section, with Pete in front, almost standing their Spitfires on their tails as they came in terrifically fast from below. We in Blue Section had given up playing tag with the Focke-Wulf 190's, and we, too, were trying to get within range, but finally we reluctantly gave up the chase with the Hun bomber hell-bent for Berlin, black smoke streaming from its engines and some fifteen Spitfires on its tail, each of them trying to get into position to make the kill.

During this period of high speed maneuvering, we had to ignore the anti-aircraft guns, and we actually flew through our own barrage twice. Flak from our own surface ships burst very close, but fortunately none of us was hit.

We were all twisting and weaving like mad because the Germans were attacking from above, coming in as fast as a bomb, simply whizzing past us, firing as they went. Sometimes they were in range and gone before we even saw them. But sometimes we saw them coming and managed to fire a burst as they went past. In all this fighting many planes were shot down. And we of the Eagle Squadron, all of us Americans, were particularly cheered by the news that American Flying Fortresses with all-American crews had gone over that morning and knocked out the Abbeville drome, rendering it useless to the enemy during the day, forcing him to base his fighters at some more distant field. One of the boys who had flown over the Abbeville drome said it wasn't anything but a bloody great hole; he said the Fortresses had simply wrecked it. We Americans were all mighty proud of that.

By this time the air battle was nearing its maximum intensity.

It reached that maximum as our third sortie arrived off Dieppe. We got there just in time for the fiercest combat of the day, just as our forces were beginning to withdraw.

This was the time, of course, for which the Luftwaffe had been waiting, because the concentration of troops at the time of withdrawal would present the Hun his best target of the day. After having spent more than nine hours ashore, our Commandos and shock troops were coming out, and the Germans were flying everything they had to make the attack. Ju 88's and additional Dorniers were brought up. Squadrons of German fighters had been brought from far distances. The air was simply filled with planes marked with the Maltese cross and the swastika.

The Red, White, and Blue sections of Eagle Squadron were terribly busy. We attacked again and again, attacking the German fighters and shooting our way through to get

DIEPPE SCOREBOARD: The score was kept throughout the day on the end of the dispersal hut. "Visitors—Them Guys" refers to the Germans. The point was that the Germans and not the British were the visitors at Dieppe. The latest score showed the number of visitors the RAF had shot down: 92 destroyed, 27 probables, 117 damaged. "Our Team" showed a loss of 56 pilots missing and 96 "prangs" (96 planes crashed, 40 of the pilots being saved). 71 Squadron's score was 1 bike, 1 Ju 88 destroyed, 1 FW 190 damaged, and 4 Ju 88's damaged. The squadron's casualties were one Air-craftsman Leader, the telephone orderly at dispersal, who in riding the bicycle —shown in the picture—had crashed into a telephone and broken his arm. Then, of course, the great news of the day came at 8:45 and the presses had to be stopped to announce that the commanding officer was safe, that Peterson had been fished out of the drink.

WING COMMANDER DUKE-WOOLLEY, DFC AND BAR: "Our winco and one of the absolute best." This photograph was made late on the day of Dieppe after Duke-Woolley, tired and worn, had led his wing since daybreak four times into battle.

at the bombers that were being escorted out to bomb our ships. The Eagles that day shot down two bombers and damaged a number of others. Gus Daymond's Red section of four Spitfires attacked a formation of fifteen 190's and simply chased them out of the sky, Gus calling to them over the R/T and telling them they were yellow sons-of-bitches not to stay and fight.

Our successes were sadly overbalanced when we heard that Squadron Leader Peterson had been shot down. Pete had last been seen closing in on a Ju 88 until he was at point blank range and then letting the bomber have it. But in the fight the German tail gunner managed to get in a burst that blasted Pete's machine, and he called out over the R/T that he was baling out. I felt my guts sort of tighten in me when I heard old Pete saying he had been hit and was hopping out into the drink.

It seemed we were getting our bad luck all at once, because it wasn't long before I heard Mike McPharlin crying out for a homing, for directions as to how to get back to England. Then pretty soon he said there wasn't any bloody good in giving him any directions, that he was out of petrol and he was stepping overboard.

I felt mighty unhappy as I turned back home after this sortie and headed for England, knowing that two of my best pals were struggling down there in the Channel somewhere below me. I looked down at the sea, and everything I saw on the water I imagined was Pete or Mike. Anyhow I sincerely hoped it was and that they hadn't got tangled in their 'chute harness, or had their dinghy punctured, or any bad luck like that.

We were refueling and rearming for the fourth sortie when the Air Officer Commanding sent the signal: "Though I know you are tired from a long day of fighting, I request that maximum effort be exerted for a few more hours. A great Air Victory is in sight!"

We gulped some more tea, and swallowed some more sandwiches, which the WAAF's kept prepared throughout the long day. We took off quickly, and the wing, Duke-Woolley still leading, steered again for Dieppe.

About mid-channel we met our forces, homeward bound now with the wounded ahead, the damaged craft immediately behind, and the Navy deployed far behind, patrolling and guarding the rear.

The wing commander held us in a fairly tight wing formation. Enemy fighters were about. A squadron of them appeared. Gus Daymond, now that Pete had been shot down, was leading 71. Always looking for a fight, Gus maneuvered us for the attack, but the 190's would not accept the challenge. They made only a feeble attempt to harass us, and once more Gussie screamed his contempt of yellow bastards who flew around in the sky just to look pretty and wouldn't fight.

We did not know at this time that some two hundred and fifty of the German fighters and bombers had been destroyed, or damaged. We did not know that the vaunted Luftwaffe had suffered a telling and most humiliating defeat.

From up above we looked down and watched our convoy pushing its way homeward. Minesweepers were far out in front. Corvettes were twisting around, leaving queer patterns in their wake. Rescue launches were speeding about in search of pilots in the drink. I was thankful that the sea was calm, and as I flew in formation, weaving and twisting and watching for enemy fighters, I still had time to wonder about Pete and Mike.

Low clouds and rain squalls were approaching from the direction of the Isle of Wight. The sun was sinking fast, and we knew that soon the ships below would be alongside the cliffs of England and under full protection of darkness.

Remnants of Luftwaffe fighter staffels still circled very high above us, but none of them would come down and fight. They stayed far out of range, just perched in the sky, slowly circling like birds with outstretched wings riding the high currents.

It was dusk when we finally glided into our small drome near the Thames after our last patrol. Not knowing we weren't going out again, the mechanics quickly rearmed and refueled while we stood by in readiness, waiting to be ordered out once more. But even before darkness had completely enveloped the Estuary and the coast of Kent, it was apparent that for the remainder of the nineteenth day of August the crack staffels were incapable of further effort. Any further bombing attacks by them could be handled by the RAF's normal complement of night fighters.

We were finally released off the station with a signal of congratulations from the Air Marshal.

Eagle pilots move fast when released by operations. To us "release" means "vamoose." Thus, it was not very long until, by devious routes through the blackout, we all arrived, a tired bunch, at The Black Swan.

Most of us were there having some pretty long drinks when the message came through: "Squadron Leader Peterson and Flying Officer McPharlin saved from the Channel and well!"

I can tell you that our cheers fairly lifted the roof—almost as high as our big naval guns had lifted those German buildings that day back in Dieppe. We were mighty glad to know that good old Pete and Mike were out of the drink and safe.

16

The first "Personal Combat Report" of August 19th, the day of the Dieppe battle, was made by Strickland:

> I was Blue III and airborne at 0450 with 71 (Eagle) Squadron. I set a course from Beachy Head after which I lost contact with the Squadron through Blue I having turned off his navigation lights soon after the take-off.
>
> While flying alone about ten miles west of Dieppe off the French coast, I saw four FW 190's in line astern patrolling from East to West at 5,000 feet. I attacked the last one, attacking from 45 degrees astern and firing a 1½ second burst of cannon and machine-guns, opening at 275 yards and closing to 200 yards. I saw strikes on the enemy aircraft, which immediately dived steeply. I claim one FW 190 as damaged.

The next report is by Peterson. It tells of his first fight of the day:

> While I was patrolling above Dieppe, five Ju 88's were reported coming toward the beach

at 7,000 feet. I spotted them about 3,000 feet above me, and saw Spitfires attacking them.

As one Ju 88 broke away downward nobody was after it so I intercepted it over the town of Dieppe. I fired about six seconds in short bursts at about 500 yards as I could get no closer and was already drawing sixteen pounds boost.

The aircraft jettisoned its bombs on the town as I fired. I saw cannon strikes on the fuselage and wings, and the motors began smoking badly. There was no return fire and I presume the rear gunner was killed. I broke away about eighteen miles inland and went back on patrol.

The Eagles' next fight of the morning was at eleven-twenty. This is S. M. Anderson's report:

I was flying in White Section, and we were patrolling the southeast end of the convoy when we saw FW 190's at 5,000 feet, and we advanced to engage them. They seemed reluctant to fight.

About that time Squadron Leader Peterson called that three Ju 88's were on our port. McMinn, flying in front of me, broke away to the left and advanced to the attack. I crossed over to McMinn's starboard and fired at an 88 from above and behind. Flying at 4,000 feet I fired a 3 second cannon burst, opening at 400 yards and closing to 350 yards. I then closed to 250 yards and on to 200 yards, firing another 3 second cannon burst. I then broke away. I think I hit the rear gunner as he suddenly ceased firing at me.

The combat started at 4,000 feet and ended at 1,500.

Then came Pete's second fight of the day, the one in which he destroyed a bomber and was himself shot down:

While patrolling at 4,500 feet near Dieppe I saw three Ju 88's about 2,000 feet above and to starboard. They were two miles away and were just starting their bombing run on the southern end of the convoy.

I attacked and they sheered away and dived. I fired at one of the 88's, diving at him and opening fire at 300 yards astern. I saw cannon strikes, mainly on the starboard wing, and his starboard motor emitted puffs of black and white smoke.

As I closed to 200 yards the rear gunner started shooting and hit my aircraft. I knew I was hit and that I would have to bale out anyway, so I kept firing up to 150 yards, then I had to quit as there was so much steam and smoke in the cockpit.

I could not see what happened to the enemy aircraft, but Wing Commander Duke-Woolley saw him crash into the sea on his back. I subsequently baled out as my motor was on fire. I saw my Spitfire hit the water with a great splash.

Then came a fight in which Coen and McPharlin, who love so much to fight together, probably knocked down a German.

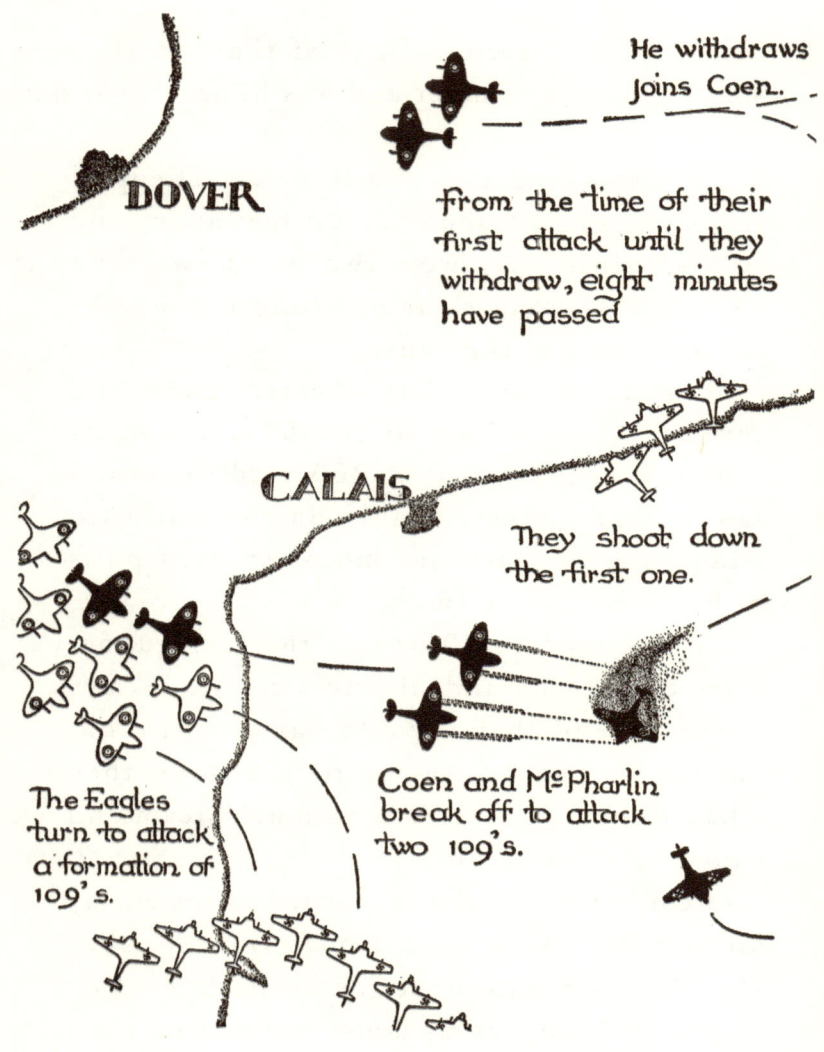

He withdraws
Joins Coen.

DOVER

From the time of their
first attack until they
withdraw, eight minutes
have passed

CALAIS

They shoot down
the first one.

The Eagles
turn to attack
a formation of
109's.

Coen and McPharlin
break off to attack
two 109's.

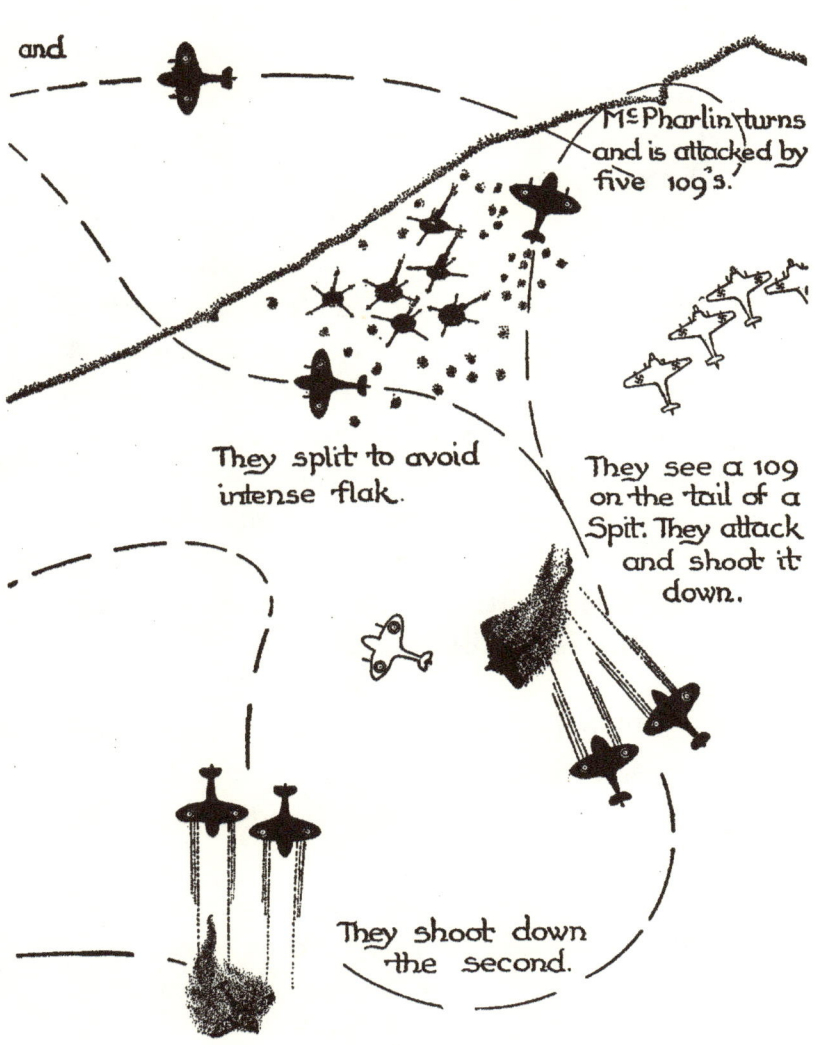

and

McPharlin turns and is attacked by five 109's.

They split to avoid intense flak.

They see a 109 on the tail of a Spit. They attack and shoot it down.

They shoot down the second.

COEN AND McPHARLIN GET THREE

This is Coen's report of the battle:

> I was flying as Blue I on the port side of the
> White section. We were patrolling east of the
> convoy when three Ju 88's came into view
> heading west.
>
> I pushed the tit and caught up to one of
> the bombers and gave a 2 second burst of can-
> non and machine-guns at about 400 yards,
> but observed no results. I then closed to 200
> yards and fired the remainder of my ammu-
> nition. His port engine began to belch black
> smoke and pieces came off his wing and en-
> gine. Pieces also came off his fuselage, but I
> do not think these pieces were from my fire,
> as there were others firing at the same air-
> craft. McPharlin was firing at that time from
> the Blue II position. I was forced to break
> away as I was out of ammunition.

This is McPharlin's report of the same fight, and notice
how Wee Michael was following his usual battle tactics,
climbing slightly above Coen and firing down past him:

> I was Blue II when at a height of about 6,000,
> feet Blue I attacked a Ju 88 which immediate-
> ly jettisoned its bombs in the sea and did a
> violent diving turn to the right.
>
> Blue I followed, firing as he dove. I saw
> pieces flying off the port engine and smoke
> coming from it. Just before Blue I finished fir-
> ing, I got above him and opened with cannon
> and machine-guns, firing a six-second burst
> from 400 yards to 150 yards. I concentrated

on the fuselage, and while I was firing I saw pieces flying off it.

As I continued my attack, the smoke from the enemy aircraft became thicker, and flames started between the engine and the wing root on the port side. I fired my cannon with machine-guns synchronized before breaking off. I broke off because I was about to be attacked by two FW 190's that had dived on me. As I slid out from under their attack, I saw the Ju 88 in a straight shallow dive. We were then about 1,500 feet and some five miles off the French coast.

After he was bounced by the FW 190's, knowing that his ammunition was practically exhausted, Michael headed into a cloud and hid. When he came out and looked round, he saw that he was over France. He also saw that the German fighters were waiting for him, and he scurried back into cover again. Feeling his way through the cloud, he thought he was flying toward England; but each time he came down, he saw that he was still over France. Then he climbed to 16,000 feet and called for a "homing," for the course he was to fly in order to get back to his home station.

But after receiving his homing from the ground station in England, Michael discovered it was of no use to him: he discovered that in the battle his compass had been hit and rendered "u/s/"—unserviceable.

He then set a course for home by the sun, but soon realized that in his flying in and out of the clouds, playing hide-and-seek with the Hun that had bounced him, he had practically exhausted his petrol and would be unable to make the English coast. Preferring to take his chances swimming in the Channel to landing on German-occupied territory, he prepared to bale out. When there were only three gallons of petrol left, he lowered the door at his side. When the last drop of petrol was gone, Michael jumped.

He was in clouds at four thousand five hundred feet when he left his plane, and he soon lost sight of it, though he heard the crash as it hit the sea. As he floated down below cloud level, he saw a patch of oil on the sea where his plane had gone in.

When Mike himself was in the sea, he took off his boots, inflated his dinghy, and climbed in. He happened to have some Benzedrine tablets in his pocket and decided they would give him extra energy for the long, long paddle back to England. He gobbled down enough of the tablets, the doctor discovered later, to do serious harm to a less sturdy man, but Michael said they only made him feel swell.

Settling himself in the dinghy for the long paddle ahead, Mike went to work. After paddling seven miles he came to a lighthouse. From there he was taken off by a rescue launch, and shortly afterward landed in England at a town that was being heavily bombed at the moment by the Germans, who were trying to get revenge for the defeat the Luftwaffe had suffered that day.

"I was taken in by some naval officers," Michael said later, "and they were mighty nice to me. They not only outfitted me with clothes but they plied me with whisky until I was in a happy daze. Altogether it was a very pleasant experience. The fighting during the day was grand and the evening was marvelous, as the navy men handed me one glass after another: 'Just to knock off the chill of the Channel waters,' they said."

But back at the Eagles' station there was not such jollity, at least not with some of the boys. Through all their bombings and fighting the Eagles have come to know and to appreciate each other, and there have been formed friendships that will last always. One of the finest of these friendships is between Oscar Coen and Mike McPharlin. On the ground and in the air these two boys like to be together, and some of the most brilliant fights in the history of the squadron have been fought by Oscar and Wee Michael. One day in particular they fought with magnificent courage. In ten minutes they fought three different battles and sent three German aircraft down in flames.

In the closeness of their friendship with each other, they made a deal. Mike had a pair of boots that Oscar particularly coveted. Mike had brought them from the States with him, and they were the very finest boots. Oscar had tried to buy them, trade for them, or get them in any way he could. But Mike wouldn't part with them. He did, however, eventually make a contact with his pal.

If Mike went out some day and didn't come back, Oscar got the boots.

If Oscar went out and didn't come back, Mike got Oscar's cigarette case and all the cigarettes he had in his room at the time he was killed.

On the night after the Battle of Dieppe, the boys at the Eagle mess were a sad lot. Two of their number had gone into the drink that day. Oscar was particularly low. His pal Mike had baled out into the sea. Oscar was mighty unhappy.

Then the telephone rang.

The messenger came.

"Some one to speak to you," the messenger told Oscar. Oscar went to the telephone.

"Oscar, you old son-of-a-bitch," said Mike, thus announcing his return to the land of the living, "you take off my boots."

British Combine

WATCHERS BY DAY: Scattered over England are hundreds of these posts where the observers are on constant watch, forever searching the skies for enemy planes.

17

It was Oscar Coen who was bounced out of bed one night by the German bombers. It was Oscar who had gone around the mess screaming for his airplane, demanding the privilege of getting into the air and having a go at the beggars. Oscar's anger, and the anger of all the other boys, was considerably accentuated because of a frightful insult suffered only a few days previously.

On the morning of that particular day the Eagles' airdrome was absolutely fog-bound; the weather was definitely on the deck. The pilots waked early, looked out, then went back to sleep. Most of them slept until around noon, then began to straggle downstairs. They sat around the mess, reading the papers, playing the gramophone, swearing at the weather.

"But it's lifting," some one said.

"Bloody little," some one else said.

Anyhow, it lifted about three hundred feet. And that was enough for a Ju 88, a German bomber, to dart down out of the fog and make a trial run across the airdrome. Then he came back and went just above the hangars, and this time he meant business: he dropped his bombs with a seven second delayed fuse on them. Because of the delayed action of the fuses, the German was away from over his bombs before they began to go off, lifting parts of

233

the hangar and scattering it as they exploded. Then Jerry turned again and started back.

But this time he made his turn to the right!

"Did you see that!"

"The crude beggar!"

"No one makes a right-hand turn over an airdrome!"

The Hun was making another run, this time over the mess. He was dropping his bombs when one of his gunners saw a group of officers standing on the edge of the field. The German gunner opened fire, and the officers fell flat on their faces like wheat bending before a strong wind.

As they lay on the ground, the mess blowing up behind them and the machine-gun bullets whizzing over them, the boys were expressing their opinion of any flier so ignorant of all aerial courtesy as to make a right-hand turn.

"Silly bastard, somebody ought to teach him better."

After the German had blown up everything he could, the boys went over to see the havoc he had left. They looked at the hangar that was wrecked and the mess that was flattened, and they said: "By God, that's a bloody insult, all right. The idea of his coming over and making a right-hand turn over our airdrome!"

After suffering such an indignity the Eagles were quick to demand the privilege of going up to attack the Hun bombers who came over a few nights later and tumbled them out of their beds. And when they were refused this privilege by men older and wiser in the ways of modern fighting, particularly modern night fighting, the boys called a meeting. They decided they would tolerate no further insults: they would not have Jerries bombing them, day or night And since they didn't know much about night fighting they decided to train themselves so they would be prepared next time the Hun came over after dark. The decision was made, of course, when the Eagles were an inexperienced lot, before they had any knowledge whatever about the curious and extremely difficult science of modern air fighting at night.

In the old days, when the Hun was coming over regularly at night and bombing in force, then night fighting was good sport, but when only half a dozen planes trickle across the Channel to North England, and only three or four come across to drop the odd bomb in South England, then the night fighters have no fun at all. They lie around their dispersal huts night after night waiting, hoping for an order to go up and intercept, but the order seldom comes, and the defensive night fighter leads a comparatively dull life.

On the other hand, the intruder, the offensive night fighter, is more fortunate. While never getting so much action as the men who fight by day, the intruder lives a strange, almost bizarre life, fighting his battles in the dark and seeing planes suddenly burst into flames and go down like meteors before his guns.

There was a period in the early part of the war when the intruder crossed the Channel solely on "spec," on speculation, of finding a Hun and shooting him down. But this haphazard way of hunting was not profitable—it was too difficult to locate the Hun at night, and "spec" flying is now seldom permitted. Now when the night fighter goes out, he goes on a specific mission.

When the Hun is up at night in any force at all, the British send out their fighters, sending them in relays to each area in France, Belgium, and Holland. These chaps, flying alone, one to an area, patrol that area, stooging around waiting for any luckless Hun that might happen to come their way. Knowing that the night skies over Occupied France are filled with these intruders, the Germans are terrified whenever their bombers return after a raid

International News Photograph

WATCHERS BY NIGHT: One of the innumerable searchlights in England, ready throughout every night to seek out the enemy and "hold" him until a fighter plane can come and shoot him down.

over England. If they believe a particularly strong number
of intruders are flying over France that night, the German
controllers order their bombers to go on to some airdrome
in Belgium. But the intruders in Belgium promptly cluster
around, and the Germans, now afraid to land their aircraft
in Belgium, send them on to Holland.

The intruders in Holland immediately take up the cat
and mouse game and begin their patrol of the Dutch airdromes. By this time the signal officers of all German
landing fields in Northern France, Belgium, and Holland
are in a flap, are excited because they know their planes
are running low on petrol and they must be landed somewhere and soon. But they can't land because there are those
damned intruders circling around and around in the dark,
waiting for their chance.

The Hun, of course, would like to turn on the lights
along the flarepath and bring in his bombers, but he dare
not because the lights would betray the exact location of
the runway and the intruder could blast it with bombs.
The Hun, too, would like to turn on his searchlights and
spot the intruder, but he can't turn them on because they
might show the position of his own planes and the intruder could then shoot them down. Finally, he would like to
open up with his ground guns and destroy the intruder,
but he dare not fill the sky with flak because he might
destroy his own bombers along with the intruder. He is
simply in a very bad way. Finally, though, in desperation
he orders his planes to come downstairs. It is then that the
intruder collects for all the trouble he has been to.

Short of petrol, knowing that they must land immediately, the landing bombers come swopping along the
flarepath, the runway lit with dim lights on each side of
it, two parallel rows of lights that show so faintly they
are little more than dull orange glows in the night haze.
But any light strong enough to show the bombers how

to land is strong enough to betray the bombers to the intruders. Therefore, as the big planes come in, losing their speed and wavering uncertainly just before they touch the ground, the intruder hurtles down upon them and sprays them with machine-gun and cannon. Then, just to make assurance doubly sure, he drops a bomb or two in the center of the flarepath, opening up craters into which the bombers turn over and catch fire.

Frequently the intruder does not actually attack; he simply forces the bombers to destroy themselves. I was talking with a night fighter ace only the other evening who destroyed three German planes without firing his guns or dropping a bomb.

"It was wonderful fun," he told me. "I was directed to patrol a certain airdrome in Holland. I went there and flew near the station but not near enough for them to get at me with their guns. I found the bombers were going to another drome. I followed them but again they changed their course. Again I followed them. This kept up until I thought I was going to end in Berlin. I began to get worried about my own petrol, but fortunately theirs gave out first, and three of the beggars crashed and caught fire. I didn't get the fun of actually shooting them down, but I did get to see three of them blazing on the ground. It was a grand sight."

Not all planes are destroyed at night as they come in to land; many of them are shot out of the sky by these intruders, who have developed remarkable night vision. Even in the dark they see the enemy, maneuver into position, and shoot him down.

Regardless of how extraordinary a man's vision may be at night, his eyes do not instantly adapt themselves to the darkness after he leaves a brightly-lighted room. Therefore while waiting to go on a mission some of the night fighters wear black glasses that cut out virtually all light. They sit around the mess talking with their friends and are themselves in almost total darkness. Then time comes for them to leave. They go out into the night, take off their glasses, and climb into their planes. Their eyes are already adapted to the dark, and the period of slow adjustment, varying in different individuals from ten minutes to an hour, is avoided. With their eyes accustomed to the night, they are ready immediately to begin their search for enemy planes.

"But there's no use just riding along looking in front and to each side," one of the greatest of the night fighters told me. "Of course on a bright moonlight night when you can see easily, any one can understand how enemy aircraft are spotted; in the moonlight it's not difficult to find them. But on dark nights the finding of a Hun is damned difficult. The best way is to sit low in your plane and lean back. Then you look above you. You just ride along and look up, watching for anything that's moving."

"Yes," said another night fighter in the room. "But while you're looking up, don't forget occasionally to look down over the sides to see if anything is sneaking up from below, coming up to shoot you down."

"Of course, you do that. Naturally you protect yourself; you take care that you, yourself, don't get shot down. In this game while you're hunting, you must always remember that you're being hunted. As you fly along you watch out for the enemy about to attack you as well as the enemy you can attack. Then you see something moving. Of course in the dark you can't tell immediately whether it's a Hun or a friend, but you always presume it's a Hun and you streak up as fast as you can to get in position to fire. Once you're close enough to determine that the plane is an enemy aircraft, you put on a little extra speed, get in position, and let go with cannon and machine-guns. And when you shoot them down in flames at night—my word, it's something!"

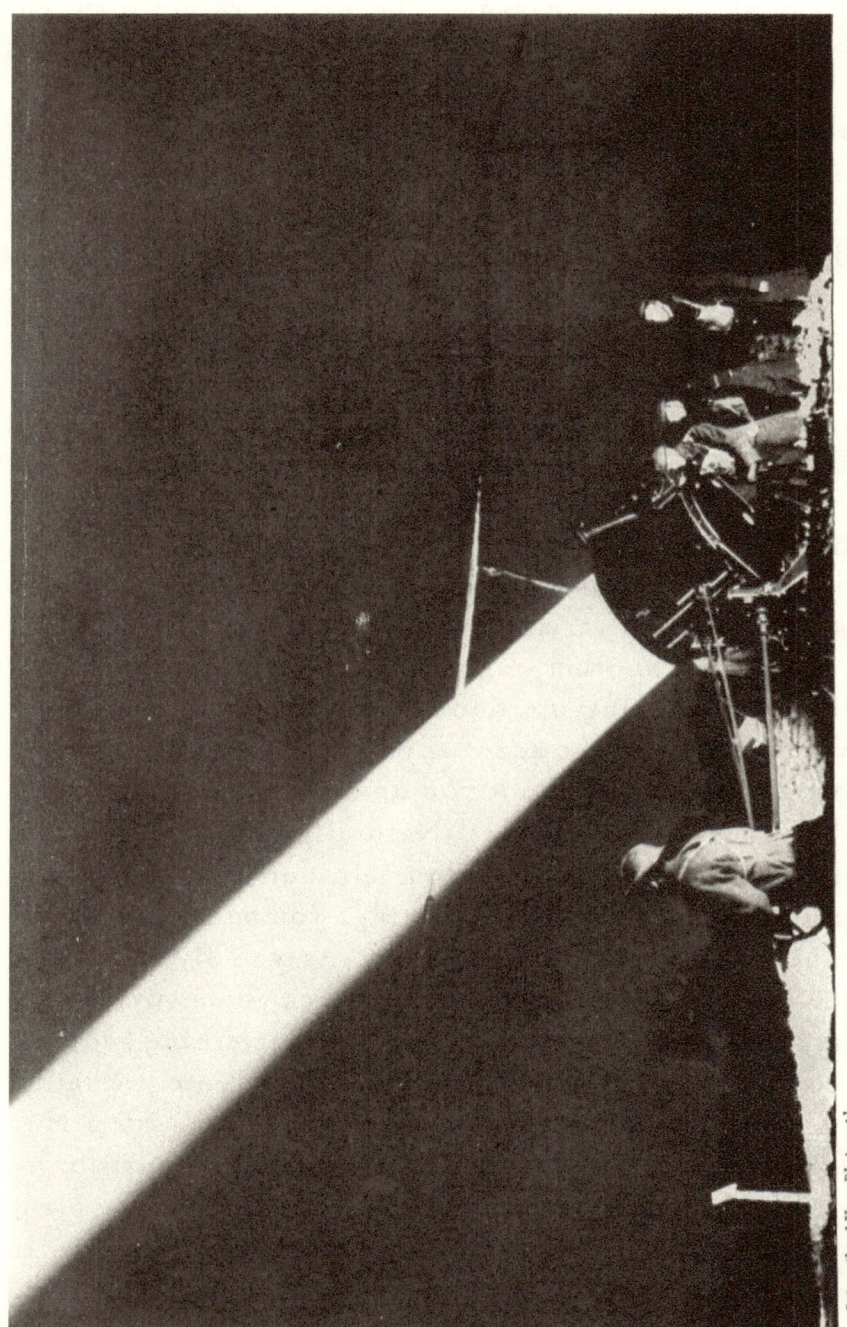

THE EYE OF NIGHT

International News Photograph

"But seeing a plane at night must be extremely diffi- cult," I said. "Do you believe your eyes are different from mine? Do you think you're gifted in some way that enables you to see in the dark?"

"No," he said, "we're not gifted; we're trained, that's all. Before any pilot goes into intruder flying, he has a lot of night flying, a lot of experience in the air when it's dark. In this way his eyes get accustomed to seeing at night, and the more he flies in the dark, the better he's able to see when there's no light except a few stars.

"But even then, with all our experience, we sometimes make mistakes. Dick here"—he pointed to a slender boy of possibly twenty years who was lying on the cot—"Dick didn't see too well the other night and he almost got into trouble. He spotted a Hun bomber and got into position to attack. When he was just the right distance, so he thought, he opened with everything he had. The Hun immediately burst into flames. But Dick had misjudged his distance. In the dark he had gone so near the bomber that when Jerry exploded and began to blaze, Dick had to fly through the flames. He came back with the paint scorched off his wings and fuselage. Fortunately he didn't catch fire."

"I was really frightened that night," Dick said quietly. "I mean to say I really was. One minute everything was just right. Then I pressed the button and the next minute I was in the middle of this bonfire. I mean it was rather breathtaking."

So the Eagles decided they would not sit on the ground and be bombed, even if it was night; they held a conference of war and decided to learn night flying. They were deter- mined to defend themselves next time Jerry came over for a night attack. Accordingly, when the moon period began again, four of them went up to practice.

The only trouble was that, unaccustomed to the laws of flying at night, they had forgotten to notify the searchlight batteries and the ground guns. So they were hardly in the air before the searchlights came on and the long white fingers began to move through the sky, feeling for them, moving slowly as they swept the heavens until one of the lights fastened to the plane that Ed Bateman was flying. Then another touched him. And a third. He was flying at the tip of a cone of light that followed him wherever he turned, or climbed or dived, while the guns blazed at him and the shells exploded all about him.

Recognition at night, determining visually whether a plane is a friend or foe, is extremely difficult, and, as Bateman discovered, the night fighter runs the constant risk of being shot down by his own guns. After dodging all over the sky, Bateman finally slid out of the cone in which he had been "held" and managed to get back to earth without being killed. He came in saying he'd had a wonderful time. "This night flying is the stuff," he said. "You don't even have to fly over France to get shot at. Get it right on your own doorstep." The other boys were jealous of Ed's fun, and they announced their determination to go up and see for themselves.

Next evening six pilots went up. But they had rather a dull time because the guns had been warned and they kept silent. The pilots were bored with the whole show. Merely flying around in the moonlight was no fun. So they came in to land, the six planes, one behind the other, making the usual circuit of the field before landing.

Only instead of six planes, there were seven!

"We'd been watching from the ground," a WAAF officer told me, "and we counted seven airplanes in the circuit. We wondered where the extra plane had come from. We soon found out, because as two of our boys were coming in to land, there was a burst of machine-gun fire from a German intruder who'd got into the circuit. He not only had

British Combine

SEARCHLIGHT BATTERY

a squirt at our chaps, but he obligingly dropped a couple of bombs at the same time just to make the landing a little more difficult.

"Keith Alexander came down quacking like mad, profanely declaring the whole thing was a personal attack on him and he thought it pretty contemptible. 'Why doesn't the guy come around during the day and fight like a man when you can see him?' Keith said. The attack actually had been made on George Brown. Fortunately, George hadn't been hit and his plane wasn't badly mauled, so nothing serious had happened. Anyhow, George was quite brave and calm, as if the whole thing was merely part of the night's work."

Still not satisfied about night flying, the boys went up again the next night. They flew until they were getting short on petrol, then they came in and were making the circuit before landing.

"I decided I'd go along and see them come down," Robbie said. "So I took three pilots in my car and we started out from the mess to the landing field. But a Jerry had again got into the circuit, and he not only had a long squirt at some of the boys in the sky, but he dropped three bombs across the mess. We heard them come whistling down behind us, and I trod on the gas and caused my car to show an amazing burst of acceleration in getting out of the way.

"After the bombs had burst we looked back and saw that all the windows and doors in the mess had been blown out and that our rooms were an awful shambles. Furthermore, a big fire had started on the heath in the dry bracken, and it lit up the whole airdrome. Going out to fight the fire was terribly dangerous, because we were well silhouetted for any stray Jerry to have a squirt at us, but we finally managed to get the fire out.

"When we returned to the mess we were met by the station commander who informed us in positive language that the Eagles would discontinue their practice in night flying since it was accomplishing nothing except getting the airdrome gradually demolished."

That was the end of the Eagles' interest in night flying. Indeed, in the future they shunned it because they feared they might learn enough about it to be assigned as night fighters, and that to them would have been a tragedy. The night fighter, even the intruder, may go for weeks without action, without even seeing an enemy aircraft. And when he does see him, the attack is over in an instant: the enemy is shot down or he dives into the darkness and is lost from sight. The air battles so beloved by the day fighters, the far-off glimpse of the enemy, the swift maneuvering for the attack, then the melee of the dog fight, the tremendous thrill of aerial battle, are all lacking. The Eagles wanted none of the long defensive patrols by night, nor were they interested in the lonely flying of the intruder. They wanted only to go on flying by day, forever seeking out the Hun and blowing him out of the sky.

Indeed, they came in time almost to have sympathy for the night flier, even the Hun.

One winter night a formal dinner was being given at the officers' mess where the Eagles were stationed. All the officers attended, and the WAAF officers were invited. The dining-room was beautifully decorated with candles on the table, and flowers, and the station orchestra provided music. In the midst of the five-course dinner, the siren announced that the enemy had chosen this occasion for a raid. In accordance with station custom, the electric lights were cut off, and the dinner was continued by candle light while the enemy aircraft flew overhead.

"Nobody cared a damn about the prospect of an attack," Robbie said. "And while poor Jerry stooged around

looking for us, all the boys could say was, 'What a wonderful time we're having down here. I bet that poor blighter
on top is mighty cold. I bet he'd envy us if he knew what
we're doing down here.'"

18

After the period of bad weather there is no more welcome sound than the call over the loud speaker: "All pilots report to the briefing room immediately." The call means that a show is on, that the boys are to get cracking again.

They tumble out of the mess, and there's a mild scramble into the waiting lorries. As they ride along toward the station intelligence office, the fighters glance at the sky and nod approval. All right upstairs. Good day for a show, good day to fly off seeking battle.

As the cars and trucks arrive at the intelligence office, the boys pile out and crowd into the large room with maps covering the walls, some of them marked particularly for that day's operation, heavy red lines showing the routes to be flown to and from the target and lighter red lines showing the flak along the route and in the vicinity of the target.

The whole wing is to participate, and the wing commander arrives wearing the ribbon of the Distinguished Flying Cross and holding several pages of typed instructions from Fighter Command. After he arrives, a moment is necessary to get things quieted down so that he can be heard; then he begins briefing the crews, giving them the information they need for the days operation.

"All right, chaps—we are to escort the Hurricane bomb-ers again." He pauses for a minute and once more reads the instructions in the combat orders sent down from Fighter Command. "The target," he says, "will be this power sta-tion. We'll enter here"—he points to a place on the French Coast—"and fly low."

"Flak!" whispers someone.

"Quiet, chaps," say the winco, though he smiles at the pilot who had impulsively spoken of the flak they all knew they would encounter on a low level attack. "We will turn left here and follow this road." He was pointing out the route on the map. "There's a canal here—notice? And a large forest there. No one should have any trouble follow-ing the route.

"The first squadron will fly in and attack with the Hurricanes, using their own cannon. The other squadrons must keep on their toes because as soon as the attack is ended, we will then turn left and keep close to the deck, withdrawing with the Hurricanes to this point—here—on the English coast.

"Now there's one other thing. We'll have no more clut-tering up of the R/T with unnecessary talk. We must stop this unnecessary radio chatter. On the last show over St. Omer when things were getting hot, somebody had the au-dacity to say: 'Brave and calm, chaps. Whatever happens, brave and calm.'" Lulu sits there with a face like an angel, though all the other Eagles are looking at him and grinning.

"It is now," says the winco, looking at his watch, "ex-actly 1312 operational time." The pilots synchronize their watches. "First squadron will take off promptly at 1352. The second at 54. The third at 56. We will rendezvous over the Channel with the Hurricanes at exactly 1415." He lights a cigarette. "Any questions?"

The room is thick with tobacco smoke. The location of the target and the part that each squadron will play in the

attack are well understood. There is no need particularly
to worry about navigation, because that will be handled
mostly by the Hurricanes: the fighters will merely follow the bombers' lead. Some pilots—the new boys—look
sort of homesick. Nobody blames them, because this is
their first low-level attack, and thoughts of this particular
operation make even old, experienced pilots wish they
were home. As usual after a briefing, there is a moment of
subdued tension as the boys sit still, many of them looking
down at the smoke twisting up from the cigarettes they
hold, turning them in their fingers, studying them and not
seeing them at all.

"Very well, chaps," says the winco. "That's all."

Another mild scramble into the lorries which speed
away from the station intelligence room to the dispersal
shacks around the field, each squadron going to its own
particular dispersal. In less than forty minutes the wing
must be airborne. Every one hits the small locker room at
the same time. Flying equipment soon clutters the tables
and shelves.

"Who the hell's got my gauntlets?"

"Listen, you ape, those are my goggles and you damn
well know it."

Once boots and Mae West are donned and all personal
equipment is collected, there's a rush to the Spitfires that
stand widely dispersed around the field so that no well-
placed bomb or low-flying fighter could destroy a number
of planes in a single attack. Standing in their blast shel-
ters, protected on three sides by solid walls, the Spitfires
wait for the pilots that quickly leap into them. A complete
check is made. Fighting harness is tightly adjusted.

Then, after all preparations have been completed,
there follow a few minutes of quiet over the field with all
pilots sitting in their cockpits watching the minutes
slip by. During these minutes of waiting there's time for

reflections about the plan of attack. The Hurricanes and the Spits will skim in just over the treetops, going in low all the way until they reach the target. There the Hurricanes will bomb, then turn, dive, and zoom around the power plant, firing with their cannon from many angles and directions. The bombs will have an eleven second delayed action so that the planes can drop them carefully, lay each egg full in the nest, and get away before the bomb explodes. And while the bombers are doing their work, the fighters too will be blazing away with their cannon.

About one minute before start-up time a great stillness comes over the squadron. Most eyes are on the leaders Spitfire marked with the Eagle Squadron marking, "XR," and with a "V" for Victory.

The minute hand reaches 49. The squadron leader presses his starter button. Immediately thereafter eleven other engines throw fire from their exhausts. There's plenty of noise and action now. Every one taxis rapidly to the take-off position.

1351—the squadron leader's arm is raised high.

1352—he circles his arm with a clenched fist, then drops his hand on to the throttle. "V" for Victory begins to roll.

The first squadron, 71 (Eagle) Squadron, is airborne.

Four minutes later the entire wing of Spitfires is climbing fast and shifting into battle formation.

Squadron Leader Peterson heads for the Estuary. Back in England only a few minutes before, the skies were clear, but out over the Channel there are many rain squalls about. Flying low, Peterson leads the Eagles just above the water, right down on the deck with the roll of the sea seeming almost to come up to them.

A convoy is passing into the Thames. Barrage balloons are flying from the coasters and from the North Sea tramps, the great "pigs" waving above the ships to tangle and drag down any Hun who attempts to come in low and attack. Pete sees the balloons in time and leads the Spitfires around the last vessel in the long line. It is a collier, loaded to the water line with coal from Newcastle-on-Tyne. Soon the wing arrives near Ramsgate, and the Spitfires find the Hurricanes at the rendezvous circling low, just above the water, flying around and around as they wait.

Now the rain is pouring down. The Spitfires fly line astern, close behind each other over the water, with the raindrops flattening instantly against the thick bullet-proof windscreen and in the driving rain the Spitfire immediately ahead alternately being blurred and distorted like a huge fish in deep water. Every one holds exactly to his place, because to lose position or break formation in a time like this would be to invite collision.

Flying in line astern the fighters close in, wrapping themselves about the Hurricanes while each pilot glances frequently at his watch, waiting for the zero hour, the instant at which the whole formation will leave the rendezvous and sets its course for the target.

Precisely as the second hand crosses the mark and the zero hour arrives, the Hurricane bombers turn slightly and head out to sea. It is still raining hard as the formation passes a lighthouse that is their exact "departure point."

Like good sailors, careful airmen never expect to make real and accurate landfall unless they have also made accurate departure from a known position. The careless airmen will go upstairs and, once he is there, set his course when he may be as much as two miles from his airdrome; but the good navigator, the pilot who always finds his target and always finds his way home, unfailingly takes the center of his airdrome as his departure point, hovering over the center of the drome and setting his course from there.

The Hurricanes lead out over the sea, steering a magnetic course of 210°–220°. They are flying directly above

SPITFIRE DIVING TO ATTACK

DORNIER 217: Primarily a bomber this development of "The Flying Pencil" has been used by the hard-pressed Germans as a reconnaissance plane and as a night fighter. The first German bomber shot down by the Eagles was a Dornier: Gus Daymond shot it and its crew of four into the sea.

S P I T F I R E : "Clean and swift and beautiful like a bird."

M E S S E R S C H M I T T   1 0 9 F : Before the Focke-Wulf was sent into combat in the Spring of 1942, the Messerschmitt 109 was the best German fighting plane. The Eagles have had many fights with the Me 109 and have shot down a good number of them. This photograph of the Me 109 does not show an actual plane, but a model like those used in all training courses of aircraft recognition.

the waves, and the little fighters spread out in a wide echelon to avoid the bombers heavy slipstream. No one wants to drive headlong into the heavy blast back from the bombers, and the Spitfires move out to avoid it and to enjoy the speed of low flying over the water. When one flies directly above the waves there is a noticeable increase in speed. The closer the water, the more effective is the "ground pack"—a phenomenon caused by the increased compression below the wing, giving the pilot a feeling almost as if he were riding a surfboard.

The rain squalls become fewer, and over toward the southeast the skies are clearing. Visibility is improving, though the salt spray still shoots up from the sea and blurs on the glass. The Hurricanes do not rise even inches to avoid the spray; nor do they deviate from their course as they fly on toward France.

Then at last the low coastline by Le Touquet looms up ahead. Steering straight for it, the pilots get set for flak. The Hurricanes push their throttles open to the gate, the pilots driving their planes forward under increased power. Peterson correspondingly increases the speed of the Spitfires, and his calm, even voice comes into the earphones of the other pilots:

"Hello, Stardust Squadron. . . . Stardust leader here. . . . Get weaving, chaps."

Then the Spitfires begin their dance. They "jink," turning and twisting with swift changes in direction, one plane behind the other, flying fast with their wingtips close to the sea. Then they leave the sea and cross the coast and hurtle over the German gun emplacement| with the flak guns blazing at them.

On past the forward line of guns they fly, and soon they find the road the wing commander has described at the briefing. They follow it, low and fast, just missing the tree-tops. They come to the canal and cross it. They fly above the forest. They find their target, and, turning left in a quick climbing zoom, they position themselves, then dive to the attack, hurtling down until they are in exact position; then they let go their bombs that eleven seconds later explode, and great columns of dust and smoke spurt up from the plant. Then Spitfires and Hurricanes together are milling around the plant like angry hornets, attacking from every angle and direction, blazing at it with their cannon.

Quite as suddenly as they arrive, the planes depart, leaving behind them the Tingry power station and transformer plant shattered and on fire.

The attacking bombers leave France and cross the coast still very low, flying fast. The Eagles climb to cover them better. Just off Le Touquet, 109s intercept. They come down fast, from above. It is essential that the Spitfires remain with the Hurricanes, because the bombers have exhausted their ammunition in the attack on the plant. Without drawing away from the Hurricanes, without ever leaving them exposed, the Eagles deflect the 109's by quick, sharp attacks that last for a second only; then the Spitfires dart back into position once more, hovering over the Hurricanes that fly so close to the water that they are almost invisible. Their camouflaged backs blending into the sea, and flying so low that they make no shadow, no tell-tale marker, on the sea to betray them, the Hurricanes race for home.

Unable to vary any appreciable distance from their set position, the English are at a tactical disadvantage. Realizing this, the Huns begin to indulge in their old dive-and-zoom tactics—coming down fast, then zooming up out of danger, on each attack firing short squirts from their Mauser cannon that shoot through the propeller hub while two machine-guns pour incendiaries and armor piercing bullets out to the point of harmonization two hundred

British Official Photograph: Crown Copyright Reserved

HEINKEL 111: German bomber.

FOCKE-WULF 190: This little German fighter has a wing span of only thirty-four feet. Weaving and twisting at two, three, four hundred yards distance, or diving at a speed above six hundred miles an hour, it is the target the Eagles must hit—as they have hit it repeatedly and sent it down in flames. This is a photograph of a captured FW 190 that was landed on an English airdrome by a German pilot who had lost his way and thought he was coming down in France.

JUNKERS 88: An all-purpose German plane, though used chiefly for bombing. A Ju 88 with its crew of four was the plane that Peterson shot down a moment before Pete himself was shot into the sea.

and fifty yards ahead, the point where all the bullets converge and are most destructive.

Strickland, Roscoe, and Mauriello are each attacked.

Then Roscoe cries out: "Stardust Leader. Stardust Blue IV calling. I've been hit."

"Badly?"

"Maybe. Anyhow, I'm bleeding badly."

The 109's poise for another attack. And down they come, firing once more with their cannon and machine-guns, then zooming up once more.

The fight continues until mid-channel is reached. There the 109's become wary. They are afraid of flying into a trap. They are afraid the Hurricanes and their escort may be leading them under a withdrawal wing of British planes, a wing flying high above and patrolling the Channel, waiting for pursuing Huns to come under and thus expose themselves to attack.

After Roscoe has cried out, the other Eagles close in about him. Those who fly close to him see that he is acting faint, that he is having difficulty holding up his head. They keep talking to him:

"Hi, Art. Hold it up, old boy. And stay back of Stardust Blue III. He's steering for the nearest emergency base. He'll lead you home. Follow him."

"Don't go to sleep, Art. Hold up your head. How are you feeling?"

"Not so good," comes the weak answer.

Down come the 109's, blazing with their cannon and machine-guns, then zooming up again.

"You sons-of-bitches, wait until we don't have these bombers to get home. Wait until we can get loose and kick your Heinie butts."

"Listen, Art, listen. Listen to me!" Pete is having trouble of his own, trying to drag home a Spitfire with a great hole in its tail. "Art, listen. Can you hear me?"

"Yes."

"If you're feeling too bad, for Christ's sake climb up and bale out!"

"I think I can make it."

The 109's have made their last attack. They turn tail and are flying back toward France.

The rain squalls have come up again, and it is raining hard as the formation returns to its departure point, crossing the lighthouse from which they left the British Coast.

Roscoe makes a landing at a forward base. The RAF surgeons take him away in the ambulance. At the hospital they get most of the shrapnel out of his leg, but when he is finally returned to his base, Doc Osborne digs out some additional pieces. And even Osborne can't get out one piece that is too deeply embedded.

Anyhow, Roscoe doesn't mind. He rather likes to carry around that fragment of shrapnel. It reminds him of what the 109's did to him on that low-level attack. And it acts as an incentive as, day after day, he goes up against the Jerries seeking to increase his revenge, to add to his score of Huns destroyed, probably destroyed, and damaged.

"ANDY"

19

There was a boy in the squadron named Newton Anderson. I met him the first time I visited the Eagles' station. There were some Belgian and Polish officers visiting the station that day, and the mess was a confusion of talk as the English, Americans, Belgians, and Poles had their pink gins before lunch. Later, at the table, the station commander, Group Captain Peel, led a fascinating conversation in which the men of the RAF told of air battles over France, the Belgians told of fighting in Flanders, and the Poles bitterly recited their experiences in their own country, telling how the Germans had marched into Poland to kill soldiers on the battlefield and had remained to murder women and children in surrendered cities. It was exciting talk, but in some way the soft-spoken remarks of the boy sitting next to me interested me even more than tales of Dunkerque or butchery in Poland.

"You're English, aren't you?" I asked.

"No. I'm an American. I was born in New Orleans."

"But you speak with a British accent."

"Perhaps that's because I've been in England for some time," Anderson said. "I've been here since the beginning of the war."

"You were in England when war was declared?" I asked.

"No. But soon after war began I went to France. I joined the Foreign Legion."

An American boy born in New Orleans, who had been in the French Foreign Legion, and who was fighting in the RAF—I turned slightly so that I might see him better. He looked older than most of the other pilots in the room, and he wore glasses with noticeably thick lenses. For the first time I really saw the thickness of the lenses. And I wondered about a fighter pilot wearing glasses; I wondered about their sending a man into air battle unless his eyes were keen and swift as a hawk's.

Newton Anderson was born into a family of wealth. He was educated in the United States and in the schools of Europe; particularly he was educated in France. Then came 1929 and the financial crash which left this nineteen-year-old boy with almost no money. So he went to Chicago and became a newspaper reporter. He was a good reporter and was getting on toward the top when France was threatened, when Hitler first marched his armies toward the French border. His beloved France in danger, Anderson took the first boat and offered himself to the French as a pilot. But he was then almost thirty, too old for air fighting, so the French said. Besides, he had unusually weak eyes. They refused him as a pilot. But there is one part of the French army where no man is refused, and Anderson joined the Foreign Legion. In time he rose to be a sergeant, and those who know the Legion know that only strong men become sergeants in this polyglot collection of men who have no past and no future.

Then came the great catastrophe. France fell, and Anderson fled the country. The United States was still not in the war, so Anderson went to England and once more offered himself as a pilot. At this time the British were so hard pressed that any man who had ever flown was wanted. Anderson had had some experience in the air, and he was taken in, despite his years and his eyes, and sent to a school as an instructor. There he taught the fundamentals of flying to boys just beginning their air training.

But instruction was not good enough. Anderson wanted above all else to be a fighter pilot. It was his dream. He talked with his commanding officers, pleaded with them, until in time they sent him to a training school and eventually posted him to the squadron of his choice, 71 (Eagle) Squadron.

Quiet, unassuming, he made no particular impression at first. At night in the mess he would smoke a pipe or two, perhaps have half a pint of beer; then he would be off to his bed so that he might be first up next morning, hoping that the weather would be clear and the squadron could sweep out over the Channel looking for trouble with the Hun. Actually at this time he was not an exceptionally good pilot. He had particular difficulty whenever the squadron flew into clouds.

Tight formation flying in clouds is not easy for any pilot, yet frequently the tactical necessities of war require that squadrons, even whole wings, must climb, cruise, or descend through solid clouds without breaking formation. As the planes pass through, only the Flight Leader concentrates on instrument flying; it is his responsibility alone for steering the flight; the responsibility of the three men behind him is to "pack in" close and follow, to fly with their wing tips almost touching his fuselage.

In really heavy clouds, visibility is sometimes less than twenty-five feet, and the Spitfire just beyond your wing is only a faint ghostly outline, a silhouette that bobs and bounces in the air currents while the water covers your windscreen and your hood. Flying with vision so greatly dimmed, the pilot often has false messages communicated to his brain, creating illusions that his plane is standing on its tail or rolling on its back. Thrown about by the

invariable rough air in clouds, unable to see, and fearing
collision any moment, the inexperienced pilot sometimes
lands, after his first flight through clouds, with his face
slightly pale and perspiration soaking his scarf so thoroughly that it can be wrung out like a wet towel. Numerous practice flights for this kind of flying are needed
before a pilot overcomes his confusion in dense clouds and
learns to keep his exact position, but once he has mastered
the trick of tight formation flying, then only an implicit
confidence in the instrument-flying ability of his leader is
necessary for him to enter the thickest cloud, fly through
it, and come out in proper position on the other side.
Experienced wings—three squadrons, thirty-six aircraft—
have been known to climb through fifteen thousand feet of
cloud and arrive on top with all units intact.

Handicapped so seriously by bad eyesight, Anderson
found that in clouds his eyes failed him almost completely. He would enter the cloud in his proper place, packed
in close behind his leader, but inside he would get out of
formation, and the squadron would fly from the cloud in
ragged line, would need to close in again before continuing its course: Some of the younger pilots were impatient;
some of them criticized Andy. "What do you expect," they
would say, "with a guy with eyes like that?" But the older
men saw in Anderson a great sincerity, a fine loyalty, and
they believed that his flying would improve.

Strangely enough, it did not improve in the ordinary
way; he did not become a good flier through practice
alone. It was responsibility that made Anderson into so
fine a flier that eventually he achieved an honor no other
American has ever known.

In the beginning of his days with the Royal Air Force,
Andy held the rank of pilot officer, the rank corresponding to second lieutenant in the American Air Force. Then
he was promoted: he was given the job of deputy flight

commander and was raised to a flying officer, corresponding to a first lieutenant. Still quiet, still unassuming, but
tremendously proud of his success, Anderson began to fly
with a surety and an aggressiveness that he had not known
before. Soon even the younger pilots recognized his ability, and they changed their feeling about him.

"Old Andy is pretty damned good," they said. "He's
O.K."

But he had bad luck. While some of the chaps would go
up and draw Jerries like honey attracting flies, Anderson
would go up day after day and never fire his guns; never
see a Hun in the sky. He would go over on numerous operations, but nobody was ever home on the days Andy went
calling. Until finally the great day came and he made contact.

On that day the squadron ran into a hornets' nest, and
the Huns came buzzing out to give battle. Andy promptly
picked out one of the Me 109's and dived on it. Bravely he
held his fire until he was well within range, then he opened
with machine-guns and cannon. Bits of the wing and tail
of the German plane flew off. Still Andy followed pouring
lead into the falling plane. He riddled it, shooting pieces
from it until it was plummeting down and almost certainly
the pilot was dead because he made no effort whatever to
bale out. Once Andy was positive the plane was headed
for the crash, he pulled out of his attacking dive and knew
the thrill that he had been waiting for: at last he had destroyed an enemy aircraft. No longer would there be only a
blank space opposite his name on the bulletin board in the
dispersal hut. Now there would be credit for one German
plane destroyed. He was a fighter pilot who had proved
himself. He had met the Hun in battle and destroyed him.

Then, at the instant of exultation, another plane darted past, and Andy's number two man, his pal who had
followed him down, opened fire on the shattered German

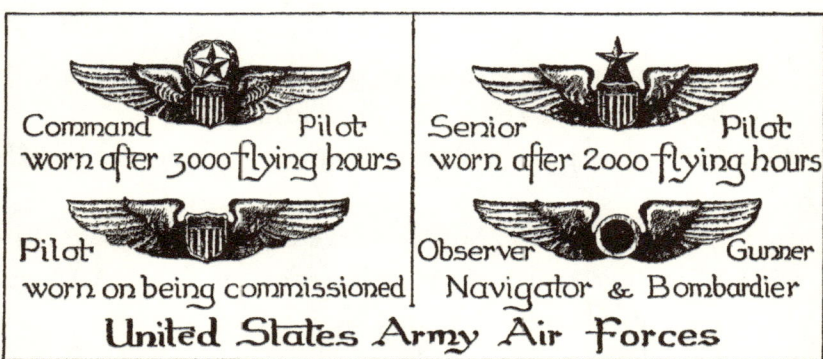

Command   Pilot
worn after 3000 flying hours

Senior   Pilot
worn after 2000 flying hours

Pilot
worn on being commissioned

Observer   Gunner
Navigator & Bombardier

United States Army Air Forces

No equivalent rank			Marshal of the Royal Air Force
	General [silver]		Air Chief Marshal
	Lieutenant General [silver]		Air Marshal
	Major General [silver]		Air Vice Marshal
	Brigadier General [silver]		Air Commodore
	Colonel [silver]		Group Captain

Pilot

Observer & Navigator

Air Gunner

Radio Operator

Royal Air Force

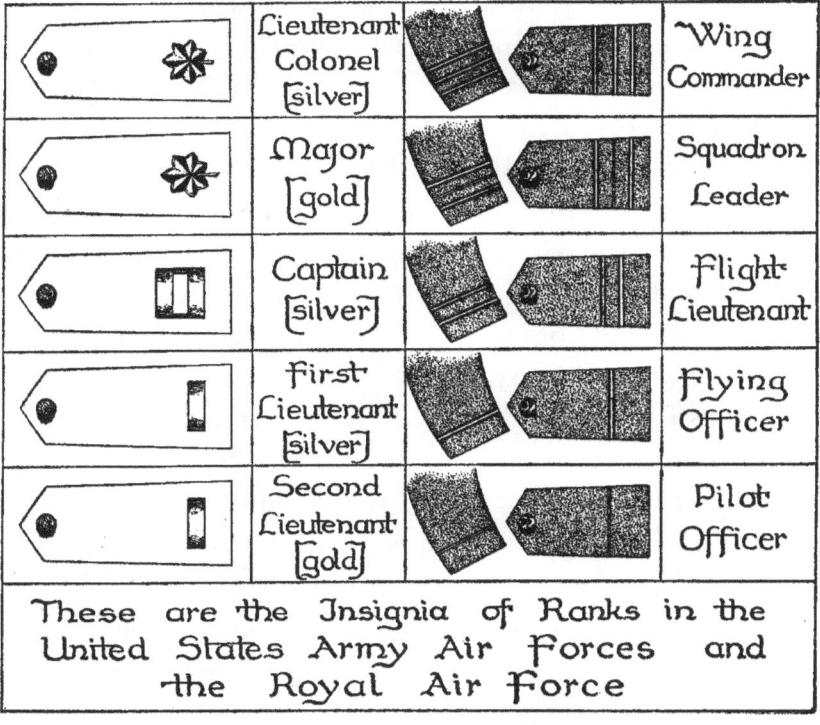

	Lieutenant Colonel [silver]			Wing Commander
	Major [gold]			Squadron Leader
	Captain [silver]			Flight Lieutenant
	First Lieutenant [silver]			Flying Officer
	Second Lieutenant [gold]			Pilot Officer

These are the Insignia of Ranks in the United States Army Air Forces and the Royal Air Force

INSIGNIA OF RANKS

aircraft. *Brrrrrut!* went the guns as the number two man fired a quick squirt at the wreckage a moment before it crashed and burst into flames.

So Anderson's bad luck held. That one quick burst from the guns of his pal had taken away full credit, and now he must share his victory; now instead of a plane destroyed, his record would show only half a plane destroyed. Today in the dispersal hut opposite his name there is recorded that this man flew on ninety sweeps over France, yet has credit for only half a plane shot down. There are any number of the Eagles who would gladly have given Andy one, two, three of their victories. They knew how conscientious he was. They knew how his heart was wholly in his job, and how he rambled through the skies day after day looking for battle, and how day after day he came back with the tape still sealed in front of his gun muzzles.

But the fine qualities of this modest, shy fellow who loved poetry and music were proving themselves on the ground and in the air, even though his score in battle was low. The commanding officer saw in Andy a gentleman and a determined, persistent fighter, braver even than his comrades, because Andy could not see at the speed and the surety that fighter pilots need to see, and Andy knew his handicap might mean his death, yet it never kept him out of the skies, never caused him to stay on the ground when there was a chance for battle with the Hun.

With all his fine qualities, Andy had a weakness: he loved France perhaps too much. His senior officers were disturbed by his love for everything that belonged to France, everything that had ever been a part of the country where he had lived and studied as a boy; they wondered if Andy could bring himself to fire on targets in France, even though now they were owned and controlled by the Germans.

One night as some of the Eagles were drinking at The Thatched, they decided they didn't like an order that had come down from high quarters. At the time it was forbidden to fly over enemy territory and attack a goods train if it was moving. The boys argued that the trains were being operated by the Germans and for the advantage of the Germans; they declared that even though a few Frenchmen might suffer, perhaps even be killed, the German trains in Occupied France should be destroyed. They argued that flying along behind a goods train, waiting for it to stop before attacking, was a foolish idea. They declared that in total war, when hundreds of British men, women, and children were daily being killed by German bombs, they had the full right to destroy German trains, even though the destruction might entail the loss of French lives.

Determined to disorganize enemy communications and transportation of supplies in Northern France, six Eagles flew out next morning before dawn. It was that morning that Peterson and Fletcher destroyed the ammunition train and Eddie was himself knocked down. On the same raid some of the other boys had good luck and destroyed three other trains. After landing back in England, the Eagles left their airplanes and sauntered into the mess as the other pilots were coming in for breakfast.

"Where the hell have you been?" the other pilots asked.

"Out having fun," the returning fighters said.

As soon as the report of the day's activities reached higher commands, the telephone began to ring. Who ordered the attack on French trains? Who had given authority for the Eagles to go over and shoot up trains in France?

"What do you mean by such attacks?" was the question repeatedly asked over the telephone.

Soon an officer of high rank flew to the station and demanded an explanation.

"Do you not understand that you must wait until a train stops before you can attack it?" he asked.

"If we did that," the boys answered, "we would be detected and attacked ourselves, perhaps shot down."

"But you might kill some of our gallant French allies who happened to be passengers on the train."

"We attacked only goods trains, sir."

"But you attacked while they were moving, when perhaps some Frenchmen were riding on them."

"That is possible, sir, but would you have us spot a goods train, follow it for miles and miles, calmly waiting until the driver stopped for a cup of coffee or to relieve himself?"

"Hmmm," said the officer, and went away.

A few days later an order was issued that fighter pilots of the Royal Air Force were allowed to attack the engines of goods trains in Northern France, even when they were moving.

That night there was a great celebration in the mess. The Eagles had started a new kind of fighting, and now it had been sanctioned. Now they could go over and shoot up German trains in Occupied France whenever they wanted. They had a new and exciting target.

But there was one of the Eagles who was not happy. Anderson could not forget that the train was running on French soil. He could gladly shoot down a German plane over France, but to him there was something horrible in attacking anything that moved on soil he loved so dearly. So his commanders were worried about him.

Then came the morning that Anderson landed and climbed from his plane. He walked into the dispersal and said quietly: "This morning I destroyed a train in Northern France. I attacked it with cannon and machine-guns. The engine blew up."

He made his report and went away. For the remainder of the day he stayed in his room, and that night in the mess he was even more quiet than usual. One of his senior

PILOT OFFICER FENLAW AND HIS BRIDE:
Only a short time after Fenlaw married this English girl he was
shot down in a battle over the Channel. It was the day the Eagles
were attacked by more than seventy Germans. "Red" Tobin and
Nichols also went down that day.

officers remarked that Anderson looked tired, as if he had been through a trying experience.

"He has," another officer said. "Anderson is a terribly sensitive fellow."

Then Squadron Leader Meares was killed. And Peterson was promoted to the rank left vacant by Meares' death. Along with Peterson, Anderson was moved up; he was given the job of flight commander and raised to the rank of flight lieutenant, a rank corresponding to a captain in the American Air Force.

"I've never seen any one so proud as Andy when he got his two stripes," Robbie told me. "Yet on the night of his promotion he came into my room and sat on my bed to talk with me. In his quiet way he sat there smoking his pipe and saying little disconnected things about this and that, commenting on happenings at the station and on the kind of flying weather we'd been having. Then he knocked out the ashes of his pipe and got up. 'Robbie,' he said, 'it's wonderful to be a flight commander in the Royal Air Force. But it's hell to get it through the death of another man. How gladly I'd give up my new stripe if only Meares were back with us again. He was a fine man and I admired him.' Then he went out of the room, and I lay there wondering how many chaps would forget promotion and distinction in their sorrow for a companion who had gone down."

Andy was the junior flight commander of the squadron. Gus Daymond was his senior. But one day a signal was received saying that Gussie was to be sent to America on a special mission. His departure left Andy senior flight commander. This meant he was only one step from the realization of his dream.

Then came the day his dream was actually realized: Peterson announced he was leaving for forty-eight hours. In Peterson's absence, Anderson was to lead the squadron.

This man who had been told he was too old to fly, that his eyes were too weak to fly, was to lead a squadron of fighter planes on a sweep over France.

He did lead them. And he led them well. The wing commander complimented him. The next day he led them again. And now at last the boys, even the young impetuous ones, knew that Andy was good. Because of his character and his bravery, they came to respect this quiet fellow who was somehow a little different from the rest of them, who read so much, and who, when the mess was almost empty, put fine music on the gramophone and sat close and listened.

Finally came the day that no one believed would ever come. At the beginning of this war no one could have believed that the Royal Air Force, proud and justly proud of its British tradition, would ever call upon an American to lead a British squadron into battle. An American had led 71 (Eagle) Squadron, but the Eagles themselves were Americans. Squadron 222 was British, all British, Oxford men, sons of British peers, and an American was to command them. Called on because of his character and his ability, Newton Anderson of New Orleans was named to lead the British fighter squadron. No other American had ever been so honored.

Still quiet, still unassuming, Andy took over his squadron with an inward exultation comparable to that of Napoleon when first he drew his sword at the head of the armies of all France. Loving England as all men love England who truly know the country and its people, this American led his British squadron with a fervor that made him tireless in his search for the enemy, and he commanded when on the ground with a firm gentleness that won the respect and the affection of the men serving under him.

For weeks Andy led a British squadron, *his* squadron, into battle, and he believed he had known his greatest happiness. He was mistaken. He was yet to realize an ambition that had been only a faint hope, a vague dream impossible of attainment.

There were more picturesque and spectacular fighters in the Royal Air Force. There were fighters far more widely known than Anderson. Indeed, the reticent, retiring American was known to only a comparative few. But those few who knew him well recognized his bravery and his qualities of leadership. His own wing commander was one who saw in Anderson a man with a stout heart and a clear head. And the day came when the wing commander granted the accolade.

"I'm taking a week's leave," he said. "You will lead the wing while I am gone."

The next day the American led a British wing over France. Thirty-six British planes followed this American into the air, seeking battle. He was their commander. And Napoleon himself after Austerlitz, or Jena, or any of his greatest victories could not have known such happiness as was Newt Anderson's when he looked back and saw the British planes—thirty-six of them!—in the sky behind him.

Robbie and I visited Andy on the day after he had led the wing for the first time. It was a lovely summer day. He came out of the mess to greet us, and he was smiling like a boy who has done something of which he is tremendously proud but, being a well bred boy, is too modest to mention.

"We heard about it," Robbie said, offering his hand.

"It's great, Andy," I said. "I think it's wonderful that you've led the wing."

He stood there for a minute in the sun, looking out across the airdrome, and then he said: "It was. It was wonderful. I shall never forget it."

Then he told us about it. He told us every detail of the sweep. And Robbie and I were proud with him. In our hearts there was exultation with him as he told of how he had led them over France seeking battle. He spoke very softly; there was a blending of British and Southern accents in his speech as he looked out over the airdrome and told how he felt when in the sky at the head of the wing. Then suddenly he turned to us; impulsively he turned and laid his hand on Robbie's arm.

"Just think," he said. "A whole wing. I've led a whole wing!"

It was Goethe writing his autobiography, Leonardo in his old age telling of his magnificent successes. It was every man who has achieved greatly saying that he has tasted the rare wine of full achievement.

Those of us privileged to know Andy hope that the wine was still sweet on that July afternoon when he attacked head-on and was himself shot down into the English Channel.

Perhaps the toughest assignment a fighter wing can draw is that of "target support." On the afternoon in July that the Hazebrouck marshaling yards were to be bombed, Newt Anderson's wing was sent over the target well in advance of the bombers that would come later. Andy's fighters were sent in to stir up the Jerries and engage them for as long as possible. Then, after they had exhausted themselves in battle, and while they were due to land for petrol, the Boston bombers would arrive over the target with their fighter screens; the marshaling yards would be bombed, and the bombers and fighters would encounter less opposition than if they had proceeded without the advance diversion. After bombing at fifteen thousand feet the Bostons would withdraw to the coast. There they would meet a "rear support" wing, fresh and patrolling to cover the withdrawal.

Success depended very much upon Andy and his boys making that initial penetration exactly according to plan.

They did their work well. They went roaring in over the target, and many German fighters came up to intercept. There was a dog fight over Hazebrouck. Spitfires went down. Focke-Wulf 190's went down. After this first fight was ended, Andy led his wing out over Cap Gris Nez and there met other 190's that had come up to intercept, joining in the battle against the greatly outnumbered Spitfires.

Anderson led his men in a head-on attack. There's nothing that requires more courage than a head-on attack. Two pilots look squarely into each other's blazing cannon and come in fast, neither swerving if both have the guts to fly into each other's cannon.

That's how Andy died.

20

Not all the boys in the squadron were so even-tempered as Newt Anderson. Some of them at times, fed up by inactivity, rather broke out of bounds. One of the most unpredictable of the "wild men" was Leo ("The Chief") Nomis.

Nomis was an Indian whose father had been an ace with the Escadrille Lafayette during the war of 1914-18. Like his father, Leo loved airplanes and loved to fly. But above all else he worshiped guns. While most of the other fellows were lying around dispersal, the Chief would be out with the armorers, personally synchronizing the Hispano cannon and the .303 machine-guns on his Spitfire. To him guns were everything; he touched them as most boys touch a girl they truly love.

During the fall of 1941 there were many days when the clouds were over France and the squadron could not attack without coming in low, offering itself a perfect target for intense and accurate antiaircraft fire. Those foggy days with the windy mist and the cold rain were days that made the Chief swear. Some fliers teach themselves to relax completely during spells of bad weather, but not the Chief. Nervous, restless, he would pace about the mess each day until he could endure the indoors no longer; then he would be off to the armorers and to his guns.

The fall of 1941 was bad, but the winter was worse. In December the sea fog blew in and the rains came until the tarmac at the airdromes resembled duck ponds.

The dispersal shack reeked with the dampness that soaked into the bunks and furniture. Then January brought the snow; day after day it fell. Weeks passed without an airplane leaving the ground. At night the gales whistled across England, rustling the blackout curtains and sifting fine flakes of snow under the sills. The Eagles, most of whom were from California or some part of the southwestern United States, were forced to hibernate like bears. Some of them spent their time wrapped in blankets in bed, but not the Chief. He stalked about the mess, saying little but stopping often to peer out at the persistent cloud ceiling that hovered just above the trees.

Throughout all January and February the thick clouds hung low. Activity over the Channel seemed forever ended. The Chief became positively morose as he watched the rain squalls moving toward the sea.

Then finally, after the dreary winter, came the warmer days of spring, and the squadron was ordered into action again. True, the action was only patrolling convoys, but that was better than nothing; at least a man was up in his airplane once more. Eventually, though, the convoy patrols became a burden, as the pilots flew in relays from early dawn until they returned to the flarepath at night. Day after day they flew over the ships, moving in long, single file through mine-swept channels in the sea. And never a sight of a Jerry, never a chance to fire a gun.

On one of these monotonous days of routine flying, the Chief and a boy named J. J. Lynch were dutifully patrolling their Spitfires over a convoy plowing its way through the North Sea. Around and around they cruised, Chief following Lynch in line astern. They waved at the escorting destroyers. They zoomed at a seaman who had playfully shaken his fist at them from the deck of one of the coasters. Then they climbed upstairs, and around and around they flew their dreary patrol.

"Kinda dull," said Lynch over the R/T.

"Ugh!" said Chief. One of his favorite tricks was to play Indian, to call attention to his heritage by talking and acting in the exaggerated Indian manner so beloved by Hollywood directors.

Around and around they flew. Chief watched the breeze pick up. He counted the red dusters, the flag of the Merchant Navy, waving from the sterns of the coasters. He saw the ships pushing their stubby noses full into the rising swells. It looked to him like a mighty dull day. No Jerries. No chance to fire his guns. . . . The thumb of his right hand slid over and caressed the firing button.

The sun shone pleasantly. Over on the Eastern horizon the barrage balloons glistened like silver beads in the sky. Around and around flew the patrolling pilots. Line astern. Lynch in front. Around and around. . . . The Chief turned on the switch of his gunsight. Then he adjusted the rheostat, dimming it until the orange ring and bead of the sight were not too brilliant against the wind-screen. Around and around they flew. Line astern. Lynch ahead.

Chief thought about his guns. He wondered if his armorer had put in the tracer bullets as he had directed. He wondered if the starboard cannon would really fire faster now that he had adjusted the spring tension. He wondered. Would more incendiaries and less armor-piercing .303's affect accuracy of fire? Did he really have his guns synchronized at two hundred and fifty yards? He wondered.

Around and around they flew. Line astern. Lynch ahead. The orange bead in Chiefs gunsight wavered just over Lynch's right wing tip. They were far out to sea. It was a lovely day. He switched the gun button to fire. The

sun was shining brightly. There was not a cloud in the sky.
If he put the bead fifty feet above Lynch's right wing tip,
the tracer bullets should miss the wing tip by fifty feet:
provided of course the sights were properly harmonized
and the armorer had put the tracers where the Chief wanted them. He wondered if he really would just miss the
wing tip. He wondered.

Lynch lazily cruised along with the Merlin engine of
his Spitfire purring like a kitten. Nothing to worry about.
The Chief was behind, protecting his tail. Nothing to
worry about.

Until over his right wing, tracer bullets streaked and
cannon shells left their smoky trail. He whirled to look for
the Hun that must suddenly have dived upon him, dropping out of the clear sky to attack.

But instead of an attacking Hun, Lynch saw the Chief's
two cannon and his four machine-guns blazing away at
him.

"*For Christ's sake!*" screamed Lynch.

"What the hell's the matter?" replied the Chief. "I'm
missing you, ain't I?"

This Lynch himself was no meek member of society.
One morning he returned from France with two feet of
a French telephone pole embedded in the entering edge
of his Spitfire's wing. He had dived and blown up a locomotive, but in pulling out had crashed into a pole and
brought back part of it as a souvenir. Nomis was a great
admirer of "J. J.," and the two boys often flew together.
And when they did, neither the Luftwaffe nor the RAF
knew what to expect.

After the flight on which the Chief had tested his
guns over Lynch's wing, there came a spell of weather that
grounded the planes. Rain fell, and more rain. The Eagles
congregated about the fireplace at their dispersal shack

and talked of their girl friends back home. Each day they talked of the sunshine in San Antonio and Los Angeles and Arizona City. They told of how, after this war was over, they would go to China for a little flying, or maybe Mexico. Day after day they sat around dispersal talking and wishing for action.

In the middle of each morning an orderly would arrive with cocoa and biscuits. Then there would be lunch. Then tea. Then dinner. And another dreary day had passed. It was the kind of life to try the spirit of the most complacent man. It was hell for chaps like Lynch and the Chief.

Late one afternoon at dispersal, Sam Mauriello said that two men from his section would need to rise next morning at four-thirty. Even though the morning would probably be rainy and nothing would happen, the section would need to have two men at dawn readiness. Sam told Lynch and Chief to report before daybreak.

Before it was light next morning, the two Eagles carried out their instructions and were at dispersal. Dressed in their Mae Wests, they waited. Their gauntlets were resting by the throttles of their Spitfires. Their oxygen masks and helmets were at the ready. Their gun sights were set.

The morning was not too bad, after all. The clouds were not too low. Perhaps there would be a chance to fly, to get going again. They sat there in the early dawn, frequently looking out at the sky and hoping.

Then the telephone rang. It was the controller at operations. A convoy off the coast was to be protected. Proceed to Barrow Deep. Patrol the convoy until relieved.

"Is this understood?" the controller asked.

Dawn was just breaking when the pair of Spitfires headed toward the sea. They flew low. They proceeded to Barrow Deep. Around and around they flew. Toward the west the weather improved, but far off toward the east there were heavy clouds close down to the sea. Just the kind of clouds German bombers like to use for cover, sneaking along until they can dart out, make their attack, and whip back into the clouds again.

Around and around the pilots flew.

"No fun," said Lynch.

"Ugh!" said the Chief.

And they both looked longingly over the North Sea toward Holland where the German bombers might be.

Around and around they flew, but somehow in their flying they seemed to be getting farther from the convoy and nearer the clouds. They continued making their circuits, around and around, but each time they were nearer the clouds and farther from the convoy.

"Looks like that convoy has left us," said Lynch.

"Ugh!" said the Chief.

They turned again and again and again, getting nearer and nearer the east. The clouds were low and, with the sea and the sky virtually the same color, there was almost no horizon. Because of the sameness of everything before them, the two boys didn't immediately see a camouflaged bomber, dirty colored, over beyond their starboard. Flying line abreast about one hundred yards apart, so that each could watch the tail of the other, they looked into the clouds before them and into the sea and for a time did not notice the bomber skimming along over the water.

Then, almost at the same instant, they both saw the Ju 88 making its way toward England for a quick attack. And as they saw it, they pushed forward their sticks and dived. At that moment the Jerry pilot turned and fled toward the protecting clouds.

Lynch and the Chief pulled the tit to get all possible speed from their Spitfires as they sought to close with the bomber. Speeding toward him, they were soon within long range and the rear gunner in the 88 opened fire. Lynch attacked from dead astern. The Chief came up from the beam. There was a running fight close above the water with the German gunner firing steadily.

Then Lynch, his plane badly hit, saw the glycol pouring from his radiator. But he held on the attack, finishing his burst, before turning back. The Chief kept coming in from the beam. Darting in, he would fire a squirt and turn away. Again and again he closed in until, on one of his attacks, the bomber suddenly reared on its tail, hung quivering for a moment, then whipped over and dived straight into the sea not far from the Hook of Holland.

Lynch nursed his plane back to England, where his crippled engine failed completely. Flying at low altitude and low speed, the Spit struck a tree and crashed. Lynch's head snapped forward and banged against the reflector sight, knocking out a tooth and laying open his face.

While Lynch was climbing from his shattered plane, the Chief was watching his petrol and wondering if he'd get back to an English airdrome. Flying as carefully as he could, guarding his petrol, he just made it. He landed with an almost empty tank.

"But how did you, who were supposed to be patrolling a coastal convoy, happen to attack a bomber off the Hook of Holland?" demanded the questioning officers that night.

"Sir," said the Chief, speaking for himself and Lynch, who with his face bound up was unable to speak at all, "we must have got lost."

There were some questions asked at headquarters about pilots who get so completely lost, but not much really was said. Most of the officials read the report and smiled, because beneath the braid and ribbons of air marshals there beat the hearts of men who remembered the days, some twenty-five years ago, when they, too, were young and eagerly patrolling for the Hun. . . .

Even the Chief agreed that June was a decent enough month. There were lots of sweeps and bomber escorts. To Hazebrouck. Flushing. Lille. There was lots of fun with plenty of fighting. The days were long, with double daylight-saving time, and it was light enough to fly without the flarepath from four in the morning until eleven o'clock at night. They were wonderful days for fighting. The squadron ran up a good score of victories and bravely took its losses.

Accustomed to almost daily sweeps over Holland, Belgium, and France, the Chief was enjoying himself immensely until a few days of rain kept the squadron on the ground. After three days of boredom, of no flying by the Eagles, the station fire department was suddenly waked one midnight and went charging furiously through the blackout to save the officers' mess. Smoke and flames were pouring from the windows and chimneys; explosions were shaking the place. The fire department arrived in time to see Very flares darting from the smoking windows and sky rockets whizzing from the chimneys.

It seems that the Chief, annoyed by three days of non-operational weather, had raided the duty pilot's hut and obtained a big armful of pyrotechnics. When the last Very flare had been fired, and the last rocket had roared up the chimney and exploded high in the air, Chief pronounced his studied opinion.

"Too goddammed quiet around here," he said.

Dissatisfied with only occasional battles on the Western front, the Chief finally put in for a transfer and set off for the hottest spot he knew. But apparently not even Malta was exciting enough, with its normal routine of daily fighting. So, according to reports just received, the Chief left the other morning for a patrol above the island, "got lost" again, and ended up conducting a one-man raid on Sicily.

"Goddam Sicily is no fun at all," he said, after he had landed and was examining his empty guns. "All I could find were some gun posts, a petrol dump, and an ammunition wagon."

The Chief and Lynch were not the only "wild men" among the Eagles. There were others who were not orthodox either on the ground or in the air.

There was Indian Jim Moore, for instance, who couldn't endure the sight of an abandoned and obstructed airdrome where tangled wires and posts placed at odd spots made landing, so the officials boasted, utterly impossible. Tormented by the sureness of the officials and wondering whether or not a man actually could land on the field without killing himself, Indian Jim one day swooped down in his Hurricane, darted under the wires, sideslipped between the posts and made a perfect landing. The custodian of the field came rushing out, waving his arms, shouting that no one could land on the field.

"It's impossible," he said.

"Horsefeathers," said Jim. "I've done it."

Then he walked away and left someone else to worry about getting the plane off the field and into the air again.

And there was Red Tobin, who, flying over France one morning, suddenly remembered it was Sunday and he hadn't been to mass. The mere fact that there were a flock of Jerries on his tail didn't seem to matter. He was a good Catholic, and he turned head on into the Germans, shot down one of them, and flew back to the airdrome in time to rush to the little station church before mass was over.

Then there was Helgason, who, along with J. J. Lynch, completely upset an RAF station one day in July, 1942. Bored with sitting around dispersal, they got permission to go up and fly above the airdrome. Anything, even a little local flying, was better than sitting still. Besides, they were being tormented by sight of a wing that had landed at their airdrome to refuel before going on over France.

Helgason and Lynch were flying above the airdrome when the wing took off—all except two planes, suffering from engine trouble, that didn't get into the air. Helgason and Lynch promptly moved over and joined up with the fighters, taking the place of the two pilots on the ground.

When the commanding officer of the station heard what had happened, when he saw that two planes from 71 (Eagle) Squadron had gone off, totally without authority, on a flight over France, he issued severe orders. The offenders were to report to him immediately upon their return. He would tear a frightful strip off them. He would teach them some discipline.

But when Helgason came back he made the following report of the battle in which he and Lynch had fought and had shot down a German plane:

> I was flying with the North Weald Wing accompanied by Pilot Officer Lynch when two FW 190's broke cloud and dived to break up a formation of Spitfires between Nieuport and Dunkerque. Two of the enemy aircraft came at me in a slight dive. The right hand aircraft opened fire at 200 yards. I pulled up as if to ram him, and he broke away and I fired a long burst of machine-guns and cannon, closing in to almost zero feet. I saw cannon bursts on the engine and saw a splash of oil in the sea. After a turn to witness this, I followed the second FW 190 at sea level Then my engine began to give me trouble, and I was forced to break off and head for home.

This is Lynch's report:

On July 19, 1942, I was airborne at 1440 and joined the North Weald Wing at 1503 off Dunkerque. After flying for some minutes, the wing turned to starboard through 180 degrees and flew back along the coast. At this time two FW 190's broke cloud in a dive, shallowing out as they approached us head on. When within range I fired a short burst at the FW 190 farthest from the coast. He was already firing at someone, probably Helgason. As he passed by I looked and saw him roll onto his back. When I last saw him he was still on his back and was below 500 feet. I then looked ahead and saw four more FW 190's just below the cloud approaching head on. I pulled up, firing a burst into the group which split up as they passed over me. I then had to pull into the cloud to avoid a section of Spitfires. When I broke cloud there were no other aircraft in the vicinity and I returned to base. In view of the possibility of my having fired at the same aircraft as Pilot Officer Helgason, I claim only one half of an enemy aircraft destroyed.

While the two offending Eagles were reproved, the commanding officer didn't tear a very big strip off them, particularly since the wing commander of the North Weald Wing had just telephoned and said he had never seen such a fierce attack as was made by Helgason and Lynch.

Occasionally even some of the more staid members of the squadron, those not jokingly called "wild men," broke out of bounds. Even Peterson one day blew up.

The afternoon previous, Bob Sprague, one of the best pilots among the Eagles, had gone over on a sweep and had fought magnificently. In the battle his plane had been riddled with bullets and cannon shell. Only a fine fighter could have lived through the engagement, and only an expert flier could have got his plane back to England. Even the ground crew, accustomed to wizard flying from the Eagles, were amazed that Bob had been able to return and land safely.

But there was a regulation that all damaged planes had to be reported. Furthermore, the way in which they were damaged had to be told. Of course every one knew that Bob had simply been shot up in battle, but some very official person requested a detailed report of why the plane was damaged and how.

Completely fed up with such nonsense after one of his pilots had fought so bravely, Peterson wrote the following reply to the official's request. (In order that every one may fully understand the reply, it should be known that "bumpf" is the term used for toilet paper, and for a very low grade of toilet paper.)

> "Sir: On yesterday afternoon Pilot Officer Sprague saw that the sun was shining brightly and there were few clouds in the sky. The beauty of the day caused him and two of his friends to set off for a jaunt over territory normally inhabited by the French, who undoubtedly would have received him most cordially; but the present inhabitants, seeing Pilot Officer Sprague and his friend flying around enjoying themselves, did not appear to be of a friendly disposition and such was their dislike that a number of heavily-armed fighter planes, marked with swastikas and black crosses, rudely and ungenerously assaulted

Pilot Officer Sprague and blew a large hole
in his tail, his wings and the fuselage near his
head, which action on their part almost lost
Pilot Officer Sprague his life and also caused
me the inconvenience of writing this useless
bumpf to you.

"I have the honor to be, sir,
"Your obedient servant . . ."

Peterson's station commander was a good sort and
promptly forwarded the letter. That was the last heard of
it. And, too, that was the last request for "useless bumpf"
ever made of Peterson. . . .

Occasionally even in battle the Eagles deviated from
the ordinary way of doing things. There was, for instance,
a day above St. Omer when they broke so many rules that
even the Jerries were hopelessly confounded.

There are times over France when Spitfires and Messerschmitts fly along on a parallel course, not far from each
other and yet not attacking. This outlandish condition
occurs particularly when RAF fighters are entering or
withdrawing with bombers. The Me 109's fly just out
of range, darting in occasionally in efforts to draw the
fighters off, then returning to their position out of range
and flying along on a parallel course once more. The old,
experienced Eagles have known all this to happen so often
that they are not excited, not even particularly interested,
by the proximity of Jerries; they simply ignore the incon-
gruity of the strange procession through the air.

One sunny day the Eagles were about twenty-six thousand feet up, acting as top cover for a wing on a sweep.
St. Omer was just ahead. Except for some tiny dots off in
the distance there were no enemy aircraft about. And no
one paid any particular attention until the dots grew into

Me 109's and climbed above the Spitfires. Even then no one was especially interested; certainly no one bothered to speak on the R/T. Every one, except one man, saw the Jerries and knew they would remain just above and just out of range. They knew, too, if any attempt was made to give chase, the Huns would simply turn around and head for Amiens or Lille; then other enemy aircraft would rise and wait for the foolish pilots on their way out, attacking them when they were short of fuel and could not remain for a real dog fight. Pete, who was leading the squadron, knew all this, and while keeping a wary eye on the 109's, he said nothing. The Eagles simply flew quietly on their way, ignoring the Jerries above.

The normal formation of a fighter squadron is three sections of four aircraft each, flying in line astern, one plane behind the other. The commanding officer leads the squadron from the number one position of the center section. Directly behind the C.O. is his number two, and this position is considered the safest in the squadron. New boys often make their first operational flight over France in this number two spot, and their chief job is to fly close behind the C.O., their eyes glued on his tail.

On this particular day over St. Omer, when the specks enlarged into Me 109's and the iron crosses showed on their wings, a boy from Georgia was dutifully glued in position immediately behind Pete. Then the 109's joined up with the Eagles, just out of range, and flew on with them toward the coast of Calais. It was all very normal and very dull indeed.

Between staring at the C.O.'s tail wheel, adjusting his oxygen flow, regulating his constant speed airscrew at twenty-four hundred revolutions a minute, adjusting his manifold pressure, and wondering just a little why he had ever left home anyhow, the new boy from Georgia did manage to cast an occasional worried glance around.

On one of his glances he looked off to the side and slightly above and saw what appeared to be another formation of Spitfires. Then he noticed that their wing tips were square and their fuselages had a peculiar dark camouflage. He was puzzled as he sat there peering at the strange brethren, while the Eagles flew on toward Calais, apparently blissfully unaware that something was amiss in the sky.

It was then that he saw the Iron Crosses for the first time in his life!

"Chrahst A'mighty! Chrahst A'mighty!" he screamed over the R/T. "Messerschmitts! Messerschmitts! They're fixin' to shoot somebody."

At this identical moment he hurtled straight up into the blue like a rocket, lunging away from the German planes while still screaming: "Chrahst A'mighty! Chrahst A'mighty! They're fixin' to shoot somebody."

"Shut your bloody trap," said Pete, "and get back down here where you belong."

"Messerschmitts! Messerschmitts!"

It was then that the rocketing Spitfire stalled in the thin air, hung poised for an instant, and flipped over to go plunging down.

By this time the pilots of the Messerschmitts were as astounded as the American boys themselves, and Eagles and Jerries were scurrying all over the skies, every one so confused and frightened that no one thought of attacking or giving battle.

The end of the disorganized mêlée was when Pete and Gus Daymond dove down to the still plummeting boy from Georgia and closed in on him, drawing him into their protection and shepherding him back into position in the squadron once more.

When the squadron finally landed and the boys climbed from their planes, the gentleman from Georgia who had

HURRICANES IN FORMATION

SPITFIRES IN FORMATION

"WEE MICHAEL": Flying Officer M. G. McPharlin was one of the two Eagles who bailed out over the Channel on the day of Dieppe. He jumped from 4,500 feet, landed in the sea, inflated his dingy, and paddled seven miles back to England.

caused the uproar went racing to Pete and his pals, crying out: "Good God, did you see them Messerschmitts? They were fixin' to shoot somebody."

One of the wildest of the Eagles' shows was staged on the ground.

December of 1941 was particularly cold and dreary. Before the month was out, the American boys were thoroughly brassed off with the weather. They sat around grumbling at the rain, fog, heavy clouds. They were in such low spirits that when the station commander assembled them one morning and began to talk about airdrome defense, they were only outwardly polite. To hell with airdrome defense. We're fighter pilots. We do our fighting in the air. To hell with an exercise in ground defense. The boys weren't even slightly interested.

Nor did their interest pick up when many lorries and despatch riders began to appear on the roads around the station. Then some artillery passed, and tanks lumbered by. Gun carriers rattled on to the station itself and went past the dispersal shack where the Eagles were swapping lines. They hardly looked up. Who cared about artillery and tanks and gun carriages? Airplanes. Airplanes. Airplanes were their life. Nothing else really counted.

Then the umpire came. And a general. And other high officers from the army. The exercise was to be carried out in defense of the airdrome against imaginary invaders who were supposed to have landed in the Estuary and were fanning out as they moved inland, some of them drawing near the airdrome where the Eagles were stationed.

"Bunch of Boy Scouts playing cowboy and Indian," the Eagles said, thoroughly bored as they watched the ground troops rush here and there.

That night it was pouring with rain. It was simply an awful night, storming and cold. But inside the mess things were warming up, particularly beside the bar where some of the Eagles were seeking reprieve from their boredom. After they had all been reprieved again and again, Scarborough from Arizona put down his glass and peered around him.

"Listen," he said. "Even a Boy Scout war is better than no war at all. Let's get in it."

The Eagles had a council. Pete, Gus, Humphrey Gilbert, Jim DuFour, Scarborough, and some of the others decided the time had come for action. So they moved in a body on the station armory. There they obtained tommy-guns, rifles, pistols, bayonets, and were furious when the terrified duty officer flatly refused their demands for a trench mortar.

Grumbling against the duty officer, but still reasonably well-armed with tommy-guns and rifles in their hands, pistols stuck in their belts, and sheathed bayonets swinging at their sides, the Eagles advanced in the general direction of where the Guards, who were playing the part of the enemy, were supposed to be advancing.

Soon they came upon some soldiers and, considering them to be the enemy, ordered them to surrender. They refused.

Half an hour later, some rather scuffed-up Eagles led their battered prisoners into the village pub where all prisoners were being deposited.

"Where did you capture these men?" demanded the umpire.

"We found them near the edge of the airdrome," proudly answered Pete. "They refused to come along, so we brought them anyhow."

"I should think they did refuse," said the umpire. "They are part of the local searchlight crews and are not involved in this maneuver. And, by the way, who ordered you chaps into this exercise, anyhow."

"Nobody," said Scarborough. "We're just helping on our own."

The next bit of assistance the Eagles rendered was to attack the railway station, throwing blank hand grenades that exploded with a hell of a bang, and rushing in Wild West style to overrun the station and attack a locomotive that happened to have just arrived. They shoved their tommy-guns into the face of the terrified engineer and informed him that his locomotive was captured and he must give them all a ride to the next station, which happened to be Epping, the home of their beloved pub, The Thatched.

In Epping they stuck up The Thatched, had a substantial round of drinks, and sallied out into the night again. Deciding that the police station would be worth capturing, they attacked. But the police informed them that they, the police, were all dead and that there was no station, it having been destroyed by a bomb half an hour before.

Satisfied with the havoc they had created in Epping, they went back to their train and returned to their home station once more. There they captured a howitzer which Jim DuFour proudly rode into the prison area and exhibited to the umpire.

"See what I've captured!" shouted Jim.

All the boys expected at least the Victoria Cross in return for the howitzer, but once more the umpire told them they had erred. He informed them the howitzer belonged to the defense, and its removal left open a way through which the enemy could easily pass in his attack on the airdrome.

Stopping only long enough to get another drink to bolster them against the rain, the Eagles went out into the night once more. This time they surrounded and captured a service vehicle. They pinched the uniforms of the drivers and arrayed themselves in the captured coats. Then they stuck tommy-guns into the ribs of the prisoners and ordered them to lead the way to their headquarters.

As they advanced, a guard stopped them. In answer to his challenge, Jim DuFour called out: "This is Colonel DuFour. And stick 'em up, buddy."

They tossed the guard into the captured van along with the other prisoners.

Then they drove on toward the enemy's headquarters.

Again a guard stopped them.

"What is your identification?" the guard asked.

"Don't waste time, man. This is important I'm Colonel DuFour. Take me to the general immediately."

The guard led them to the general's tent.

"Is this the general's tent?" Gussie Daymond asked. "Are you sure?"

"Yes," the guard said.

'Then stick 'em up."

They tied the guard and rushed into the tent.

The next moment, an indignant British general had a dozen tommy-guns leveled at him.

"Stick 'em up," Pete said.

"What's this damned nonsense?" the general demanded.

"No damned nonsense. This is war. I'm Colonel Du-Four, and you're our prisoner. Stick 'em up and come along."

"This is an absolute outrage. You kids can't—"

"Yes, we can. You're our prisoner and you come along. . . . Come on. . . . Come on. . . . Get cracking."

It was then that the umpire arrived, having heard of the Eagles' infiltration into the enemy's lines and of their attack on headquarters.

"See here," he said, "this is most irregular. You can't do this with a general. It's highly irregular." Then turning to the general, he said: "I'm afraid, sir, that this exercise is not going according to plan."

"Aw, nuts," said the Eagles, and went out into the night once more.

Even if they couldn't capture a general, they could look for lesser prey. They continued warring throughout the night, and when morning came it was learned that the boys had done right well: they had captured forty members of the Guards, the headquarters unit, a locomotive, two railway stations, a case of whisky, and a blonde ambulance driver who had willingly surrendered.

21

I asked Squadron Leader Osborne, medical officer with the Eagle Squadron, to tell me about these boys he had lived with and cared for, patching up their wounds after battle and keeping watch over their nerves to see they didn't crack under the strain.

"Most persons don't understand why the boys occasionally behave like wild men," the Doc said. "They don't understand that fighter pilots seldom crack because of too much flying or too much fighting; they break because of inactivity, when there's a lack of flying and fighting, when the weather forces them to sit around the mess with nothing to do. Even ordinary boys couldn't endure day after day of inactivity, and these kids who have known the greatest excitement possible, who've fired their guns in air battle, just can't sit still for a week at a time; they blow up."

An American himself, Osborne joined the RAF and served with the Eagles for a year and a half. He was with them in the early days when Kolendorski and Mamedoff and Shorty Keough and Red Tobin—all of them dead now—fought their way to sudden fame, He has been with them since Oscar Coen and Sam Mauriello, even Gus Daymond and Peterson, were young in the air; he has seen Oscar and Sam and Gus and Pete, all four of them, win the Distinguished Flying Cross, the coveted recognition

of ability and bravery awarded by the Royal Air Force to
only its greatest pilots. He has seen Daymond win a bar
to his cross, after Gus shot down his eighth Hun. He was
with Pete when His Majesty King George VI gave one of
his absolutely highest awards —the Distinguished Service
Order—to this twenty-two-year-old American boy.

"Suppose they do occasionally shoot up the mess. Suppose they do hold up a train. Or go off to battle without
orders. Suppose they do occasionally break loose. What of
it?" Doc asked. "They've made a marvelous record in their
fighting, and they've probably made more friends than any
other squadron in the RAF.

"I've been to several different stations with the Eagles.
And always at first the English resented the newcomers; the
English didn't want this mob of wild Americans breezing
into their mess and taking over. But before long the older
Englishmen on the station, the administrative officers and
signal officers and all the rest of them, were talking with
the Eagles and enjoying their crazy way of saying things;
they were watching the American boys and smiling at Red
Tobin coming into the mess wearing his flying boots with
maps stuck in them, or Sam Mauriello sitting still pretending to be reading while actually he was imitating a
bull frog. Before long, too, the English pilots on the station began to talk about the Eagles. The Americans might
be a bunch of hell raisers on the ground, but they were
marvelous in the air both as fliers and as fighters.

"As for the ground crews, they simply adored the Eagles.
You could always tell when 71 was coming in to land. Usually when a squadron was landing, the ground crew would
stand off somewhere and wave the planes toward them,
bringing the planes into position. But when 71 was landing, the ground crews, every damned one of them—fitter,
armorer, rigger—would race across the field to ask the
pilots what had happened, then hang on to the wing tips

as they themselves guided the planes to their assigned places. In return, the Eagles knew each member of the ground crew and chivied them around, calling them by name and playfully raising hell with them. These English cockneys thought it was wonderful; they'd never had officers treat them like that before."

When I asked Osborne if there was any difference between the original crowd, those who came over first, and the present members of the Eagle Squadron, he said there distinctly was. "Most of those first fellows were older than the chaps now," he said. "They were more men of the world. Some of the older ones didn't expect to live out the war, and a few of them didn't particularly give a damn. They were a wild lot, I admit it. They were out to get every possible thrill, and to them the most thrilling adventure of all was flying. Every one had flying in his blood; they were all mad about it. They came over to England to fly and to fight, and if they got killed—well, what of it?

"But the chaps who sort of didn't give a damn, who took wild chances, who wouldn't listen to instructions, sooner or later bought it." (In the RAF a pilot who is killed has either "bought it" or, more commonly, has "had it.") "By a process of inevitable elimination the wild men either were killed in battle or killed themselves in smash-ups. On the other hand, the pilots who were willing to listen to advice, who studied the art of aerial fighting and were willing to follow the general laws, lived through the early days, and now Peterson and Daymond and the others still alive are among the truly great pilots of the RAF."

The Doc said that besides being younger than the original crowd, the present Eagles are less bizarre in their behavior; they are more what the British call "the officer type." They are not like the buccaneers who came over in the early days of the squadron and blustered through the skies looking for fame and plunder.

"Don't imagine for an instant," said the Doc, "that the present Eagles are a soft, dull lot. On the contrary, they're still a picturesque crowd of lovable chaps, raising absolute hell now and then, but on the whole conducting themselves not unlike other fighter pilots of the RAF. Actually you should understand that the English pilots themselves are hardly a mild, demure lot. All these lads live under such a strain that any of them may break loose at any time, particularly after a spell of bad weather has kept them on the ground. None of the boys, English or Americans, ever beat up the mess when they're doing two or three shows a day. At such times they come in at night so tired they just drop in bed and are off to sleep. But when there's continuous bad weather and they can't get into their aircraft, then they become so tense they practically scream. I've seen them that way, seen them so damned nervous they had to do something wild, shoot up the mess or something, or they'd have gone mad."

Doc told me the Eagles drank their quota of beer and whisky, but there has never been a drunkard among them. Occasionally any one of them might drink past the center of gravity and lose his balance for that particular night, but none of them ever made a habit of drinking too much.

He said, too, that with the Eagles there was, perhaps, more than the normal amount of womanizing. "The Eagles undoubtedly did more love making than the English pilots," the Doc said. "But you must realize that the English boys were near their wives and sweethearts. On leave they could go to their homes and see their mothers and sisters; they could visit their sweethearts and meet them in town if they liked. But the Eagles were thousands of miles from their wives and their sweethearts. Naturally they were rather enthusiastic in their search for female companionship. Yet they were not really an immoral crowd, not even those wild fellows who came over first. There has been only one real lecher in the whole history of the squadron, and he didn't last with the Eagles very long; they got rid of him and sent him back home. The truth is, a man can't live a very bleary-eyed life and continue to live at all as a fighter pilot."

At times, however, the boys undoubtedly detoured from the paths of righteousness. The following letter to the commanding officer of the Eagle Squadron is shocking proof that at least once an officer of the squadron was guilty, and shamelessly guilty, of sin:

My dear Sir:

I feel it is my duty to write you concerning the conduct of one of your officers in his relations with my daughter.

I met this officer, Pilot Officer ——, some time ago and I considered him a very charming gentleman. However on a recent visit to London to see my daughter, who is in the musical play "—," I found out that there have been intimate relations between him and my poor child.

At the time of my visit I went to my daughter's flat in the early morning and to my horror I found the officer in question and my poor girl in bed, locked in each other's arms, sleeping blissfully, without apparent concern of committing sin.

I left the room immediately and attempted to telephone my husband in North England. Unable to get my husband, I determined to return to the flat and remonstrate with the erring children.

When I did return I found my daughter preparing breakfast and Pilot Officer singing loudly in his bath. They were actually living together as man and wife and to all appearances they were thoroughly enjoying themselves.

When I confronted my daughter, she showed no signs of a guilty conscience. Likewise Pilot Officer —— greeted me warmly and had the nerve to invite me to stay for breakfast.

I became very stern with them but they refused to take me seriously. Also when I told Pilot Officer —— of the serious consequences of his action he referred to me as a "sanctimonious suction pump," which is, needless to say, very much lacking respect

I must ask you to remand this officer and order him not to see my daughter again. I am not familiar with the ways of life in the United States, but you must agree that this matter must be dealt with in order to save my poor girl from complete ruin.

Thank you. . . .

I asked the Doc about the boys and death, how they felt about seeing men of their own squadron, their pals, shot down. And how they themselves felt about shooting down other men, killing Germans in battle.

"In the early days," he said, "whenever a chap was killed, either in a crash or in battle, the rest of the Eagles were rather shaken. But as they saw more and more men killed, as they grew accustomed to the idea of death; they came in time almost to ignore it. 'Damned shame,' they would say, 'that Bill had to go.' They would say that, but they didn't really feel it very much. All this stuff you see in the movies about pilots sitting around with an empty chair at the table or an empty glass at the bar, that's nonsense

and nothing else. They don't sit around at all after somebody has been killed. At night after a pal's been shot down,
the others in the squadron go to the mess just the same
as usual. Afterward, they go to the pub and drink their
beer and chatter with the girls just the same as usual. As a
matter of fact, that's all they can do. Fighter pilots live at
such a pace there isn't time for mourning whenever a pal is
killed; there isn't time to observe the customary decencies.
A fighter pilot, going up day after day to battle, wouldn't
dare sit around at night reflecting on life and death: he
couldn't stand it. He wouldn't last a week.

"Besides the opiate of living at a fast pace, there is
another consolation that comes in time, I believe, to almost every fighter pilot. In the early days of their fighting
most pilots are upset by the loss of their pals; but after
they've been though battle after battle, after they've seen
any number of their pals go down around them, they suddenly wake to the fact that they themselves have come
through, they're still alive. All these other chaps have been
killed—'but I'm still alive.' Then next day two more are
shot down—'but I'm still alive.' Until eventually the going of the others becomes almost part of a routine, something distant and impersonal. It doesn't matter such an
awful lot. Bob Smith was shot down yesterday. Bob Jones
will be here as replacement tomorrow. There will still be
a Bob in the squadron. Life goes on. And the important
fact is: 'I'm still alive. They haven't got me.' Not that they
become callous or completely unmindful of the death of
their friends, but in an operational squadron where deaths
are not uncommon, I believe that sooner or later each
pilot comes to think primarily of himself, and each time
a pal is shot down it doesn't bring so much a feeling of
sorrow for the dead as an accentuated realization that I'm
still alive. And this whisky is good. And the fire is warm.
And I'm still alive. They haven't got me!"

When I asked the Doc what he thought it meant to the boys to shoot down other boys, he said he thought it meant no more to them than shooting ducks in a shooting gallery.

"The airplane out there in front is to them just a target," he said. "They don't think anything about the guy inside it. And if they did, it wouldn't make any difference. The sport of the thing is to find the airplane and shoot it down. To hell with the guy inside. That's his bad luck. Some few of them may think it's a pretty good idea to knock off a lot of Germans—Kolendorski hated Germans so much he wasn't satisfied to wait like everybody else at the dispersal; he would actually sit in his airplane waiting, praying for a 'scramble' that would send him up against the Hun—but most of the boys have no such hate of Germans; they fight quite impersonally. They don't think so much about killing Huns as they think of the sport of hunting through the skies for something to shoot at, then knocking it down. I've had them tell me they sort of jumped and caught their breath as a Hun pilot baled out of a blazing aircraft; they had quite forgotten there was anybody inside."

22

In winter the nights in England are long, but in summer complete darkness lasts only a few hours. England is in the same latitude as Labrador, and in such high latitudes the seasonal variation in light and darkness is greater than we are accustomed to in the United States. With the clocks set ahead one hour for the entire duration of the war and an additional hour during summer months and the harvest season, day begins to break in England at about three-thirty on June mornings. It is then that the long day begins, to end only after the twilight of high latitudes descends well after sunset, perhaps as late as eleven o'clock under the double daylight saving time.

These are the days when the people of England work long hours in factory and field. They are the days when Spitfire squadrons take off early and return late. Flying to their rendezvous with the bombers or off on some convoy patrol, the fighter pilots often skim low over the rolling fields and woods. They look down and see that stone fences and hedges break up the countryside until it is a patchwork of green and yellow and brown. They see the workers in the fields, and see them stop to wave a greeting to the swift fighter planes as they go over. In return the pilots salute the workers with a friendly dip of the wing-tips, and soon disappear from sight.

Most of the field workers—like the munition work-ers—are women. Millions of the men of England are away, serving the Empire on the seas and in strange and distant lands. Their action against the enemy is made possible by the courage and the hard work of the women of England. With the men actively engaged somewhere in battle, British women have manned the plows and the machines, they have performed heavy manual labor and delicate tasks requiring the utmost skill and technical ability. Idleness today is a crime in the British Isles, and few women, if any, are guilty of it.

Besides the girls and women engaged in farm work, in factories, in munition plants, hundreds of thousands of other British girls and women actively serve in their country's armed forces. Some of them man gunsights, searchlights, barrage balloons. Some of them are on duty day and night in Air Raid Precaution section, working as fire fighters, spotters, drivers. In the Air Transport Auxiliary, women ferry military airplanes. For nearly four years, now, these British women have kept to their posts, wherever or whatever they might be. And each of them has released a man to engage the enemy in combat. When peace comes to England and one can fly across the summer fields again, without the constant need to search and look into the blazing sun, one can thank the women of Britain for a vital part in the successful defense of the Empire and of this world's civilization.

And when peace comes to England again, and English sailors and soldiers find their way back to English cities and towns and villages, they will once more drink their ale at the local pub, the pewter mugs will be filled and emptied, and many a lively story will be told of strange people and campaigns in distant lands. At such times it is not unlikely that the old trick question of the veteran will arise: who won the war? In the fellowship of the

BALLOON BARRAGE: No dive bomber dares swoop low over any British city or he would become entangled in the balloons or in the cables swinging from them. While the balloons actually have made only a few kills, they have kept the bombers high and made their aim less certain.

"BALLOONATIC": The girls who care for the balloons, sending the great "pigs" into the sky and hauling them down again, are affectionately called "balloonatics." It's hard, back-breaking work, but with their men engaged in battle, British women for four years have performed manual labor and delicate tasks requiring the utmost skill and technical ability.

British Combine

CONVOY BALLOON: Barrage balloons are used by ships in convoy
and are proving an effective deterrent to Nazi dive bombers. Swaying at the
ends of their cables, the big balloons are ever ready to snag a too-daring
bomber and drag him down into the sea.

tavern, soldiers, sailors, airmen, and civilians will argue the question . . . When I was in Tobruk . . . When we were over Berlin . . . Our convoy was in the Arctic Sea. They will talk and argue, and they'll probably demonstrate their battles, showing the placement of troops and ships and airplanes by intricate arrangements of the fish and chips, the salt cellars and beer mugs. Many will gather to listen, and the old ones will nod their heads.

That academic question—who won the war?—will flourish for many a year. And when the smoke is very thick and the cups of ale are passing, when empty tankards are rattled on the heavy walnut bar and dusty portraits of long-gone keepers of the tavern look down on the merry group, then Jock back from Singapore, and Tim from Libya, and Bill from Malta may put their heads together under the low-paneled ceiling of the Red Lion, or the Copper Kettle, or the Black Swan, and tell their stories of what happened, offering their own experiences as evidence that they are fitted to give weighty judgment on who won the war. As the soldier and sailor and airman talk, they may well be joined by a miner from Wales, a shipbuilder from Glasgow, a fireman from London. And the talk will probably go on late.

They will tell of how the Merchant Navy fed the people and supplied the forces. They will tell of the Royal Navy fighting on all the seas of the globe. Of the farmers at home doubling their acres though manpower was halved. They will tell of the factory wheels forever turning. And of Britain fighting the Heinkels and the Junkers and the Stukas, defying them as they flew over to bomb the little island and bring England to her knees.

Then finally in fairness they will come in their talk to the realization that British women had as much to do with the winning of this war as any other unit. Before the war, manpower could be tabulated and its capabilities estimated;

but no one—absolutely no one—could have estimated the contribution of the British women to the salvation of the United States, the British Commonwealth of Nations, and all peoples who believe in the simple, fundamental virtues and the common decencies in human relationships.

To defend his home is the prime responsibility of every man. Since the dawn of history that has been his accepted duty, and he performs no unusual task when he sacrifices even his life for his family and his country. But in times past, even during the most frightful wars, women as a whole only maintained their homes. Such maintenance has been their responsibility through the years, and they thought of no other. But in this war the women of Britain have joined and served in the British Army, the British Navy, and the Royal Air Force. They have worked in the fields and in the factories. They have spent years performing the most exacting scientific tasks and vital tasks of sheer drudgery.

When Americans first arrive in wartime England direct from the United States, many differences are quickly noticeable. An island country under the influence of war's many shortages and restrictions can not help revising some of its peacetime customs and altering its ordinary mode of living. Such revisions have played their part in somewhat altering the dress and appearance of the average English girl from what it used to be in peacetime, and the change is particularly apparent to any one who just left the United States.

The greatest difference, of course, is that so many of the girls in England are in uniform. And one of the most admired, most respected, of the British uniforms is the blue of the Women's Auxiliary Air Force—the WAAF.

When the Eagles first landed in England, they weren't yet accustomed to women in war. They thought the little

WAAF's, striding along in their uniforms, were just playing a game, keeping themselves amused and pretending to be helping.

But the boys weren't long in finding out their error. They saw the WAAF's performing many of the technical and mechanical jobs that are essential to keeping airplanes flying and airdromes functioning. They saw girls in the instrument section who were experts at adjusting, testing, and calibrating aircraft and engine instruments. They saw girls take an absolute wreck of an airplane, a mass of tangled wires and motors, and rebuild that airplane until it could go into the air again, until it could go back into battle. They saw the quick fingers of women packing the parachutes on which the lives of pilots depend.

They went up into the air, these American boys, and over the sea in muggy weather, above the clouds, and uncertain of their position, the leader of the Eagles spoke into his R/T, sending his voice out into space:

"Hello, Cobra . . . Hello, Cobra . . ." he called. "This is Stardust leader . . . Stardust leader . . . Please give me a homing for base. Over to you . . . Over."

And immediately came his answer. "Hello, Stardust leader . . . Hello, Stardust leader," came the voice of the WAAF. "Cobra answering . . . Cobra answering . . . Steer three hundred twenty degrees magnetic for base. Over to you . . . Over."

The surprised and somewhat dubious Eagles looked down at the gray clouds. This was the first time they had ever been controlled by a woman. But knowing that they themselves could not establish their direction from base or figure their course to steer for home, they went on to their magnetic compasses and flew for several minutes through the clouds, altering their direction occasionally on the advice of "that Cobra gal." When at last, still under her direction, they emerged from the low cloud they recognized their home airdrome, dead ahead: the WAAF had brought the squadron in.

Always when they returned from patrols, from sweeps and battles, the Eagles and the other pilots at the station found the officers' mess clean, tidy, as much like home as it could be made. The flowers always came from somewhere, and always they were arranged on the tables and here and there about the hallways.

And when the Germans came and wrecked the airdrome, no WAAF left her duty. Even when the bombs were pouring down and pulverizing the place, no WAAF so much as turned a hair. They stood at their posts, and some of them died at their posts. Since the beginning of the war these girls have collected all the honors and all the medals, and they still go quietly on their way arranging the flowers in the mess, driving the heavy lorries from before dawn until after night, answering Stardust Leader whenever he calls from out of space, seeking his way home.

Women have long manned the barrage balloons, but when it was announced not long ago that certain gun posts would be partly served by women, the Eagles quickly readied for their maps. "For God's sake mark those gun emplacements in red. We've got to stay away from them. Those women will shoot us and shoot each other and let Jerry bomb whatever he likes."

A few nights later the Germans came. They were bombing furiously, and the gun emplacements manned by the girls were under fire; stick after stick fell near them, but no girl left her post, and Jerry's fire was answered. It was answered so well by the girls that suddenly in the sky, directly above their guns, a German bomber exploded and came plunging down in flames.

The girls calmly chalked up one on their scoreboard.

The other night I was visiting the Eagles at a forward airdrome not far from the sea. Even in midsummer it was chilly as four Eagle pilots hurried out of the lorry before daybreak and made their way to the dining hall for breakfast. A convoy was in the North Sea, and when dawn broke four Spitfires would be needed to patrol it.

"Why don't they fight this war in the daytime," said Strickland.

"I wonder what Helen has fixed up for breakfast," said another. "I'm plenty hungry."

They entered the mess where the blackout curtains were drawn tight and tinted electric light bulbs spread an eerie, barely visible blue light along the hallway. Even with the blackout, no chances could be taken with regular lights at this airdrome. Since this particular drome was a most important one, the Huns were forever attacking it, and some of its hangars were always in ruins. The boys passed through the unlighted dining hall and into the kitchen.

"Hi, Helen," they shouted. "Hiya this morning? We're hungry."

"That's nothing unusual," replied a small, dark-haired girl with a Welsh accent. "And you know you're not permitted in the kitchen."

"Aw, Helen, old pal, skip it. And what you got for breakfast? And do I, or don't I, take you to the dance tonight?"

"Hey, Helen, where's that little red-headed job that used to be around here?"

"You mean Caroline?"

"I don't know what her name is, but you know the one I mean—the one who used to level off about six inches above the table and crash-land the soup."

"Caroline is not here any more." Helen spoke with dignity. "And WAAF's do not crash-land the soup." She finished setting the table. "If you'll be seated, you can have your breakfast. I've prepared some hot porridge, sausage and bacon, some fried tomatoes, and there's plenty of brown toast and marmalade."

"Aw, Helen, you're breaking my heart. Is that all! We got to work all day, honey."

"I've prepared a very nice breakfast for you. Sit down."

"And you're coming to the dance with me tonight—huh?"

Bob Sprague and his readiness flight sat down to breakfast. Helen brought them their food. Some drank tea. Some coffee. She hurried because she knew they were late. The dawn-readiness flight always seemed to be in a frightful rush. Yesterday and the day before and for months and years Helen had seen the dawn-readiness flight in a hurry, different boys each month but all of them rushing to get away to their airplanes and into the air.

"Come on, Helen. How much longer we gotta wait for toast?"

"Here it is. You don't have to wait at all."

It was not yet dawn when they rushed out of the dining hall. "So long, Helen," they shouted as they disappeared down the long corridor beneath the battle lights. "See you tonight," they called, as they raced out into the dark, slamming the door behind them.

It was just beginning to turn a faint gray in the east when Helen heard their Spitfires roaring down the flare-path. They passed directly over the mess for some reason. The dishes rattled on the pantry shelf. She smiled and wondered why they flew so low and so fast. She would ask them about that. She would ask them that night at the dance.

During the morning as she worked she heard the first Spitfires return and another flight take the air. The planes were taking off in relays to patrol the convoy.

DAYMOND IN FULL BATTLE DRESS: Just before he steps
into the cockpit, closes the side door, and takes off.

"DOC" OSBORNE

Some persons have worried about the behavior between men and women in the armed services. Since most of the men and women in the service of their country are from the average home, it should be expected that generally the average standards of conduct would be observed. And while it is true that a man and a girl wanting each other can usually find a time and place, it is also probably true that the discipline at airdromes and other military installations forces a standard of morality as laudable as that maintained at winter resorts, on ocean liners, on the campus of coeducational institutions, or anywhere else that men and women away from home live in daily proximity to each other.

The first part of her day's work done, Helen went to the WAAF's quarters to make up for the sleep she lost in rising so early. But she was back on duty long before the last flight had glided on to the flarepath at dusk. She was on duty because there was so much that Helen, and all the other WAAF's, had to do to make things ready for the boys returning from their patrols. The silverware had to be polished. The curtains had to be arranged in a slightly different way, and with fresh, different-colored tie-backs. The wall paper, too, needed to be cleaned and brightened. On the crisp white tablecloths alternate baskets of roses and Flanders poppies had to be arranged, and all very skillfully, so that the mess would look bright and cheery, just like home, to the boys who had been flying all day, perhaps some of them in battle.

There was soup and mutton, some roast potatoes and boiled cabbage and rice pudding for supper, all tastily prepared and served by the WAAF's. And the Eagles did nobly by it.

"Hey, Helen, me and you're buddies, you know, honey. How about scrounging me some more meat? How about it? And how about the dance tonight? All set?"

Helen smiled. "All set," she said, rather proud of herself for being able to answer these Americans in their own peculiar talk.

The dance that night was held in one of the large buildings that the dive bombers had missed. There were many nice looking WAAF's there, but the Eagle pilots who had flown on dawn patrol thought that by far the cutest of them all was Helen.

I've heard the Eagles often compare English girls to the girls back home. When measured by standards of Hollywood glamour there is undoubtedly a difference between the girls of the two countries. But if one may judge from the talk of the Eagles, if one may accept their talk as expressing the feelings of American soldiers, then woe to the gorgeous gal back home when after the war she has to admit she merely kept on being gorgeous, and did nothing useful for her country.

23

Suppose spies and agents report that Germany is getting short on some particular necessity of war—motor transports, for example. Suppose information from other sources indicates that German factories are not able to meet the demand of their military leaders for motor transports. Suppose the experts in the Allied war council agree that evidence points strongly to a genuine transport shortage in Germany. Then, obviously, good strategy would be to strike at the German source of transports, to make the shortage even more acute by bombing all factories in Germany and the Occupied Countries that produce either the completed transports or any part used in their manufacture. So the order goes down from the strategists, the planning board, to bomb these factories. The job is then out of the hands of the strategists: it becomes a problem in tactics.

The tactical commanders, the actual military commanders, are not concerned with why they are to bomb certain factories. It is not for them to ask why these targets have been assigned to them, why they are told to destroy transport factories, or power plants, or railway stations; theirs is simply the task of executing in the most effective manner possible the plans of the strategists.

On the Western Front the master tacticians of the Allied Force and the Luftwaffe are forever matching wits. Both are constantly studying every factor as they seek to concentrate their blows under conditions most advantageous to themselves, and at times and places the enemy is least prepared to withstand an attack. Years of technical study and much practical experience in total war have made them super chessmen, adroitly moving whole air armadas through the heavens by day and night, attacking, defending, feinting, ambushing from treetop level to the stratosphere. Squadrons and wings, *Staffeln* and *Gruppen,* are their pawns and bishops and kings. The stake they play for is the world, with you and me—our lives, our possessions, our freedom from degradation—as part of that stake.

Having received instructions to center their attacks on factories making motor transports, the allied tacticians then make their plans. Which factory will they attack first? Will they use high explosive bombs only or mix them with incendiaries? And what proportion of H.E.'s and incendiaries will they drop? What type and how many bombing planes will be used? How many fighter squadrons will be required for escort? What feints and diversionary raids will be made to draw attention away from the raid on the main target? What false information will be sent over days or hours before the attack in order to mislead the Germans and confuse them? All these, and scores of other questions, must be answered by the tacticians as they plan their attacks.

Besides answering all questions pertaining to the offense, they must plan their defense as well. In particular, they must take into account German flak, barrage balloons, and, if the mission is at night, German searchlights.

Flak—*Flieger Abwehr Kanonen,* meaning literally "Flying Defense Cannon," antiaircraft guns—is usually of two types: light or heavy. These terms refer solely to the caliber of the guns and are not to be used when describing the rate of fire. The rate of fire is to be designated as "intense," "medium," or "slight." Owing to carelessness, pilots sometimes report flak erroneously, referring to a certain barrage as "heavy," when actually it was light flak in caliber but intense in rate of fire.

In its most accurate form, light flak is encountered below eight thousand feet; above this height the thirty-seven millimeter Bofor guns become increasingly inaccurate. Armor piercing, incendiary, and explosive projectiles, with tracer rounds intermingled, are thrown up by the Bofors, and at the top of their rise the shells can be distinctly seen against a dark background, the burning fuses streaking up red or green like fire balls from a Roman candle. The shells from the Bofors explode either on contact or at the termination of their fuses.

In order to avoid light flak, a pilot should fly either well above eight thousand feet or just over the treetops. If for any reason he must fly under eight thousand and above treetop level, he should never fly straight or remain at a set altitude; he would then be an easy target for the Bofors. If he absolutely must fly in the danger zone of light flak, he should fly as fast as circumstances permit, and he should engage in the most fancy "jinking" possible, constantly and suddenly changing his direction and altitude.

Heavy flak is thrown up by guns of three inches, or even more, in caliber. The aiming of these guns is not visual but mechanical, and they can be fired at unseen targets, at night or through solid clouds, up to perhaps fifty thousand feet. Very accurate fire can be expected up to twenty thousand feet. But since the hitting of a weaving, twisting aircraft twenty thousand feet in the air would be an extremely difficult feat of marksmanship for a single

British Official Photograph: Crown Copyright Reserved

GERMAN FLAK: This photograph, made from a raiding British plane, shows the flak bursting slightly in the rear—"opening suddenly like great black flowers in the sky."

THE GREEN FIELDS OF ENGLAND:
In woods, besides hedges, out in the open fields, anti-aircraft guns like these wait to welcome any of Goering's boys who happen to come over.

British Combine

gun, heavy flak usually is thrown up as a barrage, a number of these big guns rapidly pumping their projectiles into the area in which the enemy planes are flying, hoping to bring one of them down.

Upon exploding, a heavy flak projectile leaves a dark circular ball of smoke some twenty-five feet in diameter, and in its center is the dull red glow of the burning explosive. With the Bofor shells streaking up red and green, with the heavy flak opening like great black balls encircling a deep red center, there is small wonder that Peterson spoke of the heavens over Dieppe as looking like fireworks on the Fourth of July.

Heavy flak when exploding is dangerous within two hundred feet because of the numerous particles of metal which the exploding projectiles scatter at high velocity. The most effective evasion against such flak is to change altitude quickly and fly directly away from the area as fast as possible.

An even better way to avoid being shot down by flak is not to fly over the antiaircraft batteries. Even though each side is constantly changing its gun emplacements, moving them from one area to another, concentrating them first in one district and then in another, and always hiding them under camouflage, still the other side has a pretty good idea of where intense flak is to be expected and where the guns are few and scattered. In this war each side keeps close score on the other; each side knows amazingly well what the other is doing.

If the Germans shift their guns today, if they move their flak from one town to another, the Allies almost surely know all about it before tomorrow. Unfortunately, the Germans, too, have ways of finding out. Amusing proof of this fact is to be found in a strange attack made by a German bomber in the early days of the war.

II. Schwerste deutsche Flak

British Official Photograph: Crown Copyright Reserved

FLAK GUN: The translation of the caption is: "Heaviest German Anti-aircraft. If one should like to get an idea of the size of this piece compare the length of the barrel with the size of the gun crew." This picture was taken from a German magazine.

One of the favorite tricks of each side is to build dummies of all kinds. Dummy lakes and forests and roads are built to mislead the pilots and cause them to fly off their course and miss their objective. The Germans build whole dummy cities to confuse pilots and draw their attack, coaxing them to unload their cargoes on the imitation city while the actual city is several miles away. An often used trick at night is the dummy fire. These fires are kept ready and are lighted when the first bombers pass over. Then as the other bombers arrive they may well unload their incendiaries and high explosives in the roaring flames, thinking they are adding their destruction to the burning city that is their target for the night, when actually they are dumping their bombs on fires the Germans have lighted in open fields.

A favorite dummy is the fake airdrome. All kinds of camouflage are used to make a meadow or a pasture appear, from the air, like an airdrome. False runways are laid down. False hangars are built. The whole area is camouflaged. The enemy is supposed to believe that this is the true airdrome, when actually the serviceable airdrome in use is a mile or more away and is most carefully hidden.

One of these dummy dromes was built by the British early in the war. They were extremely secret in preparing the field, taking the greatest care that no one should learn where the dummy was and where the true field. Then, on a certain day, after every precaution had been taken, the dummy field was exposed.

On that same day the Germans flew over and bombed. The true field they blasted with high explosives. They flew over the dummy field and solemnly dropped two sticks of bombs on it. But the bombs on the dummy field were dummy bombs! They were only wooden bombs with no explosives in them whatever. Furthermore, the German pilot who dropped the wooden bombs on the most secret British airdrome flew back over the field after he had unloaded. On this second trip he lowered the window of his cockpit and threw out a map. When it was picked up the exact location of both fields, the dummy and the real one, was marked in red ink. Furthermore, just to add more gall to the bitterness, a route was carefully traced around all the gun emplacements in the district, emplacements that the British had believed were known only to themselves.

A somewhat similar map, though obtained in far different circumstances, hangs over the fireplace in the mess of one of the bigger RAF stations. This is a map printed in Germany and showing the route from a German airdrome in France, across the Channel, and to this particular British fighter station. It is the route followed by the German bomber who used the map. And the map itself was taken from the body of the German navigator after the bomber had been shot down and its crew killed in the crash. . . .

Besides the danger of the flak there is the constant threat of the balloon barrage. Pilots flying through clouds never know at what height the balloons are waiting that day to trap them, to tangle them in heavy cables and drag them down to earth. The Germans have flown their balloons as high as twelve thousand feet, and as one goes through a cloud, or dives out of it suddenly, one never knows whether or not one of the great monsters will be there, swaying slightly in the air currents and waiting with infinite patience for its prey.

For the night fighters and the night bombers there is an added danger that the day raider does not encounter. At night there are the searchlights.

Effective up to twenty thousand feet, the long, slender fingers of the searchlight reach toward the heavens, endlessly groping for enemy aircraft. And when one searchlight finds an enemy plane, others quickly put their beams

on it until the plane is at the apex of a cone of light. Totally blinded by the fights, the pilot is unable to climb,
or dive, or sideslip out of them, because every move he
makes, everywhere, he goes, they follow; he is "held" until he is destroyed by the flak, or, more often, until some
night fighter comes and attacks him, blind and helpless,
and shoots him down.

One of the most weird uses of the searchlights is playing them against the lower clouds in such a way that their
light is diffused and reflected until it illuminates a whole
area of the heavens, quickly betraying the presence of an
enemy aircraft and making it an easy target for the guns
of a night fighter.

Searchlights also are used to guide home a friendly aircraft in distress, making a cone of light that can be seen
for miles like a great beacon. They are used, too, for illu-
minating a landing field for some aircraft that has been
badly shot up and is staggering in, unable to keep itself in
the air long enough to make the usual circuit of the field
and land on the flarepath properly.

But with all its friendly uses, the searchlight, like flak
and the barrage balloon, is primarily a weapon of offense,
prowling through the sky to find the enemy aircraft and
"hold" it until it can be destroyed.

Against all these instruments of offense, the pilot in
the air must defend himself. And except for the actual
defense with the guns, perhaps the most interesting of all
aerial defenses is the pilots' "weaving," when every plane
keeps squadron formation yet zigzags through the air with
quick turns and sudden skids. Whenever it is flying, over
enemy territory, the squadron invariably weaves, dancing through the sky so as to present a difficult target for
the flak or for enemy fighters that might suddenly hurtle
down from above. Experienced squadrons fall into a sort of
cadence when weaving and proceed in this manner for

more than a hundred miles while under threat of attack. Then, just before the enemy fighters come in for the actual raid, some one calls: "109's coming down!" and the tempo of the weaving is greatly increased, the turns being executed with a snap and a skid that presents a bobbing, twisting, and most difficult target.

In battle formation the three sections of a weaving squadron might be compared to three snakes, writhing through the sky on parallel courses. At the head of each snake is an individual who can fly, who can shoot, and who has the temperament to strike . . . to attack . . . to destroy. Behind each leader are three men: No. II, No. III, and poor old Tail-end Charley, the unsung hero of the Allied Air Force.

We hear much of those brilliant leaders who attack and shoot down the Hun, but the pilot who receives the brunt of Jerry's attack, who usually begins the battle by looking into the four blazing muzzles of a Focke-Wulfs cannon, is poor old Tail-end Charley, the chap who flies at the end of each section, who has the doubtful honor of flying in the position commonly spoken of—particularly when Charley is listening—as "coffin corner." It takes a rugged yet careful pilot to fly No. IV correctly, to keep up, to remain on the alert, and to evade the numerous attacks that occur when the Hun dives down from the sun—always striking at coffin corner and Charley.

On long flights deep into enemy territory many attacks will be received, and whenever, for any reason, a No. IV drops behind, he is almost certain to be bounced. Sometimes his pals see him shot down. Sometimes he just disappears, and when the squadron returns to its station back in England, Charley isn't there. No one has seen him killed, no one has seen him crash; he's just gone, that's all.

Any man who flies No. IV must be an exceptionally good weaver, alert to danger from behind and able to stick on No. III's tail even when the flight is twisting through the air at tremendous speed. If he gets out of position, if he allows himself to be left on the flank, or if he lags behind, he is simply inviting destruction, because the enemy is always hovering above waiting for any straggler who gets off alone and exposes himself to swift attack: half a dozen planes streak down on him and fire on him from half a dozen angles, simply blasting him out of the sky.

During battle, when the squadron is weaving furiously, when the three flights coil and uncoil, diving, zooming, twisting, turning, so that each whirling plane is the most difficult target possible, poor old Charley is cracked around like the tail of a frantic snake—while the head strikes at the enemy, thrusting and counter-thrusting until an opening is found and the death thrust is made.

Then the squadron weaves on its way again, the three snakes racing and twisting through the air until they are out of enemy territory, away from enemy fighters and enemy flak, when they settle down to straight and easy flying, steering a direct course across England toward their home station. . . .

It was a bright and sunny day. Three wings of Spitfires—nine squadrons, one hundred and eight planes—made rendezvous over the Estuary and set course for Ypres on a typical fighter sweep.

While all three wings were of the RAF, the bottom wing was made up of Poles and the top squadron of the top wing was American, the Eagles of 71 Squadron. The formation headed out toward Nieuport, its landfall on the Belgian coast, and began to climb fast over the North Sea, seeking the initial Advantage of height. Flying across the sea, the formation climbed steadily as it swept on toward enemy territory in its search for battle.

Soon the coastline appeared, eighteen thousand feet below. There was Ostend, with its small fleet of fishing boats just outside the harbor, the fleet that is always there and that is never attacked, because while one or two of the boats surely are German and carry radio transmitters, most of them are manned by our unfortunate Belgian friends out trying to get something to eat. The planes flew over the harbor and over the large, pear-shaped lagoon, like tidal flats, where the Nazi seaplanes so often anchor. They flew on through the flak that was coming up. They flew on southward, and the pilots could look far ahead and see Dunkerque, Calais, Cap Gris Nez. Directly below were the lowlands of Belgium spreading toward the hills of Ypres and Armentieres, the soggy lowlands rich green in color, with canals crossing and recrossing them, the marshy land spreading on toward the low, rolling hills where there were patches of yellow hayfields.

Only one or two woolly cumulus clouds were in the sky, and they were far below, dropping their shadows, splotching the green of the lowlands.

Flying at eighteen thousand feet above Belgium, the wing commander called the controller standing before his huge plotting board back in England: "Hello, Cobra . . . Hello, Cobra . . . Bantam leader calling . . . Bantam leader calling . . . What's the news? Over to you . . . Over."

"Hello, Bantam leader. Cobra answering. There are twenty plus"—twenty-three, twenty-four, some number slightly above twenty—"bandits over St. Omer and ten bandits over Lille. Ten thousand feet. Climbing. Listening out."

"Thank you, Cobra. Listening out."

The fighters closed in somewhat and maintained their course for Ypres. Each wing steadily climbed until the Eagles, flying top cover for the topmost wing, were at twenty-eight thousand feet.

"Hello, Bantam leader . . . Hello, Bantam leader . . . Cobra calling . . . Cobra calling. Bandits are southeast of you. Fifteen thousand feet. Climbing. Listening out."

Ypres appeared ahead and far below, at first almost invisible, detected chiefly by the twisting roadways that converged into the town. Sweeping on nearer and then over the town, the pilots could see that none of the tiny specks, the roofs of houses below, appeared to be painted. Like so much of northern France and Belgium, the houses had an untidy appearance as though the people had little means or little ambition for keeping their places neat and spotless like the houses of Holland or Normandy. What would be the use of tidying up our houses, the people of Flanders seemed to say. Tomorrow the armies may march again and destroy everything as they pass. What is the use in maintaining our homes when they are west of Germany, on the highroad of the marching horde?

"Hello, Bantam leader . . . Hello, Bantam leader . . . Cobra calling . . . Cobra calling . . . Bandits are dead ahead. Approaching you and climbing. Listening out."

The wing commander turned the formation slightly toward the right, tilting his squadrons to get full advantage of the sun. At extreme heights the sun is much more powerful than at lower altitudes, instantly blinding those who look into it. At these heights, too, it seems much larger than from the earth, its size apparently increasing until it affords a natural cover for many airplanes. The wing commander led his mass formation of planes into the sun, taking care that he would be able to use it most and the enemy use it least.

Flying as bottom wing, the Poles saw the Huns first and prepared to engage. Immediately the Poles moved out to attack, the middle and top wings began to search the skies, peering out anxiously, to see if any German planes had climbed unseen into the sun and were waiting until the Poles were engaged below, when they would dive in swift attack.

The Luftwaffe leaders on operations have great ability and practice in the use of ambushes and foils to catch the overenthusiastic and inexperienced. A trick that is frequently successful is the use of "bait" or "sitters" for the unwary of the RAF. German fighters often fly along below an RAF formation, gliding along, in an ideal position to be jumped. Frequently, though, these stooging planes are only a trap, bait for an overwhelming force of Hun fighters waiting above, hoping some stupid pilot will leave his formation and go down to attack the sitters.

Sometimes, even when there are no fighters above, the sitters are bait of another kind. They stooge along until they are attacked, and then they put on their "panic stricken" act, fleeing as fast as they can and welcoming pursuit as they retreat. They delight in making the acquaintance of a new boy who seeks to chase them while they retreat toward Berlin or dive toward their home base. Eventually there comes a time that the ignorant new boy must turn back toward England, and then, low on petrol, unable to engage in high-speed maneuvering because of the rate of petrol consumption in such maneuvering, the new boy must fly head-on into the swarm of Huns that have risen to cut him off from home and shoot him down.

Failing to find any "Hun lurking in the sun," believing that there was no trap in the approach of the Germans from below, and knowing that an attack from the impetuous Poles was impending, the middle wing spread out to afford a wider umbrella over the Poles; they formed a triangle with a squadron at each apex ready to dive in support of the lower wing wherever and whenever aid might be needed.

The Eagles, and the rest of the high cover wing, remained in position above. In a big air battle it is always best for the top cover to remain in position and not get tangled up in the fight below. Usually the top wing is not needed below unless there is an absolute mob of enemy planes, and then the wing commanders may call for help. Otherwise the pilots downstairs much prefer the top cover to remain aloft, watching and guarding while the planes below deal with the enemy without any worry of attack from above. If they know they will not be bounced from above, they can fight with more freedom and more confidence and can give more attention to shooting down the enemy. But if in their attack they are not certain about what's upstairs, then their attack is only partially effective, because the pilots must look up occasionally to make certain they themselves are not about to be bounced and shot down.

Once the Germans came within range, a Polish squadron broke out from the wing and charged into them. The Poles are probably the most ferocious fighters on the Western Front. They take long chances, and they fight to a finish. It is extremely difficult to keep Polish squadrons intact or in place whenever Germans are about. Whenever "109's at three o'clock" comes over the R/T, all the Poles start a sort of rat race to see who can get there first. They often simply disappear in the direction of "three o'clock," or "nine o'clock." They charge into Germans as their cavalry charged into German tanks, and it doesn't make the slightest difference whether there is one 109 or one thousand; they attack, always attack, and fight to the last bullet or the last drop of gasoline. Their fiery hatred of the Germans may last forever, because they solemnly swear before the altar that they will not forget, or let their children forget, Warsaw and Nazi brutality.

After the first batch of Poles swept in to the attack, a German staffel broke off formation and struck at the Poles from the beam. Then an English squadron from the middle cover dived and joined battle.

In an instant there were a dozen individual fights in progress, planes whirling around and around in pursuit of each other, moving so rapidly they looked from above almost like hoops rolling through the sky, until suddenly one part of the hoop would explode or burst into flames, or would break off combat and dive, quickly disappearing from sight, its camouflaged wings and fuselage almost instantly merging into the landscape as it went down.

"Hello, Bantam leader . . . Hello, Bantam leader . . . Cobra calling . . . Bandits approaching you from the north. Climbing. Listening out."

Below and slightly to the east the battle ended as suddenly as it had begun. Most air battles end in less than a minute. Even a battle that may require thousands of words to describe will be fought in less than a minute, all the multiplicity of happenings beginning and ending so swiftly that they are not recognized at the time; they are merely recorded in the brain and are brought to full realization only in recollection.

In modern air battles the fighters who have the advantage have it for only an instant; if they don't use it in that instant, it is gone. Just as tactical advantages must be seized in a flash, so unfavorable tactical positions must be abandoned as quickly, the plane rolling off in a swift, twisting dive, hurtling down to blend into the landscape and avoid destruction. The terrific fire power of modern fighters brings sudden and total destruction, and the plane that crosses a line of fire for a second only is simply wiped out of the sky.

"Hello, Bantam . . . Hello, Bantam . . . Cobra calling. Bandits from the north are near you . . . Listening out."

The battle below had ended. Six German planes had been destroyed and three Spitfires had been shot down. The "gaggle," the formation of fighters, was withdrawing from Ypres with the Polish wing below in some disorder after its fight. With bandits approaching from the north, and with the Poles disorganized, the Eagles and the rest of the top cover moved to the north to meet the Germans head-on or to force them to fly under the top cover if they sought to get at the Poles.

Then the Eagles saw the enemy, six of them flying along like easy prey. Blue Section was ordered down and peeled off for the attack when suddenly the wing commander ordered the section back into position—he had seen the heavy formation of fighters flying even with the horizon and blending into it, waiting until the top cover dived to attack the six stooges and left the disorganized Poles unprotected from above and in no proper formation to protect themselves.

Quickly climbing back into position, Blue Section took its place with the squadron once more, and the Eagles, along with the other squadrons of the wing, held the umbrella above the Poles while they regrouped and the entire formation withdrew safely, crossing the coast by Ostend and setting forth for England. . . .

Well planned and well carried out, this fighter sweep did not have the ending that sometimes mars a withdrawal from enemy territory: it did not end in a disorganized beehive, a strange formation in which a hundred or more individual planes join up for mutual protection in a swarm which resembles bees moving across a field in summer.

Separated as the result of battle, the planes of different squadrons and wings begin to swarm and then like a swarm roll over land and sea toward England. Invariably following a large air battle where many individual dog fights have occurred, and squadrons and wings have hopelessly lost contact, the beehive is formed of planes that are merely seeking companionship and are making no attempt to group themselves or achieve formation.

After a battle when many fighters are far over enemy territory and retreat is a necessity, one or two fighters join up with the remnant of some squadron that has managed to stay together. Then two or three other fighters join. And others. And still others. The beehive grows and starts for the nearest coast at a point where flak is not intense. As it moves, the hive still grows, steadily enlarging in size as more and more planes join up. There is considerable talk over the R/T as some one tries to reform a squadron or even a wing; but no one really listens to the talk, and certainly no one carries out any of the confused and conflicting orders. The beehive, like a huge body without any brains, moves in its own peculiar and ambling fashion, always toward home.

Within a gigantic beehive many complicated motions occur. For example, one half of the ball-shaped mass may decide to fly north of an area of intense flak; the other half may decide just as firmly to fly south of the area. At such a time the beehive may elongate—like a gigantic dumb-bell—before a mass decision is arrived at by the scores of individual pilots, all of whom are most urgently concerned with getting home. Most of them are low on petrol and ammunition. Many of them are trying to lug home damaged aircraft. And all know that terribly lonely feeling which is part of being deep in enemy territory after strong fighter opposition has been encountered and more is to be expected.

As the beehive makes its lumbering and unorthodox progress, like some monstrosity of the skies, the pilots flying in front try to stay there. Those in the middle try to join those in front. Those behind fly fast to keep up. Those on top—who don't feel equal to another dog fight with the probability of fighting odds heavily against them—try to get into the center and thus surround themselves with a shield of friendly brethren. The result is a mass of planes nudging each other, pushing each other aside and wedging in, a mass forever burrowing into itself.

The rolling, swerving confusion of buzzing Spitfires moves out of enemy territory and across the Channel, invariably flying low because the intruding planes from above have pushed their way in and pushed the beehive down. On across the Channel, the mass moves toward England, and when it has made landfall, the planes begin to separate themselves, to drop out and head for their home stations. Wing commanders, sergeant-pilots and squadron leaders untangle themselves, and the beehive is no more; there are only individual planes flying toward home. And no pilot, not one, could tell who guided him and all the other pilots in the beehive, out of enemy territory, across the Channel, and back to England again.

ARMORERS LOADING THE CANNON

FITTERS AND RIGGERS: The fitters look after the engine. The riggers do general duty around the airplane, keeping it clean, watching the flying controls, etc.

24

Included in the personnel of the RAF are the Gremlins. These little—I was about to say men, but you can't say men because they aren't really men. And you can't call them gnomes or elves or leprechauns, because the gnomes and the elves and the leprechauns are only fabulous little people. And you certainly can't say the Gremlins are fabulous; at least, you'd better not say it to any pilot in the RAF or any gunner or navigator or member of the ground crew in the RAF. You better not say it to a WAAF, either. Because, you see—or maybe you wouldn't see. Maybe you're one of those unfortunate persons who wouldn't be able to see a Gremlin even if he was turning handsprings on your wing tip as you flew through icy clouds at thirty thousand feet, or was climbing through your gunsight as you were trying to hit a Jerry, or was running ahead of you moving the lights off the flarepath and getting you all confused as you were trying to land at night. Maybe you wouldn't see the Gremlins even if you had a whole family of them living behind your instrument panel, as Gussie Daymond has.

I first heard about the Gremlins—this was before I had seen them—one night in London. I was first told about them by some pilots who are experts on photographic reconnaissance.

One seldom meets these pilots. They are a top group of operational fliers, and their assignments carry them far into enemy territory, sending them as deep as even the bombers go. They range over much of Europe, carrying tremendous loads of gasoline and flying great distances to some place that has been named to them. And when they get there, they circle the target and photograph it from thousands and thousands of feet in the air. Then they fly back home, over the flak and through the area patrolled by enemy fighters, safeguarded only by the speed at which their stripped-down planes can travel. When they land at their home fields, they casually hand over the films, which are then rushed to the laboratories and developed and printed.

The most valuable single source of information in this war is this photographic reconnaissance. Before a raid is planned, a pilot is always sent out to photograph the town or area that is to be attacked. He returns, and his pictures are printed and sent to the experts who put them under the stereoscope and study them. These experts have so trained themselves that they can point at what looks like only a dot to the inexperienced eye and say: "That is a gun emplacement." They point at what looks like a thick forest, and they say: "This is no forest at all. It is a camp where thousands of men live under camouflage that looks like a forest." They study the photographs of a city, like Hamburg, for instance, and say: "This area, that looks like an industrial area, is all faked. These are only dummy factories, despite the smoke pouring from the chimneys. Ignore this district. Here is your target. Here under this dummy lake the actual factories of Hamburg are turning out the materials that Hitler so much needs. You see, the Germans have simply switched the landscape, building a dummy lake over the actual factories and building dummy factories over the actual lake."

With this information, the big bombers are then sent to Hamburg, and they ignore the trick; they send their bombs crashing down through the dummy lake, the lake of camouflage, and on into the factories beneath, blasting them and ignoring the false factories so busily pouring out their synthetic smoke and fully offering themselves as targets.

After the bombers return and report that they have smashed the factories, the pilots are again sent out with their cameras. They fly over Hamburg, and they photograph the city once more. Again their photographs are printed, and now the experts lay the print made after the raid beside the print made before: they see how the false lake has been blown away and how the factories, now uncovered and exposed, have been battered. These experts are so experienced that they can look through their stereoscope at the pictures and tell almost exactly what damage has been done to the factories of Hamburg, tell how successful the raid has been. Then this information is passed along to other experts, industrialists and economists who know the history of German production and the capabilities of German factories, and they estimate, with remarkable precision what the damage to the factories of Hamburg will mean in Germany's total output of war supplies; they estimate that Germany's capabilities of production has been slowed down just so much by the damage inflicted during the raid.

The estimate is then passed on to the strategists, the war planning board, and this board determines whether to strike again at Hamburg, or shift to Cologne or some city of the Ruhr, or go to Central Germany and blast a city there. But wherever they determine to strike, you may be sure that they will first send out a pilot to fly over the target under consideration, and photograph it, bringing back pictures of gun emplacements, camouflage, troop concentrations, rolling stock, and all the evidence and

FLIGHT LIEUTENANT OSCAR COEN, DFC: Immediately
after landing from a battle in which he shot down a German. A WAAF officer
told me: "Sometimes when they land from battle their faces are gray and
there's a yellow froth about their mouths. It's then that a woman knows she's
superfluous . . ."

OSCAR

proof of what the Germans are doing in that district. And
the whole routine of getting the information is so fast that
the board need only ask for the information in the morning and receive it before nightfall: which means that a
pilot has flown to Germany, taken his pictures, and flown
back to England, and the facts shown in the pictures have
been studied and reported—facts that may well determine
whether next night the bombers will take off in the dark,
hundreds of them, and fly north to Emden to strike at the
submarine pens, or cross sharply over the sea to pound
once more at the steel works in the Ruhr.

The RAF world is divided into "fighter types," "bomber types," "brown jobs"—army officers—and "dead beats,"
the dead beats being the wingless wonders, the keewees of
the station, the controllers, administrative officers, and
all officers who don't fly. Even the RAF itself has no slang
classification for the photographic pilots. They are not
fighter types or bomber types, certainly they don't wear
the army brown, and goodness knows no one could call
them dead beats. They are simply in a group apart, flying
their dangerous missions, carrying on their essential work
as they race through the skies to far-off points with the
sole objective: get the picture!

I had been in England for some time before I met any
of these pilots. Then, through good luck I did meet one of
them, late one winter afternoon at Liverpool Street station
in London.

I was standing in the cold outside the station, shivering and praying for a cab, when an old one came rattling
around the corner with the cabbie wrapped deep in a dark
and ancient greatcoat. I made a quick start and reached
the doorlatch a second ahead of an officer in the RAF.

The cabbie, sitting back far behind the square windshield, opened the door and asked: "Where to, sir?"—then
quickly retracted his neck into a heavy scarf.

I turned to the tall chap beside me and asked to what part of London he was going.

"Grosvenor Square," he replied.

I invited him aboard "my" cab, explaining that I was going to Charles Street, just off Berkeley Square, and assuring him I would be glad to have him come along. I would have been glad to have him regardless of where he was going—one gets that feeling of respect for the men of the RAF, particularly after one comes fully to know how these fellows saved England and saved the United States—but it happened that our destinations were in the same neighborhood.

The pilot swung his parachute case into the cab and climbed in with me. We detoured slightly around some blitzed areas and in the gathering blackout drove along the Thames past St Paul's and Waterloo Bridge.

"On leave?" I inquired.

"Yes," he said.

We drove along, looking out at the heavy snow that was falling. We began to talk about the Royal Air Force and the American Air Force and about our fighters and bombers now flying together on their raids over enemy territory.

"Yes," he said, "we're in the same war now, aren't we?"

I replied that in my opinion we'd been in the same war for a long time, though some of the folks back home hadn't fully realized it until the Japanese explained it so clearly at Pearl Harbor.

He wanted to know much about the States, and I told him about New York night clubs, and tarpon fishing off Dauphin Island in Alabama, and oil wells in Oklahoma, and about the truth in *The Grapes of Wrath*. We talked until we passed Pall Mall, and I said I'd come back from a nasty job up north, and for my first evening in London I was looking forward to a hot bath, a good dinner, and a bottle of wine.

"I was just wondering," I said, "if you'd care to join me at dinner. I'd like so much to have you."

"Well," he said, "I'd like to. But, you see, I'm to meet some pals at nine o'clock and we—"

"Bring them along. We'll have a party."

"Well—I mean to say—I think that's a grand idea."

And that's how I first came to hear about the Gremlins.

A little before nine we met at the bar for our sherry, and Herbert introduced me to Freddie and George. All three pilots wore the diagonal purple and white ribbon of the Distinguished Flying Cross.

"I say, George, when did you get back?" Herbert asked.

"Last week."

"Any luck?" Freddie asked.

"Yes. Except those fighters near Turin got troublesome again. Those chaps in that part of Italy can be rather a nuisance."

The waiter came in, and I asked about wines. The old, fine wines of other days are not too easy to obtain in England now, and the waiter's face clouded slightly. But it was for an instant only; then he assured me he had two bottles of really good claret he had saved for some one who could fully appreciate them. Even though we suspected he probably paid all his clients the same innocent little compliment, we ordered his claret.

"But Turin is a long way from here," I said. "Why go all the way to the Mediterranean? Can't you get enough action over France?"

"I had to go take some pictures," George said.

The claret arrived and was poured. Glasses were lifted amid a chorus of "Cheerio's."

"I say"—Herbert looked around very pleased—"but this is a good wine."

Inevitably the conversation turned to flying, and soon Freddie, the youngest of the trio, was telling about a trip he had made not long before.

"I had a devilish time getting to Gibraltar," he said. "But the Gremlins met me by the Balearic Islands and rode with me all the way back to the Rock."

"The what?" I asked.

"Gremlins," Freddie said.

The look of perplexity on my face was unmistakably genuine.

"Gremlins," Herbert said. "Haven't you ever heard of the Gremlins? There are male Gremlins and female Gremlins? Sometimes they're green, sometimes they're fiery red."

"Whoa!" I said. "Perhaps it's the sherry. Perhaps it's this claret."

They laughed, but still they proceeded to talk about the Gremlins. They told of how the acrobatic ones could hang on to the propeller tips, while the aged sat dejectedly on top of the fuselage.

The waiter brought our salad and we were busy with it when Freddie began to talk again about his last trip. "I'd waited two weeks on weather so I could photograph a place; but it wouldn't clear, and things were pretty foul when I took off, but I went anyhow. I climbed through clouds and leveled off at twenty thousand and dead reckoned toward the Ligurian Sea. I met some fighters, but I scuddled into the clouds and lost them. Then I ran into ice and had to climb until I was way upstairs and needed a lot of oxygen. Then the sky cleared and I had to stay high because there was no cloud cover of any kind. I was on oxygen for about two hours when finally I made landfall and fixed myself thirty-five miles off course."

"Did you see any Gremlins?" I asked.

"No," he said. "But I was expecting them any minute. I was watching for them to hoist themselves any second over the leading edge of my wing."

George put down his wine glass and said it was too bad about the female Gremlins; he felt sorry for them because they found such difficulty getting on to the wing."

"It's the slipstream, you know," he said. "It's almost too strong for the females."

"I suppose," I said, "that if the wings are badly iced, the Gremlins wear skates."

"Oh, no," he said. "When they're airborne, they all wear boots with suction pads on the bottom so they can run along the wings, or over the fuselage, or wherever they like, and the suction pads hold them on."

"Gentlemen," I said, "would you mind doing me a great favor? Would you mind telling me what a Gremlin actually looks like?"

"It all depends," Herbert said. "Take the Malta Gremlins, for instance. They're quite different from those here in England. In Malta the Gremlins—"

But the waiter arrived with the other bottle, and at the same time the orchestra let fire with their interpretation of American boogie-woogie. For a moment the noise level was exceedingly high. Herbert was stopped dead in his attempt at describing a real, honest-to-goodness Malta Gremlin. By the time the boogie-woogie had got away from the blare of the trumpet and had modulated to the slightly less offensive saxophones, Herbert was busy with his meringue glacée and Freddie took up his story again, illustrating it with such intricate arrangements of the silverware that the head waiter moved over our way and watched.

"By the time I was here"—he moved the dessert spoon— "I was on course, but I had been on oxygen so long I knew I needed to conserve it, and I turned it too low. Without enough oxygen I was getting mighty browned off and was taking a pretty dim view"—of everything, the RAF takes a view: "dim," "keen," "weary," "foggy"—"of the whole operation. I was making some rather rude remarks about Whitehall, Brass-hats, Capitalists, Socialists, the Food Ministry, and even my corking good C.O. for sending me on such a blasted operation. And to make things doubly bad, after I had pin-pointed my position over Genoa, what do you think there was just ahead of me and square over the target?"

"Male Gremlins!" answered George emphatically. "Hanging on to the windscreen."

"Gibraltar Gremlins!" insisted Herbert. "Tugging at the ailerons!"

They debated the kind of Gremlins and where they were, and in the midst of the debate I attempted for the third time—and for the third time without success—to obtain an actual and authentic description of a Gremlin. Unable to get any information that satisfied me, I propped my elbow on the table like Rodin's 'Thinker" and tried to remember whether the oleomargarine represented Sicily or Corsica and whether the tablespoon or the coffee cup was Rome.

Freddie banged on the table for silence. "Men," he said, with the full dignity of considerable sherry and considerable claret, "there weren't any Gremlins at that time; the Gremlins didn't appear until later. But right on the target area was a bloody great rain squall. I had to circle and circle for more than an hour nearly twenty thousand feet high until that rain squall would move out of the way and let me get my picture. I was plenty browned off because my oxygen was really low and I was feeling the lack of it when some fighters came for me, and I had to climb up again and go into clouds. When I came out I was passing Mount Cinto on Corsica, and from there I dead reckoned for Gib. I let down to five thousand and took some coffee and biscuits, still feeling the lack of oxygen and still furious at having had to come on such a mission. Then all of a sudden right in front of me—"

"Gremlins!" I said.

"No!" he replied and shook his head positively. "No Gremlins! Not yet. Ahead of me was a heavy and solid wall of rain that reached down to the sea. There wasn't anything else to do, so I went on in and began to fly on instruments. After about an hour of staring at the gyros my D.R. position put me off the Balearic Islands and I tried to find the sea below, to spot the islands and get a fix.

"It was raining hard, and the water kept trickling through the hatch and splashing on my neck. I knew my petrol was getting low, and I knew I couldn't correct my altimeter; I couldn't tell if the sea was far beneath me or I was about to plow into it. I was wet through and shivering with cold, and I couldn't find a shoreline to guide me to Gib. Any old shoreline would have done, but I couldn't find one anywhere."

"Was it then you met the Gremlins?" asked George.

"No," replied Freddie. "Not then. But after nearly five hours at altitude, after the ice and the rain squall over the target, after the fighters, and being on instruments and short of oxygen, and that confounded water hitting my neck—it was then that the Gremlins from Gib climbed on board, hoisting themselves over the leading edge. And in less than a minute after they came aboard, the Balearics loomed up off to the starboard. So I set my course and—"

"Freddie," I interrupted, "won't you please tell me what a Gremlin from Gib, or from anywhere else, really looks like."

Freddie laughed and said he had made it all right. He had landed at Gib with enough petrol, fifteen gallons to be exact.

By this time the orchestra had finished. The diners were preparing to leave. Our waiter was tapping his foot and glancing at his watch.

George answered for Freddie. "It's, like this," he said. "There are really no words to describe the Gremlins. You have to see them yourself."

George looked at the other two, and they solemnly nodded agreement.

At the checkroom we slipped into our greatcoats. We slung our gas masks over our shoulders and stepped from behind the Blackout curtains to feel our ways in the sudden and total darkness of the street. There were some "Cheerios" and "All the bests" and we parted to go our different routes among the bombed buildings by Hyde Park.

Any one would long remember those pilots. Freddie, with his square jaw and broad shoulders. Herbert, tall, rangy and thin. George, stocky, built somewhat like a wrestler. Each of them had deepening lines on his face and had wideset eyes that for three years had looked down on almost every country in a hostile Europe.

As I thought about the solid walls of rain through which they had flown, the enemy fighters they had eluded, the shortage of petrol and shortage of oxygen when they were trying to find a shoreline—any shoreline: the ribbon they wore under their wings, the diagonal purple and white ribbon of the Distinguished Flying Cross, took on a new significance to me. . . .

But still I hadn't found out about the Gremlins.

I asked Robbie about them.

"Oh," he said, "don't you know about the Gremlins? Haven't you ever seen one? There are lots of Gremlins, all different kinds, and they exist for the sole purpose of plaguing the men in the RAF. They especially plague the flying types, the pilots and all members of the air crew.

"Surprisingly enough, very little is actually known about Gremlins. Even their appearance is a subject of debate. I saw in the paper the other day that Gremlins are 'bulbous little fellows with spindly legs. They have round knobby heads and stubby horns. They wear green bowlers, red jackets, and corduroy trousers.' I don't agree with that at all. It is true that they are small—about the size of an elf or gnome—but they certainly aren't spindly-legged or knobby-headed. They are much more shapely than that, and I fear for the safety of the poor fellow who described them so disrespectfully.

"The imagination of all Gremlins is unending. There is nothing to which they won't resort in order to make a pilot look indescribably foolish in the eyes of his fellow men. But they are never malicious, and so far as I know there's no record of any one ever having suffered bodily harm at their hands. They will, however, make mincemeat of one's ego, and they don't hesitate well-nigh to scare the wits out of a chosen victim.

"For instance, when a pilot is about to become airborne they'll suddenly switch his prop into course pitch and cause him to prang his kite, to smash it completely just when he's trying to make a particularly impressive take-off before some air marshals.

"Even if they let him become airborne in good style, several of them may sit on his tail when he comes in to land and then gleefully wreck a perfect, three-point landing. They'll shift the flarepath just as a night flier is coming down. They'll guide a pilot after many weary hours of flying to a dummy airdrome. They'll jam cannon when a fighter is about to get a Jerry. They'll hide parachutes and lose spares and play all kinds of tricks; there's no amount of mischief they won't do.

"I remember on one occasion Pilot Officer Billy Bograt, a particularly keen type, decided to get in a little practice, and after obtaining the necessary permission, he took off and stooged around the airdrome a bit, performing a few aerobatics just to relieve the monotony. Then to his joy he saw another crate doing likewise, and he romped over to beat it up. For several seconds he had a glorious time, diving, swooping, turning and twisting, but then he became slightly suspicions of the behavior of the other aircraft, and flying close to it discovered to his horror that there was no pilot in the cockpit. *Zip . . . !* He was off as fast as a bomb when he realized he had been beating up a remote-controlled aircraft. After he was well away he looked out, and there, sitting cross-legged on the wing of his kite, thumbing his nose and grinning, was a Gremlin.

"Some pilots have their own pet Gremlins. One fighter type I know has a Gremlin covered with mole-like fur, and whenever he is stroked the wrong way he rolls on the floor in a frenzy of rage.

"Gremlins, you understand, don't confine their activities solely to flying types. They find ample scope for their imagination on the ground, especially in such places as Flying Control, Central Registry and Equipment. Here they romp about to their heart's content, happy as moths in a mink. Messages are incorrectly addressed, files unaccountably vanish, and what happens to equipment is just nobody's business—except the Gremlins'! They feel they have scored a particularly fine point if they can get Group Headquarters to tear a frightful strip off some long-suffering and especially conscientious officer.

"The study of Gremlinology is, I assure you, altogether fascinating, but it's a study to be entered into with extreme delicacy and tact. Above all, let it be understood that any man who talks about the Gremlins, or writes about them, or even thinks about them, must never laugh at them. To laugh at the Gremlins is the ultimate sin, certain to bring swift retribution."

At a WAAF officers' mess I told them what Robbie had said. They were furious.

"Gremlins don't exist just to plague the pilots," one WAAF said. "Actually Gremlins are the friends of pilots."

"Ooh! I'd hate to be Robbie—talking that way about the Gremlins."

"So many people have mistaken ideas about Gremlins, and think they're naughty, troublesome creatures. They're not. They're wonderful to the pilots, and watch out for them and guard them.

"Whenever a Gremlin guides a bird right up to the air-screw—jumping off himself just in time—and the bird smashes into the airscrew and the pilot has to crash-land somewhere, it wasn't because the Gremlin was being mischievous; he just knew if the pilot went off on the bus service that day he'd get shot down. He was saving the pilot's life—don't you understand?"

"And if you prang your kite because of the Gremlins, you can bet your bottom dollar it was because they were saving you from some far more serious accident. Only the other day a pilot came back from a sweep over France. His kite had been all shot up, and when he landed he hit a soft spot and somersaulted on to his back. The fire tender and everybody around dispersal rushed out to help. They undid the pilot's harness, and he crawled out unhurt. Then the flight mechanics had a look at the plane and found that neither flaps nor brakes were working. If he hadn't hit that soft spot, if the Gremlins hadn't put it there and guided him to it, he'd have gone on and crashed into the Watch Office and killed himself. The Gremlins saved his life even if they did make him look silly by turning him over on his back before everybody."

"It's a real shame the Gremlins are misunderstood," another girl said. "They only want to help, that's all. Suppose a bomber is coming back across the sea after an operation, and suddenly the engine seems to take on a different note. 'Bit unhealthy,' thinks the first pilot. The second pilot gloomily mutters through the inter-com: 'Gremlins!'

They both scan the control panel and check up on all the instruments, the oil, fuel, pressure, and so on. Then the first pilot notices he hasn't turned on his de-icer, and, muttering, 'My God, just in time,' turns it on. Presently the unhealthy note disappears, but unfortunately it doesn't occur to them to thank the Gremlins for drawing attention to the de-icer, for saving their lives."

"But not all pilots are ungrateful," quickly said a little girl across the table. "Plenty of them realize that Gremlins guard them and protect them. In the early days of the war, back in 1940 I think, a bomber was returning from ops after having had a pretty nasty time. It came in wobbling a little and touched down, but just as it came to a standstill, the port wing gently tipped over and rested on the runway. When the engineer arrived he said that no plane could possibly fly in that condition, and the ground crew looked at it, and whistled through their teeth, but they didn't ask how it had been done. They knew, as well as all the boys in the bomber knew, that the game little Gremlins had simply come in vast numbers and had held that wing in place until the bomber had made its base safely."

"I would still like to know what a Gremlin looks like," I said.

"Well, there are all kinds of Gremlins. Most of them are a little like hobgoblins, but not quite. They have rather thin arms and legs, and usually they have beards, but not always. And they have bushy eyebrows and large, round eyes with the sort of mouth that can leer sardonically as well as laugh like anything. They often wear top hats and some of them smoke pipes."

"And almost always their boots are far too big."

"And those who hang on to the tail fin and perform acrobatics always wear tights."

"Mind you," said the senior WAAF officer in the mess, "I don't deny that Gremlins are mischievous. They are, but never wickedly so, and never with fatal results. Something

GREMLINS

may go wrong with your gunsights, or your turret may unaccountably stick, but never when you really need it, and then the Gremlins are only playing, only fooling for fun. And those silly accidents that sometimes happen, making you look like a goose—you can be sure the Gremlins are only teaching you a lesson. You may have forgotten to do something about your equipment or your aircraft, or you may have done it carelessly. They know that next time it might be fatal, so they let you make a fool of yourself so you'll not forget again."

One of the girls turned to me. "Maybe you don't believe in Gremlins," she said, the tone of her voice challenging me, daring me to say no.

"Oh, yes, of course," I said. "Certainly I believe in them."

"That's good," she said. "Some people don't. But that's because they don't understand. If they'd ever battled their way back across the North Sea in a bomber On a January night, with driving snow and sleet piling up on one side of the windscreen, and if they'd arrived over their base to find similar conditions prevailing, and the view of the flarepath practically blotted out with the snow piled up on the port side of the perspex—if they'd ever had to mutter, 'For God's sake move the stuff because I can't see a thing,' and the blanket of frozen snow had suddenly shifted, been whipped away upwards, leaving their vision unobstructed, I wonder if they'd have thought it was only the wind, or if they could have seen the busy little hands scraping it away, making it all clear so the boys could come in and land."

"You do believe in Gremlins, don't you?" one of the girls asked. "You really do, don't you?"

"Surely," I said.

But I was only saying it to please them. I wasn't quite positive about Gremlins until after I left the WAAF mess and went back to the RAF mess. There I joined some of the boys at the bar and fell to talking until it was late, and the face of the clock was uncertain in the haze that had risen in the room, and straight lines were wavering, and the room itself was swaying from floor to ceiling with a curious cadence.

It was then that I suddenly looked behind the bar and for the first time saw a little man with big round eyes and a bushy beard, wearing a green bowler hat, red jacket, and corduroy trousers, climbing out of the bottle.

I saw him just as plainly as he climbed out and came running along the bar toward me, his big boots flapping. And when he got in front of me he stopped and held out his hand.

"Hiya, Toots?" he said.

"Hiya, Gremlin?" I said, and we shook hands warmly.

BOB SPRAGUE: As this book goes to press, word has just come that Bob has been killed.

25

Besides meeting the Gremlins, the Eagles met any number of other interesting characters in England. Three of them one night, for instance, met Lady Screedsmere.

The boys had been in England only a short time when, late one afternoon, they set off from their station to go to London. Gus Daymond, Ed Bateman, and Indian Jim Moore from Texas set sail for their first trip to the big city, looking for the English version of the Great White Way. Robbie met them and took them in tow.

To begin with, Gus wanted to see "Diccapilly Circus."

"You mean Piccadilly Circus," Robbie said.

"O.K. I knew it was something like that."

First they wandered around from one famous bar to another and had a look at each. Then Robbie made his great announcement.

"Boys," he said, "to-night you're going to meet Lady Screedsmere."

"Gosh!" said Gus.

"You mean a real lady?" asked Ed Bateman.

But Indian Jim, calm as always, said nothing. He merely walked with loping, springy steps and, Indian fashion, reflected on life.

"Yes, a real lady, the wife of an English lord," Robbie said. "I thought you'd like to meet her. She's joining us at the Berkeley Hotel for dinner."

Lady Screedsmere had been born in New Zealand, where she won considerable fame doing the kind of dances that brought the gentlemen back the next night and caused them to buy, if possible, front row seats. Having prompted the masculine eyes in New Zealand to bulge, she had departed from her native land and tossed her hips into the English arena. One night the Viscount saw her and was willing to pay the ultimate price, and so they were married. Thus Lady Screedsmere left the stage and took her place among those who came, were seen, and conquered.

That night, as Robbie and his young guests entered the hotel, the Lady, sleek in black and brilliant in diamonds, smiled and held out a pale wan hand. And three young Americans took her hand, smelled the faint perfume of her hair, and crash-landed at her feet.

"Pleased to meet you," said Ed Bateman.

"Me, too," said Gus.

But Jim, Indian fashion, drew back into his wigwam and looked the situation over, from the slender black-silken legs that were carefully exposed exactly enough, to the black depths of her eyes that said exactly enough.

"And how are you?" she asked, with a voice like the sound of soft chimes heard far off.

"Swell," said big Indian Jim of Texas.

Then they dined. And there was champagne. And, too, there was the dark, black wine of her eyes. The music of the orchestra was something distant, soft, faintly heard beyond the music of her voice as she talked and told those American boys about England.

As she told of England and the boys listened, the actress had an audience again. With the fair green isle as her theme, and with her audience clustered so near and so tense, she talked on and on and on, while the waiter filled, and filled, and filled her glass until tears came to her eyes, and her voice broke as she told the sad saga of the passing of an age.

She told of England when bluff King Hal stalked through the court, and the knees of strong men bent, and the heads of beauteous ladies were uncertain. She told of Queen Bess, the virgin queen—"My ideal! I've often thought we had so much in common." Once more Raleigh's cloak was laid down; Shakespeare's pen moved again, and Essex laid his head upon the block while the sorrowing lady from New Zealand, distressed by memories of so much that was beautiful, sought an end to her sadness, repeatedly turning to the glass beside her, drinking the wine, and continuing to shed her tears.

She told of Charles that fateful afternoon when the hated drums rolled, and Cromwell and his Puritans tried to end the House of Stuart. She told of another Charles and of his love for Nellie Gwyn. "She was an actress, you know. I have so often wanted to play the part of Nell Gwyn in some magnificent production." She told of Charles' dying wish that the girl he loved be well cared for. "Oh, it was love," she said, "serene, kingly love." And she drank her wine to the memory of such love, and to all love.

She talked of old, unhappy, far-off things and battles long ago. She told of the Black Prince with his plumes a-waving. She told of Drake and how he singed the beard of the King of Spain. She talked of Wellington and the Old Guard shattering itself upon the English might at Waterloo. She remembered the Six Hundred. "Into the valley of death rode the Six Hundred," she murmured, looking with moist eyes into the past, and into the glass beside her.

She told of England and its glory, and she told of the passing of an age. She said in sorrow that the old English aristocracy was gone, and so were the railings from Berkeley Square.

"Here we are," she said, with a little gesture that some-how encompassed the room and all England beyond it. "Here we are, shut in this room, the windows bricked up, and outside the guns firing. And the railings around Berkeley Square are gone. Gone forever." She struggled against her emotions and, bolstering herself with wine, bravely carried on. "Do you hear me?" she said, bending nearer. "Do you understand that they have torn down the railings from Berkeley Square?"

She told of how once Berkeley Square had been the most beautiful square in all England, a place for the play-wrights to lay their plays. "I have often wanted to take the leading part in some magnificent production of that beau-tiful, beautiful play," she said, then told of the nightin-gale that once truly sang in Berkeley Square. In a low, sad voice she sang of the nightingales, until she could sing no more and lifted her glass to quiet the unhappiness with-in her. "But now they have taken down the railings from Berkeley Square. Ruthlessly taken them down, and car-ried them away to make scrap iron and make guns. So the beauty of the square is gone. The greenness of the grass is ended by a thousand trampling feet. And England is no longer England. An age has passed. The old aristocracy is doomed—doomed. And the railings of Berkeley Square are gone. Gone forever."

It was too much for her, this daughter of the New Zea-land stage bewailing the passing of England's aristocracy and the dreadful destruction of the railings in Berkeley Square. Swaying gently, her Ladyship yet again wavered up her glass, and her tears glistened above it as she quaffed the wine and stilled the bubbles winking at the brim. And two American boys, Gus and Ed, shook their heads in bewildered sympathy.

Then at last the old Indian came from out his wigwam, and he took her by the hand.

"You are my papoose," he said. "And I am your pappy."

Then, still holding her by the hand, he led the peeress from the ballroom, through the lobby of the hotel, and, Indian fashion, out into the blackout of the London night.

POTTER AND ROSS PLAY SHOVE HA'PENNY

BEFORE DINNER: Some of the boys have a beer or a pink gin before dinner. Others read. Most of them carry on the endless talk about airplanes.

26

After meeting Lady Screedsmere, the Eagles met another lady in England, one of an entirely different sort. They met Pins. Pins is an American woman, born in Des Moines, Iowa, who married an Englishman and after his death went to live with her friend, Maysie Robinson, Robbie's wife. Through the years as the Eagles cruised in and out of the big house high up on the Heath, Pins came to know the boys, and they looked on her as a pal to whom they could take their troubles and have them well listened to, and take their torn shorts and uniforms and have them well mended. Pins is that sort.

We were talking the other night, and she was telling about a big bomb that had fallen near the station where she is an Air Raid Warden.

"It was a delayed action, thank goodness," she said. "When we heard it coming we figured it had our names on it—we could tell it was a big one, and it was coming close. If it had exploded at once it would have blown us all to kingdom come, but it didn't. And now the bomb disposal crew are dealing with it."

She said that whenever a bomb is heard coming down, every one waits for it to explode, because sometimes it doesn't go off the instant it touches the ground. Sometimes it has a delayed fuse, and the length of time between the moment it strikes and the moment it explodes depends on the length of fuse the German girl in the factory back in Germany put on that particular bomb. So when a bomb is heard whistling down, making that shrill, increasing whistle as it gets nearer, every one waits for the blow off. But sometimes it doesn't come; sometimes there is no explosion. And then they know it's a delayed action, and they can't be certain when it will explode.

Whenever such a bomb hits, the bomb disposal people are notified, and a crew comes and examines the place where the bomb went in. Then they begin to deal with it. Sometimes the bomb, if it's a big, heavy one, may be as much as fifty feet down. "You see," she said, "in soft soil a bomb never rests. Its weight keeps it burrowing down and down, and since it always takes the path of least resistance, it may curve off from under the point it entered the ground and end up some place some way from where it started."

"But why bother about it?" I asked. "Why not let it peacefully alone?"

"Oh, you wouldn't dare do that," she said. "Because days, weeks, even months later it might explode. One went off in a thickly populated district of London about a year after it was dropped. No one knew it was there, and when it exploded it killed thirteen people. Why it went off at that particular time no one knows, but since any bomb might go off any old time, they must be dealt with as quickly as possible."

Robbie told me that Pins really should be something of an expert on bombs. "At least on the receiving end," he said. "She's been bombed three times."

I looked at the woman sitting there wearing the uniform of a corporal in the Air Raid Wardens, smoking and chatting with us. "And you've been bombed three times," I said.

"Yes," She reached over and patted Andy, the fat old Sealyham who had come waddling in. "Once here in this house. I heard the stick of bombs coming up the valley, and as they fell nearer and nearer I pulled the cover over my head and said, 'Well, Pins, you've had it.' But luckily the stick straddled the house and none of the bombs actually hit it. Of course, it shattered all the glass in the conservatory, and broke out most of the windows, and it sort of lifted the house and shook it the way Andy would shake a rat."

"That's why the floors creak so much when you walk on them," Maysie Robinson said. "And why the doors are hard to shut. The bomb sort of knocked the house out of line when it gave it such a shaking."

"When was another time you were bombed?" I asked.

"Up on the Heath," Pins said. "I was coming along with some milk when I heard a stick coming. I threw myself flat and waited, and I could hear the bombs in the stick coming down, blasting things, but they fell off to one side, and all that happened was that my teeth were rattled, and the milk bottle I was carrying got knocked over somehow and broken."

"And when was the third time?" I asked.

"That was in the Café de Paris," Pins said.

They had been entertaining Paul Anderson, one of the Eagles, that night. He was going home because he had been rather badly hurt in a crash, and they were giving him a farewell party.

"My wife was in America at the time," Robbie said, "and when I drove down town to get my date, the whole West End of London looked as if it were on fire. The Germans were giving the town a real pasting. Incendiary flares were streaking down, and the big bombs were shaking everything. My date told me afterward that as she had sat in her bath at the hotel, a bomb had rocked the building until the water had spilled over the side of the tub. We went on from her hotel toward the Café de Paris, where we were to meet Pins and Paul Anderson and the rest of our party, but before we got there we saw a cloud of dust, and glass and bricks were all over the street, and they were bringing the people out."

Pins said that the orchestra was playing "Oh, Johnny, Oh," and everyone was dancing and having fun when, without the slightest warning, a bomb crashed through the ceiling and exploded in the room. She said that in an instant the room was filled with plaster and shattered glass.

"The man who was dancing with me," she said, "was tall, and he put his arms around me and bent down over me, and while he was holding me that way I felt the blood running off his head and down on to my back. But he held me, and I remembered to put my handkerchief over my nose so as not to breathe the plaster dust and the fragments of glass that were in the air.

"Somehow we got out of the room itself and to the stairs, and while they were pretty well smashed, we managed to crawl up them. My partner's scalp had been cut open, but we bandaged it, and he sat down to get his strength back, and I saw a lot of beer bottles sitting on the bar, and I thought they should be opened for some reason. So I went behind the bar and opened all of them, two dozen of them, and I remember saying, 'What a handy little gadget,' as I opened them with a special kind of opener that was nailed to the wall. I suppose my opening the bottles was a kind of hysterics that took the place of the screaming of some of the other women. It's peculiar how a shock like that affects you. I remember one rather elderly woman they helped up from below. They brought up her husband whose leg had been smashed into a pulp, and they sat him in a chair, and his wife sat beside him and just stared straight ahead. She didn't look to one side or the other, and her expression didn't change; she just sat there.

"One of the strangest of them all was a woman who came up looking a little pale. I asked her if she was all right, and she said she didn't know; she supposed she was, but she couldn't be quite sure. She sat down for a minute, then she got up suddenly, and started running for the door as if she wanted fresh air. But before she got to the door, she stopped and just slumped down on the floor. When they got to her, she was dead. The blast had split her spleen. It hadn't broken her skin anywhere, but it had split her spleen, and she bled to death internally."

Pins said that of all the people who were injured or killed in the Café de Paris that night, she remembered most vividly a girl in a white evening dress. "She was a beautiful girl," Pins said, "a really beautiful girl, and when they brought her out and laid her down, I thought I had never seen any one with a more lovely face. There was the paleness of death in her face, but she had on some make-up, and in the dim light where we were working, dressing the wounds and bandaging people, she looked like a girl who had just fallen to sleep, except that one side, her whole right side, was gone; it was blown completely away."

Pins got up and got her gas mask and her helmet. She reached for her greatcoat.

"See here, Pins," I said, "just what do you do? What is your job?"

"Air Raid Warden," she said.

"But what do you do?"

"Well, I'm on duty sixty hours a week. I go on at midnight to-night, and I come off at nine in the morning. If the Huns don't come over to-night, there'll be nothing for me to do. If they do, and if they drop any bombs in this area, then I'll be plenty busy."

PETERSON AND STRICKLAND PLAY CHESS: Jerko
Gray looks on. This picture was made on the day after Jerko had shot down
his first Focke-Wulf 190.

TEA AT ROBBIE'S: Sunday afternoon
some of the boys always show up at Robbie's house for tea. In this picture in
the library are Morgan and Mike McPharlin, then Audrey Peterson—Pete at
the time was away on a mission in America—then Bob Sprague, Robbie's butler,
the incomparable Dunsford, Maysie Robinson, and Robbie himself.

She went on to tell that she has a plan of every house in her district. "Every room is marked," she said, "and we know exactly where everybody is sleeping, exactly in which room."

"Why?" I asked.

"Well, suppose this house is hit to-night. There'd be no sense in our digging at the end of the hall, if you're sleeping in that room over there. We dig wherever a person has been sleeping. If we can get him out in time, we may save his life."

She told me of one warden who saved the lives of a lot of people in her district. "The Germans were flying over, dropping bombs in the middle of a settlement. Three people in this settlement were killed: they were simply blown up the chimney—there just wasn't anything of them left, nothing at all. But no one else was lost, and forty-seven people were dug from ruins of houses. That was because the warden knew exactly where everybody was sleeping, and she could direct the crews where to dig in the debris."

Pins said that whenever there was an "incident," whenever a bomb fell, the warden in that district went as fast as she could to where it fell, and she took immediate and complete charge. She directed the work of the fire-fighting crews. She pointed out where the big demolition trucks should clear away the heavy timber. She assigned a place for the injured to be laid out, and a place for the doctors to do their work. She kept a way clear for the ambulances.

"The ambulances are always backed in toward the wreckage," she said, "so they'll be able to leave as quickly as possible once they're loaded with their stretcher patients. They must not only got their load to the hospital quickly, but they must hurry back. After a blitz, there aren't enough ambulances for each incident, and we have to run a shuttle service from the wreckage to the hospital and back again."

Pins was standing there in her greatcoat, her gas mask and her helmet slung over her shoulder.

"Maysie," she said, "do you want to go in town with me tomorrow? I've got to see that fussy old doctor again."

"Pins had bad luck in the Café de Paris," Robbie said. "She got a sliver of glass blown in her ear, and she lost her hearing on that side. And the blast did something to the sweat glands of her hands; she has all kinds of trouble with her hands."

"Inventory of damage to poor old Pins," she said, laughing. "But I got out lucky. I got out alive." She looked at her watch. "Golly, it's almost midnight. I got to hurry." She started for the door. "So long, you chaps," she said, and went on out.

Then I heard her walking on the gravel of the garden path, hurrying toward her station up on the Heath.

27

In the Battle of Britain, fought so magnificently in the latter part of 1940, the Royal Air Force kicked Goering and his gang out of the daylight skies above England. Before the battle the Luftwaffe had been coming over almost at will, flying where they wished, and almost all the day fighting took place above England. But after the battle the Luftwaffe and the RAF were no longer fighting for the air above England: that air had been won by the British. The RAF had forced back the fighting zone, and No Man's Sky was now east of England, above the North Sea, the Straits of Dover, and the English Channel.

At that time, late in 1940 and early in '41, the German aerial front line was at the coasts of France, Belgium, and Holland. The RAF entered the air above these Occupied Countries only at great risk to themselves. But risk or no risk, the RAF determined to attack that line, to pierce it with fighter planes and to engage the enemy above his own soil. So the great sweeps began: the annoying raids were initiated and fostered. The RAF was giving the Luftwaffe some of its own, showing the Hun how it felt to be shot out of bed at dawn and visited again at lunch and tea and dinner by fighter planes diving to pay their respects with blazing cannon.

And the Hun didn't like it. He began to squeal as day after day the RAF flew over and shot up his airdromes, killing the pilots before they could get to their airplanes and destroying the airplanes themselves as they sat helpless on the ground. Finally Goering declared the more advanced German airdromes to be untenable, and they were abandoned. The Luftwaffe moved back, retreating from the incessant attacks by the low-flying, cannon-carrying Spitfires and Hurricanes of the Royal Air Force.

This slow and costly and superb air victory was won when Britain fought alone. But now, each day that weather permits, Allied fighter planes can be seen climbing fast toward France and Belgium and Holland; now the Americans and British together are going over to fight for the complete air superiority that is essential before there can be victory for the Allies and peace in the world again.

The German and Italian Air Forces with their unfortunate satellites, Romania, Finland, Bulgaria, are very strong in operational aircraft, pilots, and reserves. The Axis production of aircraft is great, far greater than is commonly supposed. Furthermore, the Germans are continuously blackjacking Occupied Countries into contributing all munitions of war, especially aircraft. With vast numbers of operational aircraft already in use, with even greater numbers being produced in all parts of conquered Europe, the Luftwaffe and the Regia Aëronautica can and do mass thousands of airplanes for an offensive. And for the defense, they possess the great advantage of interior lines of communication; they can fly their air fleets to any part of Europe within a single day. Until they are over-powered they will continue swiftly to mass these fleets, the most mobile force in all history of war, in any area from which an attack is to be launched by them or against which an attack by us is expected. Before the Allies can fully carry the fight to the Luftwaffe and the Regia

Aëronautica and totally destroy them, an Allied air force so vast it has not yet been dreamed of by the layman will be necessary.

The most important prelude to complete air superiority is fighter superiority. Thousands and thousands, and still more thousands, of American planes and pilots will be required before the final Luftwaffe and Italian squadrons are blasted from the sky. Gigantic air battles already are being fought. They will continue with increasing intensity. It is imperative that American fighter planes be capable of highly efficient operation, plane for plane, against the formidable Luftwaffe. American fighter planes must be provided with all the exacting military requirements for air combat against German planes and German pilots. American fighter planes must not only possess certain flying characteristics; it is vital that they possess certain fighting characteristics as well.

Since 1936, when they sent their pilots and planes into the experimental war they had instigated in Spain, using it as a testing ground, Nazi engineers and Nazi manufacturers have been constantly changing, rebuilding, improving their fighter planes until to-day they have a truly powerful instrument of battle, terrible in destruction and swift in retreat. The British, too, have experimented and learned through years of battle experience what is required of a fighter plane that can strike and destroy utterly and can withdraw so fast the eye can hardly follow it in its downward plunge. We Americans have much to learn from both the Germans and the British in the building of fighter planes. And there is no need for us to insist that our fighter planes are superior merely because we, a nation of great engineers and builders, have made them. Laudatory adjectives about our planes will never make an indentation in the armor plate of a Focke-Wulf flying thirty thousand feet above St. Omer airdrome in France.

Bob Sprague and Gene Potter were the first Eagle pilots to do combat with the FW 190, Germany's great fighting plane of sixteen hundred horsepower. It is a powerfully armed aircraft carrying two 20 mm. Oerlikon cannon, two 20 mm. Mauser cannon, and two machine-guns. This formidable armament is further increased and made effective by the very high rate of fire of the Mausers, more than eight hundred rounds per minute. Besides its powerful armament in attack, the 190 is heavily armored in defense, carrying armor in front and behind, and protecting the pilot with a strong, bullet-proof windscreen.

Sprague and Potter encountered the Focke-Wulfs by Le Touquet. They saw the four Jerries ambling along under some low-lying clouds, flying almost on the deck. The two Eagles promptly pounced, and a fierce dog fight followed.

In the initial attack Sprague put his bullets into the cockpit of one of the 190s. It barrel-rolled rapidly three times and crashed. But there were three Huns left, and one of them got on Potter's tail. In telling about the fight, Gene said that for a while he was a mighty busy man fighting for his life, but he still had time to wonder why he had ever tangled with the 190's, why he hadn't let them go on in peace; he said he had never fought against an airplane that could do so many tricks, and do them so fast, as the plane that was on his tail with lead pouring from it and streaming toward him.

In one part of the battle, the 190 closed in from slightly above, and Gene, banking his plane steeply with the wingtip just above the sea, pulled back hard on his stick, whirling the plane on its own wingtip. The 190 attempted to follow, to do as Gene had done, but the pilot tightened too much and the plane stalled. The German boy lost control, and Bob Sprague saw him crash into the sea and his plane explode. The other two Huns promptly turned tail and scurried for home. And that was the end of the first battle between the Eagles and the famous FW 190.

Since then the Eagles have fought the 190's repeatedly and have shot down dozens of them. The Eagles have flown their Spitfires and Hurricanes against the Messerschmitt 109's, the Focke-Wulf 190's, and everything else the Germans have sent into the sky, and their judgment about the requirements of a good fighter plane is, therefore, worth consideration.

The more technical requirements need not be discussed here, because, frankly, as the Eagles sit in dispersal forever talking airplanes, they frequently become so technical that only an engineer or an airplane designer could understand them. Furthermore, the perfect balance of speed, weight, drag, wing area, horsepower, etc., is highly debatable, and even the Eagles do not agree as they discuss the fighter airplane of their dreams, the ideal plane that would maneuver and perform so wonderfully that with it they could go up and swat Jerry out of the sky. But there are other factors, other requirements for a good fighter plane about which most of the Eagles do agree. These requirements are not technical and can easily be understood by the layman.

One day at dispersal I asked the boys if they would stop their talk about "load factor," "wing loading," "power loading," and all the rest of their professional jargon long enough to tell me what they wanted most in an ideal fighter airplane.

"Good Lord," said Wee Michael, "that's like somebody asking what he wants most in a woman. There's a million qualities a man wants in a woman. There're just that many he wants in an airplane."

Off in the corner Bob Sprague stretched his long legs and said: "Just suppose you could have everything in an

382 JAMES SAXON CHILDERS

airplane you wanted. Gawd A'mighty!" He whistled softly. "What couldn't you do with an airplane like that."

Then they began to argue about what they would want. On only a few of the requirements for the perfect airplane did they all agree. But there was no question that they all want planes that can fly faster, climb faster, and climb higher than any plane being made today.

"Pretty soon," said Gus, "we'll need such airplanes as only the most daring designers have ever thought of. On the Western Front it's becoming more and more necessary that fighters fly faster than four hundred miles an hour, and climb faster than four thousand feet a minute. You got to have such airplanes, that's all. And they got to do their stuff not only at medium heights—twenty to thirty thousand feet—but they got to paddle right on up into the stratosphere."

The boys pointed out that flying and fighting at greater and still greater heights is not only to be expected; it is certain. Enemy bombers already are operating at forty thousand feet; the German Ju 86 and the He 177 are bombing from that height. Allied fighters must be built that can climb rapidly above them and shoot them down. And even forty thousand feet is not to be considered the ceiling—designers of fighter planes in Germany already are striving for a fifty-thousand-foot ceiling.

"But however high Jerry goes, we must get above him," Oscar said. "Superior height is essential."

Every fighter pilot knows what height means: he knows that height is another way of acquiring speed or tactical advantage. From above, a short sharp attack can be delivered. With the excess speed acquired in the dive, a zoom back to the original position can be accomplished. Sometimes fighters dive and zoom, dive and zoom, attacking each time they come down.

"It won't be easy to build planes that will perform and maneuver in the stratosphere," Oscar said, "but you got to build them. Everything is going higher and higher, and the pilot who gets on top is in a position to call his shot, to come down when and how it suits him best. And the poor guy downstairs can only stooge around and wait until he's had it."

Then Pete brought up the fact that in an ideal fighter plane almost all adjustments should be made automatically.

"A fighter pilot doesn't have time to be making adjustments manually, to be looking down into his cockpit and adjusting his engine, radio, propeller, oxygen control, and all the rest of it. There're occasions when you fly a long time with mighty little chance to look into your cockpit. Certainly you can't watch your instrument panel when you're in tight formation in clouds, or tight formation anywhere. And goodness knows, you can't make adjustments when you're in combat."

"As a matter of fact, you should look at your instruments mighty little when you're over enemy territory, even when you're not in combat," Gus said. "When you're over France, every second you're studying your instruments or adjusting your controls instead of watching out for a Hun, you're asking for it. Practically all planes shot down are destroyed by surprise attacks, by somebody the other guy didn't see. If you're not seeing every inch of the sky so that nothing can be there you don't detect, then you're giving the other fellow that split second advantage that's long enough for him to insert a load of lead into your backside. Hell, no, you don't want to be looking at your instrument board. Or anywhere else except the sky. Even then you often won't see him until he's shooting at you. The first 109 I ever saw, I didn't see—I've still no idea where he came from—until he was smack on my tail and pouring lead at me."

All the boys quickly agreed that the design of a plane should permit a pilot to make a quick and safe emergency exit.

"If you don't feel you can get out in a hurry," Strickland said, "you're going to be mighty unhappy. If you feel you're trapped inside and can't get out once you're on fire or after your controls have been shot away, then you don't want to fly that particular kind of airplane. You don't mind going up and fighting and risking your neck, but you don't want to die just because some dumb designer didn't give you a good emergency exit.

"Any number of pilots saved themselves from falling airplanes during the Battle of Britain, and the realization that they could get out in a hurry, that they didn't have to stay inside and go down with the plane, was a tremendous uplift to the morale of British pilots. At Dieppe the percentage of escapes from falling airplanes was even greater than in the Battle of Britain; at Dieppe nearly one-third of the British pilots whose planes were shot down were themselves saved."

"And they could never have done it if the designers of the Hurricanes and the Spitfires hadn't planned a proper exit," said Bob Sprague.

Then they began to talk about the strength and ruggedness of planes.

"They got to be rugged nowadays," Mike McPharlin said, "both in the air and on the ground. They got to be able to stand the strain of centrifugal force in high speed maneuvering. And sometimes that strain is so great that a person, even a pilot, can hardly realize it. When you're maneuvering really fast, when you're throwing your plane about, the strain on the wings may actually be ten times the normal weight of the airplane. They got to be plenty rugged to stand strain like that."

"Yeah, and they got to be rugged in another way," said Oscar. "The really good modern fighter must take all the banging it gets from cannon and flak, and still stay in the air unless some vital part is hit. It's got to stay up there even when it's been shot to hell. Like yours did the other day, Bob."

"That was a pretty good pasting, all right," said Bob in masterly understatement.

Bob Sprague has been shot up more than any other man in the squadron. But the other day he outdid even himself. He brought home a plane that no man, seeing it after it landed, would have believed could have been kept in the air for fifty feet, much less fifty miles. While Bob was on a sweep over Dunkerque the Hun gunners got him squarely in range and simply poured flak at him; they riddled his plane, but somehow he managed to keep it in the air and get it back to England.

"Mighty funny feeling," Bob said, "after you've been hit several times and your plane is crippled and you got to help it along. I was flying the old crate as fast as I dared— about a hundred and eighty miles an hour—and at that rate I thought the French coast would never leave me. I just sat up there chugging along while they kept throwing stuff at me."

"And a good bit of it hit him," Pete said. "When he brought his plane down it looked like a sieve. I still don't see how he got back."

In talking of the ruggedness of planes, the boys insist that a good fighter must be rugged not only in the air but on the ground as well.

"Hangars are out of date," Oscar said. "They were all right before the war, but you can't concentrate planes in hangars today. If you did, Jerry would come over, bomb your hangar, and you'd have no planes left."

Oscar explained that fighters today must be dispersed around the airdrome, a hundred yards apart, each in its own little protected niche, and left there, out in the open, throughout the hard European seasons.

"You've got to have a fighter plane that can stay outside and take whatever, weather comes along," Gus said. "You don't want one with a hot house history, accustomed to a flock of doting mechanics. And you don't want one that has spent its entire life operating from large velvety smooth airfields, with paved runways and large maintenance shops always within gliding distance. To hell with fighter planes like that. You got to have the kind you can land anywhere, squat 'em down in a cow pasture or a rocky field or almost anywhere at all. And take off from places like that, too, if you have to."

The boys insist that in the good fighter plane the cockpit should be comfortable.

"If you get tired or cramped, you can't fight," Strickland said. "I don't mean we expect or even want a day bed in the cockpit, but we do want more than a tight-fitting box. Furthermore, the cockpit should be amply ventilated, and it should have a controllable adjustment to withstand outside temperatures at high altitudes of sixty-five degrees below zero."

"And from that cockpit," said McPharlin, "for the Lord's sake give us good visibility. If you got a plane built so the pilot can't see, then you got a coffin. Just like Gussie says, most of the guys who go wrong nowadays get shot down by some other guy they never saw. And wherever there's bad visibility in a plane, wherever there's a blind spot, the Hun can attack at that spot, and we can't see him."

"And don't forget to place and protect the gasoline tanks so that the possibility of flames in the cockpit is reduced to a minimum," Pete said.

British fighter pilots wear long leather gauntlets and knee-length boots primarily for protection against flames. Their large awkward-looking goggles are shatterproof and are designed to cover their foreheads below the helmet and protect their foreheads from fire. Their oxygen masks with the enclosed radio microphones are also designed to withstand flames.

"But even with all that stuff on us, we don't like the idea of fire," Pete said. "I think every fighter pilot dreads fire ten times more than he fears a bullet. It's no fun to be trapped in a plane with the damned thing burning. While you're voting on what you want in a fighter plane, put in my vote for gasoline tanks that are as safe as they can possibly be made."

"And while you're protecting the pilots and the plane," said Bob Sprague, "you might as well increase the amount of armor and bullet-proof glass now being used. You might place more armor around the pilot himself and around the more vulnerable spots, the soft spots, of the airplane. More armor in a plane might save the lives of any number of valuable fighter pilots."

Then they began to argue about guns.

"With the speed of planes today, an air fight is over so damned fast," said Gussie, "that you got to have guns that can do their stuff powerfully fast. You got to get the mostest number of large caliber, armor piercing, incendiary, and explosive bullets and get them there firstest, as my old friend, General Forrest of the Confederate Army, used to say. You never have more than a mighty few seconds to shoot at any enemy aircraft and destroy him, and you don't have much more time when you're attacking a ground target, so you got to have plenty of guns that can throw big stuff and throw it mighty fast."

Some of the boys believe that besides guns, fighter planes should carry bombs.

"You see, there's two kinds of bombing," Strickland said. "There's the kind when you go in with the big bombers carrying tremendous loads of explosives and incendiaries, and carrying so many guns—like the Fortresses—that they can defend themselves. Then there's the kind of bombing the Hurricanes and the Mosquitoes are doing; you might call it speed bombing—they go in, drop their bombs, and whip out at terrifically high speed. But still they don't attack and get away fast enough. Faster and faster bombers will be needed, because the speed of bombing, like everything else in the air, is increasing. Then why not use fighter planes, like the Spitfire? You could hang a couple of bombs under a Spit and then—zip!—you'd be over the target and gone in a mighty few seconds. If a whole wing of Spitfires attacked like that I figure you'd do considerable damage."

"In other words," I said, "you want your fighter to be not only a fighter, capable of all the performance and maneuverability demanded of a fighter plane in combat, but at the same time capable of doing the work of light bombers."

"Exactly," Strickland said.

"Let me point out further," I said, "that you're asking Allied manufacturers to design and build fighter planes that will not only meet all your requirements, but that will have range enough to cross the Channel and penetrate into enemy territory, then meet a German plane that need only rise from its airdrome and go straight into battle. You're asking for a lot."

"Maybe we are," Gus said, "but still we're not asking for too much. We're asking only for a plane that will give us an even break in battle. And regardless of what it takes to build such planes in the United States and in England, they must be built. Without such planes we can't win; we

can't possibly win. But with them in large enough numbers—a whole sky full of them—we'll knock our old pal,
Herr Goering, flat on his fat bottom, and what's more,
we'll keep him there!"

PETE, COLONEL JIM, GUS

28

It was a bad day for the Germans back in November, 1940, when Gus Daymond reported to the Eagle Squadron. The entry for the seventh of the month reads: "Pilot Officer G. A. Daymond, our youngest pilot—only nineteen years old—was posted to us today." That entry is the epitaph of a good many Germans.

Daymond was born at Great Falls, Montana, in November, 1920. Even though he was only nineteen when he reported to the Eagles he had flown airplanes all over the world, having done private flying in the United States and having flown freight in South America and South Africa. Arriving in England as a member of the RAF, this nineteen-year-old boy climbed into his airplane and began his work of shooting down Germans. When the Eagles were transferred from the Royal Air Force into the American Air Force on September 29, 1942, Gus had top score of any man in the three Eagle Squadrons: he had official credit for eight German planes shot down.

Here's a letter Gus wrote Robinson a few days before Peterson and Audrey Boyes were married and while Maysie Robinson was still in the United States with the Robinson children:

Dear J. Roland:

I hear that Maysie has been delayed again.
Ain't it colossal the screwy way these jerks
operate. I'm damned sorry she won't get home
this week. Now she'll miss Pete and Audrey's
furious hitching ceremony.

Too bad I didn't see you on my last trip
to London. I imagine Pete told you what happened. Taxi trouble, ya know, so the illustri-
ous domicile of 109 [109 was Audrey Boyes'
flat] became the sole shalter for four breathing, pulsating souls. Pete was in his usual determined form and swiped the sole remaining
object of furniture in the sitting room that had
any semblance to a bed and left me performing
astounding contortions spread-eagled between
a sofa and an ever-roaming chair. For that I'm
going to bird-dog him out of every remaining
piece of pulchritude he ever acquires. [To "bird-
dog" any one is to take his girl from him.]

My charmer is back in good form and
whatever her well-kept inhibition was it
seems to have disappeared, except for that
occasional remark, casual and vague but
unmistakable, about engagements and a flat
for two and similar intimations. They fall like
sticks of 250 kilo, bombs across my burdened
shoulders. Ya see what you got me into when
you introduced me to this babe? I like her but
she acts mysterious as hell and won't tell me
what cooks in that fiercely active gray matter
of hers. She occasionally befuddles me, but
I'm still in there pitching.

Gosh, I sure miss you around here. We had
a scrap the other day that set a new precedent

for all time rugged fighting. I suppose Pete told you about it. If he didn't, here's what happened.

Our wing was sent off as high cover on a raid to Bruges, and while these damned Hurry Bombers were piddling on the target, we orbited around and around with our fingers well up at 22,000 feet while smoke trails converged on us from all directions. [At high altitudes, because of a form of condensation, a plane sometimes leaves a white streak behind it, a trail that clearly marks the path the plane has flown. Frequently from the ground the plane itself can not be seen with the naked eye but the vapor trail can be seen easily.]

When it was about time to leave the target and get the bombers back home, it happened. About fifty of these FW 190's that had been converging above us suddenly bounced on us like nobody's business. Jumping Jesus Christ, what a pandemonium broke loose. It's the first time I have ever heard of a genuine mass dog fight in this war.

To begin with, Pete sailed down and promptly blew the back porch off one of the bastards. At the same time another of them got on top of Pete and came down firing with all he had. He blew a hell of a big hole in Pete's wing, and Pete said afterward that the fellow was so near he could see the expression on his face, and the guy was looking powerfully puzzled. He had shot Pete's plane with everything and he saw the holes in it and couldn't figure out why Pete didn't go into the drink. And Pete, was mighty lucky, I reckon, that he

didn't go in, because he was terrifically shot
up, but he managed to lug the baby home and
put it down on all three feet without a smash.

Well, about the time Pete was shooting
and getting shot, three of the Jerries dived on
my section, so I turned like mad to try and
get position on them. What happened? The
dogs turned right with us. Poor old George
Teicheira was my number two. I last saw him,
unfortunately, not turning so sharp as he possibly could, and three 190's were cued up behind him shooting him until his plane looked
like it was throwing out decks of cards and
stove lids, and everything else was flying off
it in every direction. They stayed on him until they shot him down into the drink.

I then tried to attack a Hun who was on a
Spitfire's tail, but before I could get at him
five 190's leaped on me. From then on it was
undoubtedly the damnedest battle I have ever
had. These five stayed right with me attacking
furiously, never letting up a second. I could
never hope to tell you what an unfriendly
bunch of bastards they were.

About five miles off Ostend one of them
made a slight mistake and I managed to get a
three-quarter port beam shot [a beam shot is
any shot from the side] from about 325 yards
and I saw one of my cannon shells explode
on the fuselage about four feet in front of
the tail. He dived away and I never saw him
again. I thought I had only slightly damaged
him but two other chaps saw him go straight
into the drink. I don't think I hit him more
than two or three times and his plane could

not have been damaged enough to throw him. I reckon I must have hit the pilot with a cannon shot and killed him straight off. Anyhow, he's out of the way however it happened.

After this Jerry disappeared, the remaining four chased me to within five miles of Manston, attacking like mad. When I landed at Manston I had only two and a half gallons of petrol left. And believe me it took all my strength to drag myself out of the cockpit. I was wringing wet with sweat. Never in my life have I taken such a pasting. It was lots of fun, though, but at the time I was mightily in doubt as to whether I would make it home for tea. . . .

Besides flying airplanes in the United States, South America, and South Africa, Gus Daymond had worked in the art department of Warner Brothers studio in Hollywood. He had managed to get all that in and still arrive in England to join the RAF when he was only nineteen.

"He was nineteen in years when he came to us," Robbie said. "But he was a damned sight older than that in his ways. Most kids his age would have been playing and thinking only of fun, but Gus was working and thinking only of airplanes. He worked so hard that Churchill, the squadron commander, suggested I take him away for a few days' rest. Gussie wouldn't go. 'I can't spare the time, Robbie,' he said.

"In the day he flew every chance he got. And he didn't just get up there and throw his airplane all over the sky. He figured and he planned, then he went up and tried out his plan. And usually it worked. Whatever he did, he had the knack of doing it correctly. Whenever he flew a formation, for instance, he flew it neat and tight." Robbie began to laugh. "One day he flew it almost too tight. He was following George Brown, and the orders had been to close in and fly an absolutely packed formation. Gus went in so close that his airscrew shaved a bit off George's tail—not enough to throw him, but quite enough to shake him. After that George never ordered Gussie to come closer.

"When the others went up for gunnery practice, fighting with their ciné guns, they would come down with their films showing only a little airplane way off in the distance, only a dot bobbing up and down. Then Gussie's film would be shown. You could tell it every time. Right off you would see an engine or a great piece of wing. He didn't do any of this ropey firing from far off; he waited until he saw the whites of their eyes. From the very beginning he was absolutely wizard with his guns.

"Then at night when most of the boys were sitting around the mess talking, Gussie would be off somewhere studying airplanes. I would dare suggest that Gus today knows more about airplanes than any other operational pilot in the Royal Air Force. He recognizes any aircraft in a flash. He knows the wing span to the inch, the horse power, and every gun and its fire power. He's simply a walking encyclopedia on airplanes. Again and again I've heard other chaps arguing about planes, and when they couldn't agree, some one would say: 'You're wrong. Just wait until we see Gus and I'll prove you're wrong.'"

Despite his age, Gus was made a deputy flight commander soon after he joined the Eagles. He took his responsibility seriously and did his job well. Never leaving things to chance, he checked on every detail, and his commanding officers began to say that here was truly an unusual fellow. Far older than his years, they said.

Then came his first chance in battle. He was on convoy patrol when he spotted a Dornier and went for it. But the bomber was at such a distance Gus needed extra boost, and he reached over to pull the tit. But it wouldn't budge. That particular plane had been flown several times by Kolendorski, the wild Pole, and whenever Kolendorski saw a Hun, even if he was half way to Berlin, then Kolendorski pulled the tit and gave chase. Tired of working on the engine every time the plane returned, the engineers had played a trick on the Pole: they had wired the tit so he couldn't pull it. Then Gus had gone up in the plane that day and genuinely needed the boost. When he couldn't get it, he was furious. He returned to the airdrome and his propeller had hardly stopped turning when he sprang out and began such a quacking as the engineers had never heard before. He stamped around the place and said he thought that any one who would wire down the tit was a bloody saboteur.

"How the hell can we shoot them down if you don't let us get at them? By God, you should all be run away from here. We should get engineers who'll let us go up and fight What the hell do you think we're here for?"

Every one stood around in amazement. Was this the quiet, hard-working, young chap they ordinarily saw? Was this Pilot Officer Daymond who was forever studying airplanes and going up for practice flights? Who was this wildcat who'd suddenly appeared in their midst?

So they came to know the other Gus Daymond, the fighter, the absolutely fearless fighter who would dive into the midst of any number of Huns and take his chances on shooting his way out.

The boys around the mess began to play ping-pong. Gus had never played. But the game interested him. He took it up. He would play for a while, then sit and watch. He would study the play of the others. Then he would play again. And again. And sometimes he was obviously practicing one particular shot over and over. After a while, Gus was pretty good. Then he was better. Finally he was the best ping-pong player in the mess.

Then the boys began to play snooker, Gus had never played. Today he is the best snooker player in the mess.

July 2, 1941, Gus shot down his first enemy aircraft. "Since then he's never looked back," Robbie said. "He's gone on shooting them down until now he's one of the most experienced of all the pilots, and he's absolutely brilliant in battle. Now that he's fighting with actual guns, instead of the ciné guns of training days, Gussie still waits until he sees the whites of their eyes. Where the others may fire four and five seconds and get only a damage, Gus waits until he's exactly where he wants to be; then he lets go with a second and a half or a two second squirt—and that's the end of the story. He's an uncanny shot. And when he presses the button, the Hun is finished, that's all.

"The strange truth is that Gussie, who has been so successful in battle, hates war as much as any pilot I know. He has no love for the adventure or the excitement of fighting. He's got a job to do and he works like stink at it, but whenever he shoots a man down, he feels it in his belly. He hates all this shooting and killing. He wants to get it over and stop destroying things; he wants to get back to some kind of constructive work."

In December, 1941, the Americans wanted two of the most experienced pilots in the Royal Air Force to go to the United States and advise them on fighter tactics. Daymond was one of the two pilots chosen. He was flown over and fêted. He was given a private airplane, and he went here and there, a kid of twenty in years, but an old and wise man in battle tactics.

"In the midst of his tour, the squadron had a big day," Robbie said. "We shot down five one afternoon, and we

knew it would make the front pages of the American newspapers. 'Gussie will see it,' we all said. 'And, my God, how
he'll quack! He'll say we've played a lousy trick on him,
shooting down that many while he's away.' Some of us bet
he would be back in a fortnight. And we won. Eight days
after we got the five, Gus came storming into the mess one
morning, waving his arms and indulging in a typical Daymond quack. We were nothing but moldy flamingo dung,
all of us, to start the shooting season before he returned.
We were a collection of brass-bound bastards to put on a
five-Hun show while he was away."

It was immediately after he returned from America that
I met Gus Daymond. Robbie and I were dining at Josef's
on Greek Street, just off Soho Square, when this slender,
absolute boy in appearance walked in.

"Hiya, Robbie?" he said.

"Hiya, Gus? Food?"

"Steak."

He was wearing the purple and white ribbon of the
Distinguished Flying Cross. He was an ace. And yet I
could see only a boy. So long as we talked about the food,
and Hollywood, and girls, he was still a boy. But once we
began, talking about airplanes and flying and fighting,
he was a cool and calculating man, almost impersonal in
exactness.

We were talking about the effect of pressure bn the
body, both at altitudes and in dives. We talked of how
a man flying in the sub-stratosphere without a pressure
cabin, without artificial protection against the decreased
pressure of the thin atmosphere, will be troubled with
small nitrogen bubbles in the blood stream causing "the
bends"—similar, to trouble a deep-sea diver experiences
upon too rapid ascent from the ocean floor. We talked
of how, in a high speed dive, the rapid increase in air

pressure as the plane descends can burst the eardrum unless the channels, of the inner ear are free and open. And at the end of such a dive, if the pilot pulls out too quickly, the blood may be forced down suddenly from his brain and he will "black-out," he will lose consciousness and fall through the air until the blood returns to his brain or his airplane crashes.

"Remember Fessler's black-out?" Gussie asked.

"I remember," Robbie said. Then to me he said. "Fessler is one of the Eagles who was shot down and is now a prisoner in Germany. He got hit on a low-level attack and had to crash-land. The other boys saw him climb out of his plane and set fire to it before the Huns could get to him. The Jerries were shooting at him, trying to make him leave his plane, but he didn't leave until it was blazing and ruined, until it could be of no use whatever to the Germans. Incidentally, we get letters regularly from him and he says he doesn't like his new home; he'd much prefer being at the old squadron dispersal waiting for a scramble signal. We regularly write each Eagle who is a prisoner of war—there are five of them in German prisons—and we always write quickly whenever we shoot down a Hun, giving the details of the fight and telling just how Jerry got his behind shot off. We tell all the details not only for the boys in the prison but also for the Hun censor who has to read it; we like to brighten up the censor's day by letting him know how his pals are getting shot out of the skies by the Eagles."

"This Fessler was a darned good flier," said Gus, "and one day when he was in combat at twenty thousand feet, he blacked out on a high speed turn. He was plenty blacked out, completely unconscious, as he started down. And he stayed unconscious for most of the way down, but fortunately he came to in time to see the ground coming up toward him at a hell of a bat. He tried to pull out, but at first he couldn't. He pulled and pulled, and finally he managed to pull out just in time; actually when he leveled off he just cleared the treetops. He was coming down so fast he made about a 'nine g pullout.'" (The speed of his body coming down increased the normal weight of his body nine times the ordinary pull of gravity.) "It was such a terrific pullout that his seat split from top to bottom. The seat was made of bakelite, and splitting bakelite isn't easy: that'll give you some idea of the force at the end of his dive."

We talked on until it was so late that even Josef, usually a most patient host, came around and looked at us and said: "Gentlemen—?" And when I looked at my watch and saw it was past midnight, I believed my watch was wrong. I couldn't believe we had talked for three hours.

It was two days later that Gus fought the battle described in the letter to Robbie at the first part of this chapter. When I saw Gus shortly afterward I asked him about it.

"Hell of a good scrap, it was," he said. "Those four blokes who chased me home were absolutely stinkers, with their snozzles sapping at my backside all the way across the Channel. I was a mighty unhappy gent while they were squirting their pop-guns at me."

After the Battle of Dieppe, Peterson, the commanding officer of the Eagles, was awarded the DSO and was ordered to inactive flying; he was given a rest. He had been on more than one hundred operations, and he had been shot down into the sea in this last fight. Fighter Command figured he was due for a rest. So Pete was grounded. And Gus Daymond was given the squadron.

On the first operation after he took command, Gus shot down an FW 190 over St. Omer airdrome. The ciné film shows the Hun plane absolutely filling Gus's gunsights. Then the plane sort of spews up in a lot of pieces and the pilot comes tumbling out.

"It wasn't much of a fight," Gus said. "He was a weaky type and tried to get away without putting up a scrap at all. I just sort of eased in close and massaged his backside, that's all."

Old pilots who have flown with Gus and seen him in battle say he is not only brave but blessed with true inspiration. "He simply does the right thing before any one else gets started. While the others are starting to move, Gus has already moved and pressed the button, and the Hun is going down. He's always a fraction of a second ahead, and a fraction of a second is time enough for such a deadly shot as he is."

I asked Robbie if he attributed Gus's success in battle primarily to inspiration. "He has tremendous inspiration, there's no doubt of that," Robbie said. "As much as any man you'll ever meet, he has absolute genius in battle. But don't ever forget that he didn't depend on inspiration alone. Don't forget that he worked and studied and practiced and did it over again and again, forever thinking and planning and testing until he made himself a marvelous fighting machine, blending himself into his airplane and his guns until man and plane and guns flew and fought as one force, moving through the sky in an absolute union of destruction."

When Gus took command of the squadron, some of the older men on the station wondered. They remembered Gus was still only twenty-one years old.

"But we didn't wonder long," one of these older men told me. "He's making a marvelous commanding officer. He's one of the best administrative C.O.'s the squadron has ever had. And, of course, we always knew he'd be magnificent as a leader in battle. You know, come to think of it"—he thought of it, then decided he was right—"yes, this Gus is really a rather remarkable chap."

29

On the evening of the seventh of December, 1941, the Eagles were tired after a busy day. Most of them left the mess early and went to their rooms. Newt Anderson was in bed with a book by eight o'clock. Robbie was in bed by eight-thirty. Only Peterson and Strickland stayed downstairs. They wanted to finish their game of chess.

They were silently studying the board when the nine o'clock news came on the radio. They paid no particular attention to it; they were deep in their game. Peterson reached out to move a pawn—

"Bombs on Pearl Harbor! The Japanese have attacked American military installations at Pearl Harbor and have bombed the American fleet. In a sneak attack the Japanese—" But Strickland and Peterson heard no more of the broadcast. They raced out of the room and down the hall yelling like wild men.

"The Japs have attacked Pearl Harbor," they shouted. "The bloody fool Japs have attacked America."

"We're in the war!"

From rooms all along the hallway the Eagles came pouring out. In their pajamas and dressing gowns they raced along to Robbie's room where there was vast excitement.

"My God, we're in the war. Hurrah!"

The bell was rung, and lashings of rye whisky were ordered, and everybody set in to celebrate. The contempt-ible manner of the attack was the ultimate justification to these boys for all they had done. For their having left home. For having gone to fight in another country before their own country had faced the inevitability of war.

"The little yellow jerks—attacking like that!"

"We're in the war, chaps."

"Good old U. S. A.! We'll kick the literal hell out of them."

"Good old Robbie, you damned old Englishman! Here, have a drink."

"You have a drink—it's my whisky."

"Doesn't matter, Robbie. Put it on the lend lease."

"Hurrah, we're in the bloody war."

"Here's to the good old U. S. A.,
     Drink it down,
     Drink it down—"

On into the morning they drank and sang and celebrat-ed. The U. S. A., their country, was taking its place with the British Commonwealth of Nations to settle the most important issues that have been raised in world history; their country was coming in with England.

"Together we can do it, chaps," said Newt Anderson just before we went to sleep on Robbie's bed. "England and the U. S. A.—that's the way it ought to be, and for-ever."

Ten months later, on a rainy morning in September, 1942, the Eagles stood at attention at a fighter airdrome somewhere in England. Camouflaged buildings formed a quadrangle about the parade ground, where a unit of the RAF Regiment lined up in a hollow square. Sir Sholto

Douglas, Commander-in-Chief of Fighter Command, Royal Air Force, and Major General Carl Spaatz and Brigadier General F. O'D. Hunter, commanding generals of the American Air Force, stood at the reviewing platform before the microphone.

As the rain fell from the gray clouds the Eagle Squadrons—71, 121, 133—stood at attention while Sir Sholto spoke.

"I would have wished that on this my first opportunity of addressing all three Eagle squadrons together on one station that my words should have been other than words of farewell. We of Fighter Command deeply regret this parting, for in the course of the past eighteen months we have seen the stuff of which you are made, and we could not ask for better companions with whom to see this fight through to a finish.

"But we realize—as you too must realize—that your present transfer to your own country's air force is in the long run in the best interests of our joint cause. The United States Army Air Corps's gain is very much the Royal Air Force's loss. The loss to the Luftwaffe will no doubt continue as before. . . ."

The Eagle pilots stood motionless while Sir Sholto spoke. In the ranks behind them stood the airmen—the English mechanics, fitters, riggers, armorers, radiomen—who had so many times called, "Good luck, sir," as the boys set off for sweeps over France, and who so many times had come running across the fields with the eager questions, "What luck, sir? Did you get one?" The Eagles listened attentively to Sir Sholto and remembered the many times he had visited them at their dispersal hut to chat. He had always taken a genuine personal interest in the welfare of these boys. He and the other officers of the Royal Air Force had watched well over the American Eagles as their wings were slowly forged in the fiery crucible of war.

DAYMOND IN THE COCKPIT OF HIS PLANE: He is
wearing his helmet, goggles, and oxygen mask with enclosed radio microphone
—the usual accoutrements the boys wear when actually going into battle.

He had seen them, a group of sadly inexperienced boys, form and develop three of the most experienced, and most destructive, squadrons on the Western Front.

"In the eighteen months which have elapsed since your first unit became fully operational," Sir Sholto said, "Eagle pilots have destroyed some seventy-three enemy aircraft—the equivalent of about six squadrons of the Luftwaffe—and probably destroyed and damaged a great many more. The actual official total of destroyed is, I believe, seventy-three and one half, the half being part of a Dornier shared with a British squadron as a symbol of Anglo-American cooperation!

"Of the seventy-three and one half enemy aircraft destroyed, forty-one have been claimed by the Senior Eagle squadron No. 71—a record of which they may very well be proud, but one which I understand the other two squadrons are determined will not long remain unchallenged.

"It is with great personal regret that I today say 'Goodby' to all you boys whom it has been my privilege to command. You joined us readily of your own free will when our need was greatest and before your country was actually at war with our common enemy. You were the vanguard of that host of your compatriots who are now helping to make these Islands a base from which to launch the great offensive we all desire. You have proved yourself fine fighters and good companions, and we shall watch your future with confidence. . . ."

Why had they come as the vanguard of that host of their compatriots? Even more, why had they stayed during those long, inexplicable months when America was talking and talking and talking, debating the existence of the sun and the moon and the stars, the inevitability of time and tide? Hardship, danger, meager pay, the maddening boredom of bad weather, had been their portion. Oerlikon cannon shells ripping through their wings, their cockpits filling with smoke over the North Sea and the English Channel, these had been their portion. Why did they stay?

They don't know. They can't tell you. They know no more why they stayed than why they came in the first place. But whatever brought them, or whatever made them stay—adventure, curiosity, travel, fame, a love of flying, a desire to try anything once—whatever the combination of forces, the Eagles would surely return again if the chain of circumstances were to repeat itself. If the Panzers were to crash through the Lowlands again, if France collapsed and the Luftwaffe dominated the continent, if the U-boat scoured the seas and unarmed America clung to that incredible word, "neutrality"—if all these things happened again, I'm sure I know what the Eagles would do.

Pete would write his mother and Dad: "Dear folks, I guess I'll be traveling for a while." Oscar would call home: "So long, Dad, I'll be back soon." Fellows like Andy Mamedoff, Newt, Anderson, Red Tobin, Shorty Keough, Tom McGerty would just naturally disappear from American towns and cities, and you would next hear of them over the Channel flying Hurricanes and Spitfires.

"There are those of your number who are not here to-day—these sons of the United States who were the first to give their lives for their country." Sir Sholto spoke slowly. "We of the RAF no less than yourselves will always remember them with pride. Like their fathers who fought and died with that American vanguard of the last war—the Lafayette squadron—so will those Eagles who fell in combat ever remain the honored dead of two great nations."

Despite their being in uniform, when the Eagles first arrived in England they were unmistakably civilians: military courtesy or discipline had almost no meaning at all for them. Old soldiers around the station were amazed at the behavior of these young Americans who, in some cases, were plain saboteurs of military tradition. They forgot to salute. They forgot to rise when a senior officer came into the room. They forgot to stand at attention when reporting to the C.O. And as for polishing their buttons—to hell with it.

Then, too, the soft modulation of the voice, so common in the English officers' mess, was not characteristic of some of the Eagles. One Eagle like Bert Stewart could make more noise, day or night, than thirty Englishmen or ten Australians.

And English officers, reared in British army tradition or down from the Varsity, marveled at the table manners and the methods of drinking of some of the newly-arrived Eagles. Amid continuous and hilarious talking some of the boys would reach across a neighbor's platter, spear the oleomargarine with their fork, yell for some goddam water, bust the potato with their fists and gobble it down, skin and all.

Such behavior was not limited to the mess. Long before they were trained, long before they were ready to go into action against the highly experienced Luftwaffe, the Eagles were screaming for action. Having no true conception of what waited for them in the skies over the Channel, they wanted to get going, to start knocking off these here Jerry fellows.

Patiently, with infinite forbearance, the experienced pilots of the RAF restrained the boisterous Eagles. Knowing the sight and sound of lead streaming past them, and flak coming up, and 109's hurtling down from nowhere, Churchill and Woodhouse and Meares quieted their difficult charges and trained them until they were fully ready to go into battle, to sweep out on raids over Ostend, Dunkerque, Lille, to fly above St. Omer and dare the Hun to rise.

This association with the veterans of the RAF quieted the Eagles. And their experience in battle, their daily association with death, sobered them. Within a few months after they had begun actual combat, the Eagles, while still young in years, were old in experience. Each of them underwent a change, and despite the occasional outburst, when they beat up the mess or a pub, the Eagles were now a more orderly, a more gentlemanly crowd on the ground. In the air they learned the meaning of discipline; they learned it by witnessing the disastrous results of the lack of discipline. They learned, too, that there isn't room in the sky today for the stubborn individualist who insists on blazing a solo trail; they discovered that the lone fighter ace of other years has now disappeared from the daytime skies, shot down by formations of planes, by mass maneuvers that swept him totally from the air. Learning all this from their RAF leaders and from experience, the Eagles came in time to take and keep their proper places in their own formations; they grew to respect discipline and to understand obedience.

This quieting down, this sobering of the Eagles, did not mean that after a spell of bad weather they didn't occasionally blow off steam by wild and crazy flying, by inverted flying over the treetops, by flying so low they cut hay with their propeller tips, by coming out of the clouds in tight formations and screaming down until the salt spray splashed on their windscreens. They were still a wild bunch of irrepressible kids. But now they were something else as well. They were also officers in the Royal Air Force, and, as such, they quietly took their places in the officers' mess and bravely took their places in battle sweeps over France.

Aggressive and determined in attack by day, they acquired in time the calmness, the equanimity, that enables a fighter pilot at night to look back on the death of his best pal without too great emotional upset. After months of fighting, after repeatedly seeing their pals go down, sometimes in flames, they came even to achieve the restful detachment that enables a fighter pilot to look upon his own death without terror. Before a low-level attack over France, when they would be flying into the very muzzles of the Bofors, they learned to say: "Well, here goes nothing." And it was not bravado, not a bolstering of their courage, that prompted them to say it. They had simply undergone the indoctrination into the fellowship of danger and death, a purifying experience denied less fortunate men who have lived always in security.

"And now I have some news for you," said Sir Sholto. "The Air Council, anxious to give tangible expression to the gratitude which we all feel for the great work you have done, is going to ask each of you to accept a small personal memento of your services to the Royal Air Force. The memento will take the form of a medallion, and though it has not been possible in the short time available to have this medallion struck and ready by today, it is hoped that its presentation will be made in the very near future.

"I hope that these emblems will serve as a pleasant reminder of your comradeship with the Fighter Command of the Royal Air Force—a comradeship which we have been very proud to share and which I as your Commander-in-Chief shall always remember with gratitude and affection.

"Good-by and thank you, Eagle Squadrons of the Royal Air Force.

"And good hunting to you, Eagle Squadrons of the United States Air Force."

The Eagles felt the rain soaking into their blue tunics. They had jeopardized their citizenship to leave America. They had been a bunch of crazy, hair-brained kids who couldn't keep their pants on.

"And they're already in England getting killed in Spitfires. We mustn't let it happen here. It can't happen here."

Remember?

General Carl Spaatz, the veteran American flier, the commanding general of the Eighth Air Force, spoke slowly into the microphone. He would soon—only a few minutes now—be their commanding general. The beloved and honored blue of the RAF would soon be put aside. Already in the mess were laid out new uniforms, brown, with gold "US" on the lapels, with silver wings on the left breast.

"The operational experience of the Eagle Squadrons is a most valuable asset to the fighter units of the American Air Force. I welcome you with a great sincerity."

The American Stars and Stripes was raised alongside England's sky blue flag of the RAF. The band played "The Star-Spangled Banner."

Then Squadron Leader Gus Daymond, Distinguished Flying Cross and Bar, of Hollywood, California, and Carroll McColpin, Distinguished Flying Cross, of Los Angeles, California, and Squadron Leader Jimmy Daley, Distinguished Flying Cross, of Amarillo, Texas, barked commands.

The RAF Regiment and the company of WAAF's executed a smart turn.

"Forward march!"

Swinging their arms straight from their shoulders and with their heads held high, the Eagles passed smartly in review, and passed out of the Royal Air Force.

And what of the future? Could lieutenants, captains, and majors in the United States Army shoot flares out of the windows and skyrockets up the chimney of the officers' mess?

All that afternoon and that night the rain fell, until the roads were terribly slippery. Because of the slippery roads the airdrome fire department was a trifle late, sometime after midnight, in arriving to save the officers' mess.

Unknown persons had shot flares out of the windows and skyrockets up the chimney, and had tossed smoke bombs into a few odd corners.

While members of the fire department were debating with lieutenants, captains, and majors the wisdom of burning down "the whole bloody place," Robbie was broadcasting to England and to America a farewell to the Eagles:

"The sky was full of planes returning from battle over France. The ground crews, who had seen so many pilots fly away for battle, were looking at the sky and counting. 'Nine . . . ten . . . eleven . . .' counted the Flight Sergeant. Then, with anxiety in his voice, he turned to me and said, 'One of them is missing, Sir.' It was their first big action over France. The eleven planes landed, and the pilots climbed stiffly from their cockpits, their faces tense with excitement. They came toward where we were standing, and with two-handed sweeping gestures, they described the fight. They had destroyed three and damaged four. They talked in accents different from those one ordinarily hears in England. But they were accents that I knew, and had come to love.

"I am going to tell you something of the pilots of the first Eagle Squadron. These were the men whose triumphs and sorrows I shared for two fascinating years: a picturesque bunch who had answered some irresistible urge to fight. They had left the oil fields of Oklahoma, the vast plains of Texas, the ranches of Utah, and the studios of Hollywood. They were flying Spitfires instead of driving taxis and trucks in New York. They had exchanged the sunshine of Florida for the gray skies of England.

"Young America was fighting Hitler in the air.

"These American pilots came from all classes of life. It was wonderful to see how the taxi driver and the university graduate came to recognize fine qualities in each other.

It was good to see how quickly real friendship and understanding grew up between them and the Englishmen who
trained them and who led them into their early battles.

"In a few months of fighting the Eagles matured. At the
age of twenty they were seasoned veterans with nearly fifty
offensive sweeps behind them. It thrilled them when they
were called upon to fight over France two or three times a
day. They were unhappy only when the bad weather kept
them on the ground. Their list of victories grew rapidly.
Their losses mounted slowly. When one man was killed,
another eager young American was ready to take his place.
Their fighting was aggressive and vigorous.

"On one afternoon, Gus Daymond and Johnnie Flynn
went on patrol over France. On their way out they saw two
Messerschmitts taking off from a coastal airdrome. Down
they went to the attack. As they began firing, six more
took off to attack them. At this time there was no place
like home. Gussie made for the deck with four of them
giving chase. Johnnie flew at a thousand feet, with two
on his tail. Half way across the channel, Johnnie turned
at bay. He instantly blew a Messerschmitt right out of the
sky, while the other one beat it for home. Then Johnnie
went home, too, with his guns empty. Down below, Gus
was boxed in with a 109 on either side of him, and two on
his tail. Any other man would have been dead meat. But
Gus was an inspired fighter. He lost speed suddenly and
skidded to the starboard. The enemy overshot, and Gus
blew one into the sea. At the same time another shot Gus's
hood off with cannon guns. Gus said he was scared stiff.
But he was fighting mad, and he returned the compliment
by blowing large pieces off his adversary, who departed
hurriedly for home. A third likewise had no stomach for
the fight and quit. A fourth, 'a very intrepid bloke,' said
Gus, followed him to the English coast, continuously

firing short sharp bursts at him. Gus had no ammunition left, and his brilliant evasive action must have been a joy to see. Twenty minutes later a happy and excited man landed at his base. Now Gus Daymond wears the DFC with a bar, the first American to win such an honor in this war, and he leads the squadron.

"There were times when the Squadron faced real adversity. At one period, five experienced pilots were lost in ten days. It was a great blow. But C. G. Peterson from Utah provided the answer. Vigorous offensive action. When things were bad, he would invariably come back with something in the bag. His inspiration at this difficult time proved the turning point. Following Pete's example, the Eagles went out on determined, aggressive sweeps, and the following month they had the top score in Fighter Command. Pete was awarded the DFC.

"As the weather deteriorated in the autumn, there was less scope for offensive sweeps. So the boys began to wage their own private war. Every night after dinner, new plans were worked out for the next day. At the crack of dawn, pairs of Eagles took off on offensive action. They shot up enemy aircraft on the ground before their crews were awake. They blew up ammunition dumps while their guardians were still sleepy. They destroyed railway engines and oil-tanker wagons at dawn. And then, when the rest of the world was taking its breakfast, they returned for their food with a successful day's work behind them.

"The autumn weather got worse, and, in the belief that there would be no action for a week, seven of the most experienced pilots were given leave. While they were away, the Squadron was called upon for an offensive sweep. The new boys went into action, jumped a squadron of 109's and shot down five without loss to themselves.

"The old-timers were indulging in a whirl of gaiety in London. Friends congratulated them on their success of the afternoon, but they knew nothing of it. They were furious that the new boys should do this in their absence. Their indignation was picturesque. It was a personal affront to them that this should have happened while they were enjoying life in London. But times had changed—the Squadron was not dependent on a few brilliant individuals any more. Every man in the squadron was one hundred per cent.

"There was little to do all the winter, but when the spring fighter offensive began there were three Eagle Squadrons in the front line. The two new squadrons came in with the same vigorous offensive spirit as that of the first and quickly made their mark in RAF history. Their scores mounted rapidly.

"As was to be expected, on August 18, 1941, all three squadrons found themselves doing a grueling day's work over Dieppe. When the day ended, they had among them destroyed eight enemy fighters and bombers, and had another seventeen probables and damaged to their credit. One of the bombers destroyed went to the credit of Squadron Leader Peterson. He saw a Ju 88 preparing to unload its bombs on our ships. Regardless of the risk, he went straight in, determined to destroy it before the bombs could be dropped. He made a fierce attack from astern, but in doing so he had to fly right in the line of fire of the rear gunner. He saw cannon shells striking the 88, its starboard engine bursting into flame, and its bombs dropping into the sea. Simultaneously, the rear gunner of the 88 opened fire. Pete's aircraft was hit and his cockpit filled with smoke. Nevertheless, he continued his attack until he could no longer see. When he broke away, an English colleague saw the 88 crash into the sea. Pete jettisoned his hood, and the smoke cleared from the cockpit. Quietly and methodically, he prepared to bale out. As he jumped he saw his plane burst into flames and go spinning down. He himself floated slowly down to the water with not a care in the world, for the sea was full of British naval boats. Within fifteen minutes they had picked him up and he was on his way back to England. The trip home was not peaceful, for within ten minutes, enemy aircraft were strafing the ship, and he saw a new-found friend killed at his side. When Pete got home, he found his great courage and gallantry had won for him the first and only DSO of the war awarded to an American pilot.

"Now the first chapter of the Eagles' story is told. These Americans who came to fight in the Royal Air Force have gone to join the great Air Force sent here by their own country. They have changed from the blue of the RAF to the brown of the American Air Force. It is a slight change, little more than a nominal one, because while a man changes his dress and his uniform, he never changes his heart, and those stout-hearted fellows who came from America to fight for us a year and a half ago, still fight with us, alongside thousands of other American boys. As we see the planes in the sky, the American and British squadrons, flying together, there is no telling which is which, nor does it matter. We think only, as we look up at them, that there go our boys, our British and American boys.

"At this time of nominal parting, the Royal Air Force salutes the Eagles and wishes them good luck and God speed. . . ."

Three days later the newspapers carried the following story:

> Four German FW 190 fighter aircraft were destroyed and two were damaged this afternoon by fighter pilots of United States Army Air Force Eagle Squadrons.

The four victories were credited to the following fighter pilots:

> Capt. Oscar Coen, Carbondale, Illinois
> Lieut. S. M. Anderson, Indianapolis, Indiana
> Lieut. G. B. Fetrow, Upland, California
> Lieut. J. A. Clark, Westbury, N. Y. and Wing Commander Duke-Woolley, RAF (shared).

The two "damaged" credits went to:

> Major W. J. Daley, Amarillo, Texas
> Lieut. Brewster Morgan, Honolulu.

The air battles in which these victories were won occurred over enemy flying fields at St. Omer, where Flying Fortresses, escorted by Eagle Squadrons, made a diversionary sweep during the larger bombing attack upon the aircraft factory at Meaux.

The fights were described by two of the participants:

"The battle seemed to be over in a matter of seconds," said Major Daley. "It was our first since our transfer into the American Army, and I think it was almost a celebration. Anderson saw his Hun crash in flames and Coen saw his chap bale out. Fetrow set one on fire and Morgan and myself each damaged a 190."

Another statement came from Wing Commander Duke-Woolley:

"We met fifteen FW 190's over the Calais area about eight miles inside the coast at 23,000 feet," he said. "We saw six FW's 7,000 feet below us, but it was obviously a booby trap, so we ignored it Instead we attacked fifteen others which passed in front of us in straggling formation at about our own height. We waded in and the whole fight was over in about two minutes. One of the American pilots and I fired at the same time at the same 190. We blew his tail off and he went down."

The Eagle squadrons suffered no losses. . . .

Same old Eagles—

Saw him crash in flames!
Saw him bale out!
Blew his tail off!
Good hunting, you chaps!

THE OTHERS WHO WERE IN 71 (EAGLE) SQUADRON
WHEN, ON SEPTEMBER 29, 1942,
THE SQUADRON TRANSFERRED FROM
THE ROYAL AIR FORCE TO
THE UNITED STATES AIR FORCES

R. L. PRISER
56 East Congress Street
Tuscon, Arizona

W. B. MORGAN
Honolulu, T. H.

Left to right:

R. C. CARR
Angola, Indiana

G. H. WHITLOW
2404 Osceola
Denver, Colorado

V. A. BOEHLE
Indianapolis, Indiana

R. A. BOOCK
Springfield, Illinois

H. L. STEWART
1110 Harpe Street
Raleigh, North Carolina

H. L. MILLS
Leonia, New Jersey

Roster of Officers and Pilots

No. 71 (Eagle) Squadron, Royal Air Force
Unless otherwise indicated as Engineer Officer, Adjutant, Medical, etc., the following officers and pilots were on flying duty.

Squadron Commanders
S/Ldr. W. M. Churchill, DSO, DFC (Br.), *Posted**
S/Ldr. W. E. G. Taylor, *Joined U.S. Navy*
S/Ldr. H. de C. A. Woodhouse, AFC, DFC (Br.), *Posted*
S/Ldr. E. R. Bitmead (Br.), *Posted*
S/Ldr. S. T. Meares, DFC (Br.), *Killed on active service*
S/Ldr. C. G. Peterson, DSO, DFC
S/Ldr. G. A. Daymond, DFC and Bar

Officers and Pilots
P/O J. K. Alexander, *Posted*
P/O L. L. Allen, *Returned home*
P/O C. F. Ambrose, DFC (Br.), *Posted and then killed on active service*
F/Lt. N. Anderson, *Posted and then killed in action*
P/O P. R. Anderson, *Killed on active service*

* *Posted:* sent from the squadron to duties at some other post

P/O S. M. Anderson (Adjutant)

F/O T. J. Andrews

P/O R. H. Atkinson (Adjutant), *Killed on active service*

P/O J. B. Ayer, *Posted*

F/O C. E. Bateman, *Posted*

F/O W. A. Becker (Engineer Officer), *Posted*

P/O D. W. Beeson

P/O F. B. Bennett (Br.) (Engineer Officer), *Posted*

P/O F. A. Binks (Br.) (Medical), *Posted*

Sgt/P V. A. Boehle, *Posted*

F/O V. R. Bono, *Returned home*

F/O R. A. Boock

Sgt/P A. E. Brite

F/O E. Brookes (Br.) (Adjutant)

F/Lt. G. A. Brown, DFC (Br.), *Posted*

P/O R. C. Care

P/O L. A. Chatterton, *Killed on active service*

P/O J. A. Clarke

F/Lt O. H. Coen, DFC

P/O R. F. Collin (Br.) (Engineer Officer), Posted

P/O C. G. Daniel, *Prisoner of War*

P/O F. P. Dowling, *Posted*

P/O W. R. Driver, *Killed on active service*

F/O J. G. Du Four, *Posted*

P/O W. R. Dunn, *Posted*

Sgt/P J. E. Evans, *Missing*

P/O H. S. Fenlaw, *Killed in action*

P/O M. W. Fessler, *Prisoner of War*

F/O J. Flynn, *Killed in action*

Sgt/P V. D. France

P/O C. O. Galbraith, *Posted*

P/O D. Geffene, *Posted*

P/O W. D. Geiger, *Prisoner of War*

F/Lt. H. T. Gilbert, DFC (Br.), *Posted and then killed on active service*

F/O J. A. Gray, *Posted*

P/O W. I. Hall, *Prisoner of War*

P/O J. Harrington

P/O J. F. Helgason, *Killed on active service*

P/O H. D. Hively

P/O W. J. Hollander

P/O A. Hopson

F/O B. J. Hudson (Br.) (Engineer Officer)

P/O W. B. Inabinet, *Killed on active service*

F/O D. C. G. Jones (Br.) (Medical)

P/O J. M. Kelly, *Posted*

P/O B. F. Kennerly, *Returned home*

P/O V. C. Keough, *Killed on active service*

P/O S. M. Kolendorski, *Killed in action*

P/O P. H. Lechrone, *Killed on active service*

P/O J. F. Lutz

P/O J. J. Lynch, *Posted*

F/Lt. A. B. Mamedoff, *Posted and then killed on active service*

F/O R. L. Mannix, *Posted*

P/O N. M. Maranz, *Posted and then Prisoner of War*

P/O H. F. Marting, *Posted*

F/Lt. S. A. Mauriello, DFC

P/O G. S. Maxwell, *Posted*

P/O F. B. Mays, *Killed in action*

P/O C. W. McColpin, DFC, *Posted*

P/O T. P. McGerty, *Killed in action*

P/O L. J. McGinnis, *Killed on active service*

P/O R. D. McMinn

F/O M. G. McPharlin

P/O H. L. Mills

F/O E. T. Miluck, *Posted*

P/O R. A. Moore, *Returned home*

P/O W. B. Morgan (Adjutant)

P/O W. H. Nichols, *Prisoner of War*

P/O L. S. Nomis, *Posted*

P/O V. W. Olson, *Killed in action*

P/O E. E. Orbison, *Killed on active service*

F/O W. T. O'Regan

F/Lt. A. S. Osborne (Medical)

P/O W. Pendleton *Returned home*

F/O E. M. Potter

P/O R. L. Priser

P/O P. B. Provenzano, *Posted*

F/O J. R. Robinson (Br.) (Intelligence), *Posted*

F/O A. F. Roscoe, DFC, *Posted*

P/O C. E. Ross

P/O P. Salkeld (Br.) (Intelligence)

P/O D. H. Satterlee, *Posted*

P/O R. O. Scarborough, *Killed on active service*

Sgt/P P. A. Seaman

P/O W. J. Smith (Ground Defense), *Posted*

F/Lt. R. S. Sprague, *Killed on active service*

P/O H. L. Stewart

F/O H. H. Strickland

F/O R. V. Sweeney (Adjutant), *Posted*

F/O F. H. Tann (Br.) (Adjutant), *Posted*

P/O K. S. Taylor, *Killed on active service*

P/O W. D. Taylor, *Missing*

P/O G. Teicheira, *Missing*

F/O E. Q. Tobin, *Killed in action*

P/O R. E. Tongue (Br.), *Posted*

F/O C. W. Tribken, *Posted*

F/O M. S. Vosburg

F/O T. C. Wallace, *Posted*

P/O R. C. Ward, *Returned home*

P/O J. W. Weir, *Killed on active service*

P/O G. H. Whitlow

F/Lt. R. C. Wilkinson, DFM and Bar (Br.), *Posted*

P/O F. G. Zavakos, *Killed on active service*

List of Victories

No. 71 (Eagle) Squadron, Royal Air Force

Destroyed / Probably Destroyed / Damaged

	Destroyed	Probably Destroyed	Damaged
S/Ldr. C. G. Peterson, DSO, DFC	6	3	6
S/Ldr. G. A. Daymond, DFC and Bar	8	-	1
S/Ldr. H. de C. A. Woodhouse, DFC, AFC	1	-	-
S/Ldr. S. T. Meares, DFC	1	-	-
P/O J. K. Alexander	-	1	-
F/Lt. N. Anderson	½	-	1
P/O S. M. Anderson	-	-	1
F/O V. R. Bono	-	1	1
F/Lt. O. H. Coen, DFC	1½	1½	2
F/O J. G. Du Four	-	1	-
P/O W. R. Dunn	5	½	-
P/O H. S. Fenlaw	-	1	1
P/O M. W. Fessler	2	1	2
P/O J. V. Flynn	1	-	-
F/O J. A. Gray	1	-	-
P/O J. F. Helgason	½	-	-
P/O J. J. Lynch	1	-	-
P/O R. L. Mannix	-	2	-
F/Lt. S. A. Mauriello, DFC	2	-	1
P/O C. W. McColpin, DFC	6	-	-

F/O M. G. McPharlin	1½	½	1
P/O L. S. Nomis	½	-	1
F/O E. M. Potter	-	1	2½
P/O A. F. Roscoe, DFC	1	1	-
P/O R. O. Scarborough	2½	-	1
Sgt/P A. Seaman	-	-	1
F/Lt. R. S. Sprague	1	-	-
F/O H. H. Strickland	-	-	1
P/O K. S. Taylor	-	-	1
P/O G. W. Tribken	-	1	-
F/O T. C. Wallace	2	-	-
Total	45	15½	24½

In addition to the above listed victories, many ground targets such as goods trains, barges, gun posts, ammunition dumps, factories, etc., have been destroyed or damaged by the Eagles. A full list of these successful attacks is not kept by the RAF owing to difficulties of assessment.

Roll of Honor

No. 71 (Eagle) Squadron, Royal Air Force

Killed in Action

S/Ldr N. Anderson

P/O H. S. Fenlaw

F/O J. Flynn

P/O S. M. Kolendorski

P/O F. B. Mays

P/O T. P. McGerty

P/O V. W. Olson

F/O E. Q. Tobin

Killed on Active Service

P/O P. R. Anderson

P/O R. H. Atkinson

P/O L. A. Chatterton

P/O W. R. Driver

S/Ldr. H. T. Gilbert

P/O W. B. Inabinet

P/O V. C. Keough

P/O P. H. Lechrone

F /Lt. A. B. Mamedoff

S/Ldr. S. T. Meares, DFC

P /O L. J. McGinnis

P/O E. E. Orbison

P/O R. O. Scarborough

F/Lt. R. S. Sprague

P/O K. S. Taylor

P/O J. W. Weir

P/O F. G. Zavakos

Missing

Sgt/P J. E. Evans

P/O W. D. Taylor

P/O G. Teicheira

PRISONERS OF WAR

P/O C. G. Daniel   P/O W. I. Hall
P/O M. W. Fessler   P/O M. N. Maranz
P/O W. D. Geiger   P/O W. H. Nichols

A Short Glossary of RAF–WAAF Slang

There will be disagreement about some of the definitions, even some of the words, given here, because the slang of the RAF is by no means stabilized. There are marked variances between the talk, for instance, of fighter pilots and of bomber pilots; indeed, the slang of one station may differ distinctly from the slang of another, even though it is only a few miles distant.

Adj. Adjutant.

Balloonatics. Personnel in balloon command.
Beat up, to. To attack, either playfully or seriously, any place or thing.
Big noise. Important person (frequently ironic).
Bird dog, to. To steal another chap's girl.
Bit of fluff. A girl (usually the fluffy kind).
Black, a. Something badly done, a "bad show."
Blackouts, or twilights. WAAF issue panties (black in color).
Blitz, a solid lump of. Large formation of enemy aircraft.
Bog rat. Recruit (a bog rat being the lowest animal the RAF can imagine).
Blood wagon or meat wagon. Ambulance.
Bought it. To be killed.
Brassed off. Diminutive of "browned off."

Brolly. Parachute.
Browned off. "Fed up."
Bus driver. Bomber pilot.
Buttoned up. Job properly completed, "mastered."

C.O. Commanding Officer.
Civvie Street. Civilian life.
Civvies. Civilian clothes.
Clobber. To beat unmercifully, to destroy. (A plane badly
    shot up is frightfully "clobbered.")
Completely cheesed. Completely at a loss.
Completely surrounded. No hope at all.
Crab along, to. To fly near the ground or water.
Crate. An airplane.
Cyphereen. Senior Cypher Officer (WAAF).

Dead beat. RAF non-flying personnel.
Deck, to crack down on. To crash-land an airplane.
Dim. Slow-witted.
Ding bat, to go like a. To travel at almost incredible speed.
Do a bunk, to. To leave without permission.
Drill, the right. Correct method of doing anything.
Drink, in the. To come down in the sea.
Dud. Applied to weather when unfit to fly.
Duff gen. Incorrect information.
Dust bin. Rear gunner's lower position on an aircraft.
Dwaaf. Director of WAAF's.

Erk, an. Aircraftsman or Aircraftswoman—the rank in the
    RAF—WAAF corresponding to a private in the army.

Fan. The propeller.
Fireworks, Mr. Armaments Officer.
Flak. Antiaircraft fire.
Flannel, to. To toady, to seek favor by fawning.

Flap. A disturbance, general excitement.
Flat out. Completely.

Gen (pronounced *jen*). Information of any kind.
George. The automatic pilot.
Get cracking, to. To get going.
Get weaving, to. To get cracking.
Glamour badge. Brevet.
Glamour boys. Fighter pilots.
Gong. Medal.
Gravy. Petrol, gasoline.
Greenhouse. Cockpit cover.
Gremlins. The "little men" of the RAF.
Groupy. Group Captain.

Harbor Master. Commanding Officer of a Station.
Have had it, to. To have been killed, or, said ironically, meaning just the opposite, meaning *not* to have had something.
Hedge-hop, to. To fly so low the aircraft appears to be flying over hedges.
Hooch, to. To pub-crawl, drink at public houses, bars.

Jink. Sharp maneuver, sudden evasive action by aircraft.

Kee-toi'ing. Crash of any kind—usually a sudden crash in love.
Kipper Kite. Coastal Command aircraft which convoy fishing fleets in the North and Irish Seas.
Kite. Airplane.

Lay on, to. To arrange anything, to produce anything.
Land Army. RAF Regiment.
Left, right and center. All over the place.

Mae West. Life-saving stole or waistcoat, inflated if wearer falls into the sea.
Mickey Mouse. Bomb-dropping mechanism.

Office. Cockpit of aircraft.
On your knees. Too tired to stand.
One Pipper. Second Lieutenant (Army).
Operational. Anything that actually does its job: an airplane, a fountain pen, shoes, the weather, anything at all can be operational—or not.

Pack up, to. To cease to function.
Pancake, to. To land an airplane: formerly a crash landing, now any landing at all.
Peel off, to. To break formation.
Pickled as a newt. Tiddly, intoxicated.
Piece of Cake. Gift from the Gods (a Hun aircraft easily shot down, a girl easy to meet—each is a "piece of cake.")
Play pussy, to. Hide in the clouds.
Pleep. A squeak, rather like a high note klaxon.
Plonk. Recruit.
Pulchritude. Wizard Wench, a glamour girl.
Pull your finger out, to. To stop loafing.
Put your props up, to. To be promoted to Leading Aircraftsman or Leading Aircraftswoman, at which time a propeller insignia is sewn on the sleeve.
Prang, to. To crash—usually meaning to crash an aircraft, though one can be "pranged," broken up, by a girl.
Pug away, to. To continue to fire, keep after target.
Pukka gen. Accurate information.
Pulpit. Cockpit of aircraft.

Queen Bee. Senior WAAF (Administrative) Officer on a Station.
Quick squirt. Short, sharp burst of fire.

Quickie. A quick anything—burst of fire, drink, love affair, etc.

Ring the bell, to. To get good results.
Ring conscious. Conscious of rank. (Rank in the RAF and WAAF is designated by width and number of rings on the cuff of the tunic.)
Rings. Rank designation on officer's cuff.
Ropey. Uncomplimentary adjective—ropey landing, ropey type, ropey evening, etc.

Scream downhill, to. To execute power dive.
Scrub, to. To wash out.
Second Dickey. Second pilot.
Shaken. To be suddenly and severely taken aback.
Shaky do. Dangerous operation.
Shog, to. To make love.
Shooting a line. Exaggerated talk, generally about one's own powers.
Shot down in flames. Crossed in love; severe reprimand.
Show—"good," "bad," "poor." Anything can be a show— dinner party, dog fight, trip to London, etc.
Sicky-dog, to. To feel ill.
Snake about. Operational aerobatics.
Spin in, to. To make any bad mistake.
Sprog. Brand new uniform: newly commissioned officer.
Squaaf. Squadron Officer (WAAF).
Station Master. Commanding Officer of Station.
Stooge. A stand-in, a deputy, one who does something for someone else.
Stooge about, to. To patrol, flying slowly over an area, usually looking for trouble.

Tail-end Charley. Rear gunner in a large bombing aircraft, or the pilot of rear aircraft in formation.

Tapes. Non-commissioned officers' stripes.

Tear a strip off, to. To reprove severely.

Tick off, to. To reprove (less than tear a strip off).

Tiddly. Intoxicated.

Touch bottom, to. To crash.

Toys. A great deal of training equipment is termed toys.

Train, to drive the. To lead more than one squadron into battle.

Type. Classification—usually referring to people: good, bad, ropey, etc.

U.S. Unserviceable—anything at all can be U.S.: weather, airplane, etc.

View. RAF personnel always take a view of things—good, poor, dim, etc.

Weave, to. To take evasive action by aircraft—not quite so sudden or violent as jink.

Weave uneven course for home, to. To be tiddly, half seas over.

Wizard. Really first class, superlative, attractive, ingenious—anything deserving, or getting, highest praise.

Wizzed as a bee. Tiddly.

Worthy type. Said ironically and sarcastically of solemn and self-righteous individual.

Colonel James Saxon Childers, author of "War Eagles," shown with two members of the Eagle Squadron, Squadron Leader C. G. Peterson, D.S.O., D.F.C. (left), and Squadron Leader G. A. Daymond, D.F.C. and Bar. (right)

JAMES SAXON CHILDERS was born in Birmingham, Alabama. He enlisted in 1918 in the Naval Aviation and was acting as pilot at Key West, Florida, when the Armistice was signed. In 1920, he graduated from Oberlin College. He received a Rhodes Scholarship and entered Worcester College, Oxford, taking the Oxford B.A. degree in English literature two years later. After four years of residence in England, he returned to Birmingham and became a special lecturer at Birmingham-Southern College. Since then, he has occupied himself by writing novels and books about his travels; also by traveling and writing special features for a prominent Birmingham newspaper. Colonel Childers is now on active duty with the U. S. Armed Forces abroad.

BASTOGNE

The Story of the First Eight Days
In Which the 101st Airborne Division Was
Closed Within the Ring of German Forces

COLONEL S. L. A. MARSHALL

Details at
CoachwhipBooks.com

Details at
CoachwhipBooks.com

Available from your favorite online retailers

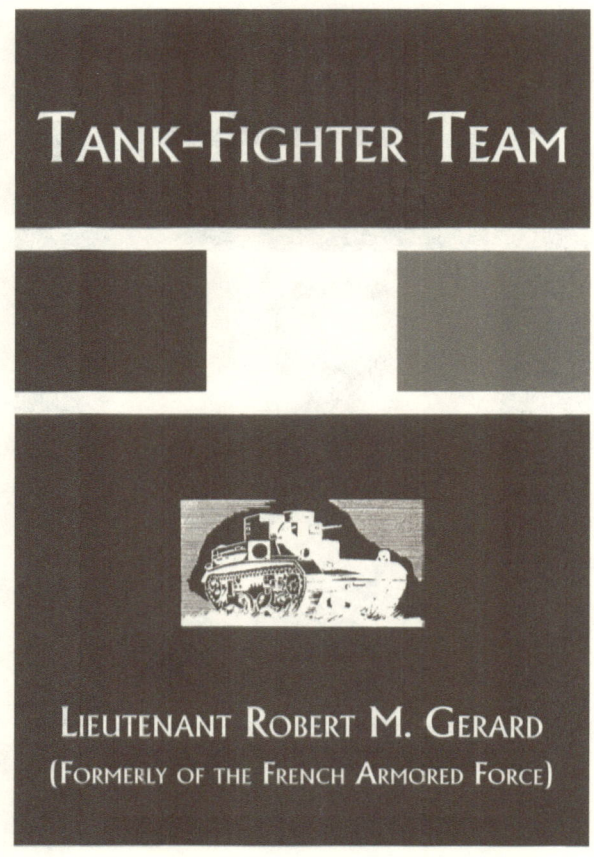

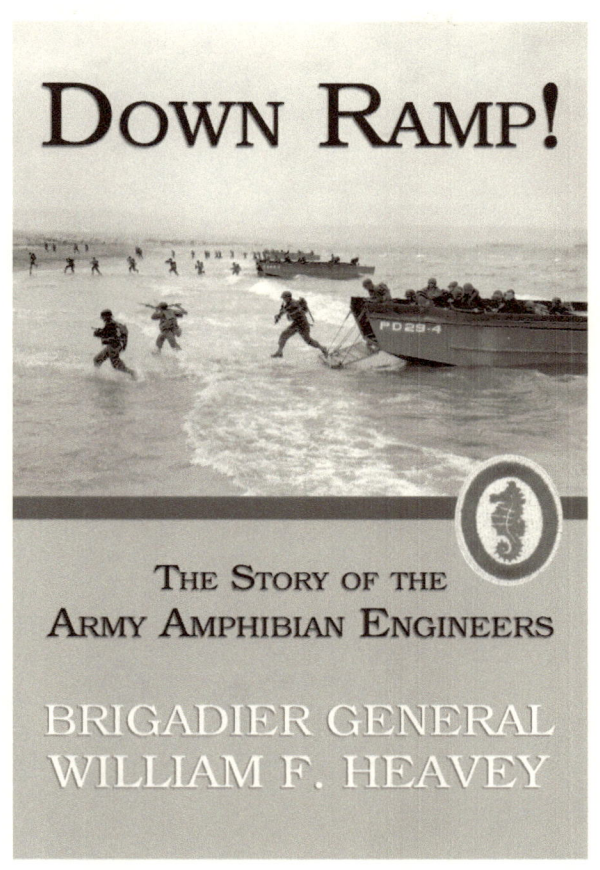

Details at
CoachwhipBooks.com

Available from your favorite online retailers

Details at
CoachwhipBooks.com

Available from your favorite online retailers

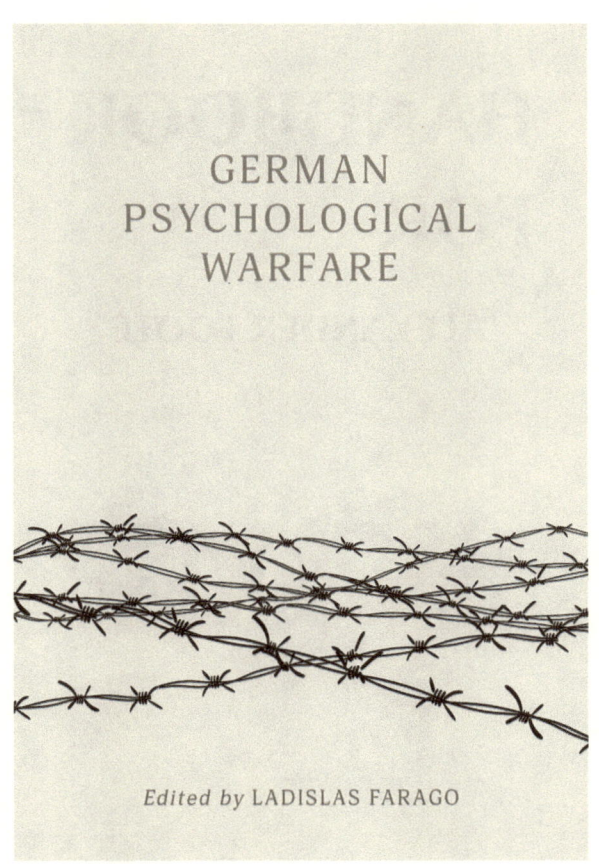

GERMAN
PSYCHOLOGICAL
WARFARE

Edited by LADISLAS FARAGO

Details at
CoachwhipBooks.com

Available from your favorite online retailers

HANDBOOK
FOR SPIES

ALEXANDER FOOTE

Details at
CoachwhipBooks.com

Available from your favorite online retailers

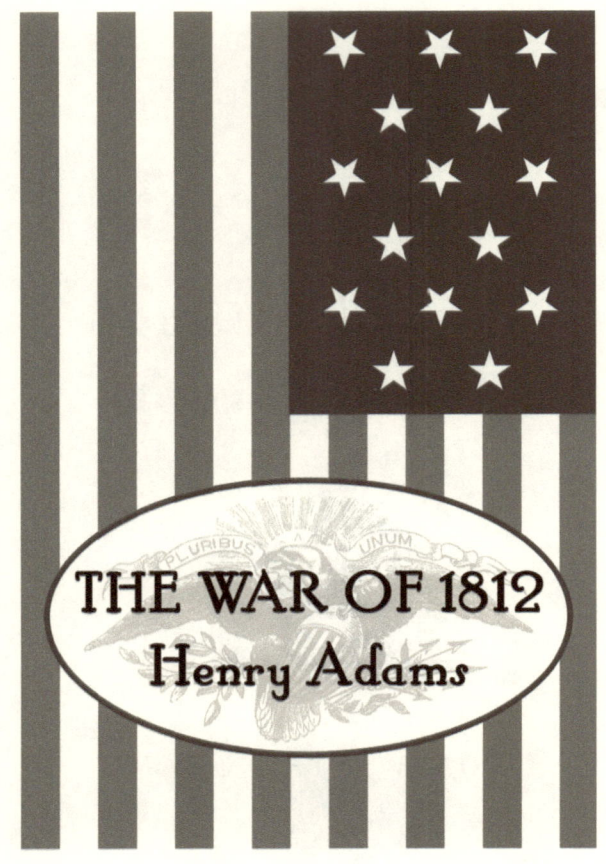

THE WAR OF 1812
Henry Adams

Details at
CoachwhipBooks.com

Available from your favorite online retailers

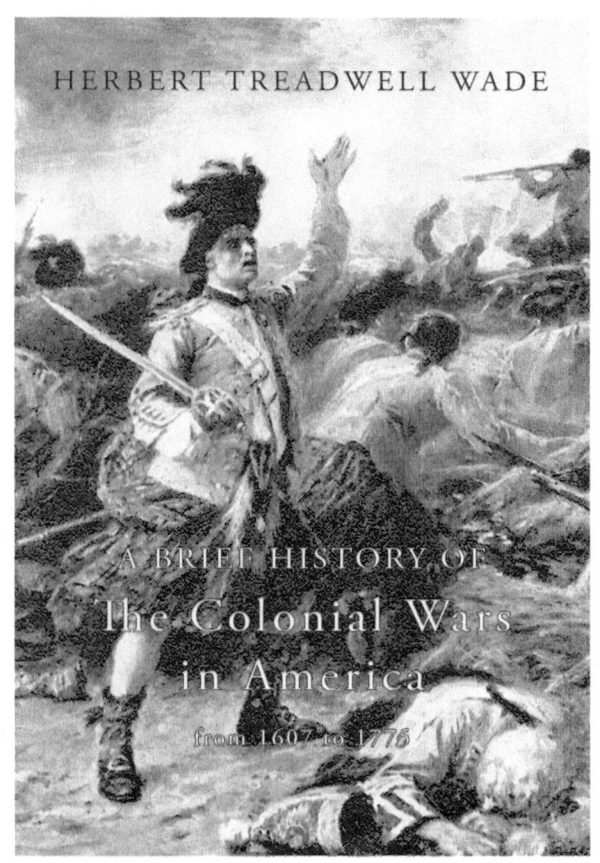